THE
Walter Hagen
STORY

Welcome to the Rare Book Collection, a unique compilation of golfing history proudly presented by Sports Media Group.

If you are interested enough in the game to be reading this page, you are likely aware of golf's matchless position within the library of sport, a standing supported by a body of international writing as richly varied as it is venerated. Indeed, with aspects as wide-ranging as instruction, history, course architecture, biographies, travel, tournament play, and all manner of fine anthologies, the field of golf literature has, for nearly 300 years, provided us with exceptional prose in areas far more diverse than any other game.

The goal of the Rare Book Collection is a simple one: To provide, at affordable prices, quality reprints of coveted golf volumes that, through scarcity or prohibitive cost, have heretofore lay beyond the reach of many readers. Our list of titles is uncommonly broad, its authors representing a veritable Who's Who from the game's long and storied past. It features many acknowledged classics but also a variety of hidden gems, overlooked or forgotten works every bit as interesting to mainstream readers as they are to serious collectors. Above all, it is our purpose to revive these great works at an attractive price, making the game's greatest—and rarest—titles available at a cost affordable to readers worldwide.

As coeditors of the Rare Book Collection, we enjoy the unique privilege of helping to select these volumes, and to reintroduce them with brief historical notes. We join everyone at Sports Media Group in hoping that you will gain as much enjoyment from reading these timeless works as we have in selecting and publishing them.

Daniel Wexler
Mel Lucas

Editor's Note

It has been some 80 years since Walter Charles Hagen battled for the 1924 Open Championship at the Royal Liverpool Golf Club, a particularly exciting event that ultimately found him facing a tricky, downhill six-footer at the 72nd green to claim his second Claret Jug. In as hot a cauldron as might be imagined, Hagen not only kept his cool but looked surprisingly nonchalant, stepping to the ball with little delay, then tapping it delicately down the shallow grade and dead into the hole. In the celebratory mayhem that followed, a British writer suggested that Hagen had looked almost too casual in making the putt, and asked if he'd known all that was at stake as he approached it.

"Sure I knew," replied Hagen confidently. "But no man ever beat *me* in a playoff."

The book you are about to read is Walter Hagen's autobiography, penned in 1956, the story of a man capable of coolly executing some of golf's greatest pressure shots, yet who is far better remembered for the legendary, almost mythic lifestyle of "The Haig." Hagen did, in fact, hole his putt to win the 1924 Open, yet he also damned well *had* been beaten in a play-off, and not in some long-forgotten backwater but just nine months earlier at the 1923 PGA Championship! But that, in a nutshell, was Walter Hagen—winning large, living larger, and definitely, as was his maxim, stopping to smell the flowers along the way.

For many years Arnold Palmer has been singled out as the patron saint of the contemporary professional golfer, and there can be no denying the impact he had on the game's growth as television brought the PGA Tour into millions of homes. But in terms of simply elevating the American professional from low-paid hired hand to affluent touring star, Walter Hagen simply had no equal. For Sir Walter was the first American to fully develop the many opportunities available to the successful professional, including personal appearances, endorsements, and all manner of additional off-course endeavors.

Becoming the first American pro to eschew country club employment and survive entirely off the fat of the golfing land, it was Hagen who maximized the concept of the exhibition tour, traveling literally the world over (often with trick-shot legend Joe Kirkwood) to demonstrate his skills for hefty fees. It was also Hagen who, like J. H.

Taylor in England, did so much to advance the social status of his fellow professionals in a class-conscious society, prompting the great Henry Cotton to observe that: "Pros today should go down on their knees and say a prayer for what he did for our profession."

Beyond such tangible accomplishments, however, what fascinates us most about Walter Hagen was his style, for Hagen lived as no other golfer has, before or since. Stories of his arrival at matches in chauffeur-driven Daimlers and Rolls-Royces are legion; yet more impressive was his habit of traveling to many mid-1920s events in his own private Pullman car. A regular among high society who counted the Duke of Windsor among his more prominent friends, Hagen was perhaps the sporting world's ultimate symbol of Roaring '20s America.

Though Hagen was known to experience the occasional financial drought (his longtime friend and rival Gene Sarazen once observing that "there were times when Walter had little to live on except his bravado") he was notoriously generous, tipping lavishly and famously turning over his entire £100 check to his 16-year-old caddie upon winning the 1929 Open Championship at Muirfield. It is true, of course, that a man of Hagen's sort was frequently America's guest, but Dan Jenkins's citing of the late, great Dave Marr as "the only Tour pro who ever picked up a dinner check" did not entirely do justice to Walter Hagen.

On the golf course Hagen's style was similarly unique, his stance inappropriately wide, his swing handsy and full of sway. He was, by most accounts, a long enough hitter but his driver in particular was prone to truly impressive bouts of wandering. Consequently Hagen was one of golf's all-time greatest recovery artists, his ability to navigate his ball back to civilization from parts unknown often breaking the hearts of more orthodox opponents. His short game also was world class (particularly from sand), and his putting—in which he held supreme confidence—was even better.

Much of Hagen's ability to walk his entertaining golfing tightrope came from his supremely measured approach to managing his game, for, unlike most, he suffered no psychological damage from his wayward blows. Indeed he once explained to the great sportswriter Grantland Rice that "I expect to make at least seven mistakes each round. Therefore, when I make a bad shot, I don't worry about it. It's just one of the seven." Of course, Rice observed that he once saw Hagen make 19 mistakes and still shoot 71, an amusing hyperbole perhaps, but hardly an impossibility given Hagen's particular brand of greatness.

Beyond his physical skills, Hagen possessed a vast reserve of what the British call "pluck," the sort of intestinal fortitude that spurs one to fight hardest when the chips are down. Nowhere is this more valuable than in golf, where even the best players in the world fail to win at least 75 percent of the time, and few ever get themselves up off the mat as well as Hagen. Perhaps the finest example of this came in 1928 when, prior to the Open Championship at Royal St George's, he was humiliated in a 72-hole, £750 challenge match with Britain's Archie Compston by the ungodly margin of 18 and 17—but typically undaunted, Hagen righted the ship in time to win the Claret Jug two weeks later, leaving the wealthy but Major-less Compston nearly forgotten in third.

And then there was gamesmanship, that subtle art of low cunning at which Hagen was the absolute master. One favored ploy involved dangling the prospect of exhibitions as a distraction, excitedly suggesting to opponents he was trailing that they might join him on a lucrative tour once they won the event in question—which, inevitably, they wouldn't after allowing their thoughts to wander to the grand paydays ahead.

According to Gene Sarazen, Hagen used an even more inventive tactic when the pair met in 1922's unofficial "World's Golf Championship," a 72-hole match-play contest staged in Pittsburgh and New York. Arriving for the New York leg of the event, Sarazen found waiting for him an expensive tie, gift wrapped with a note reading "You probably don't remember me but I'm the blonde from the Follies you met. Don't look for me in the gallery. I don't want you to take your mind off Hagen." Both the tie and the note, of course, had been sent by Hagen, and though the spirited Sarazen ultimately won the event 3 and 2, he readily conceded to having spent the morning round searching the gallery for the mysterious blonde before a laughing Hagen enlightened him over lunch.

Hagen himself will discuss the many highlights of his playing career but certainly a brief overview of his accomplishments is in order. Of his 44 victories today recognized by the PGA Tour, fully 11 were Major championships, a total that ranks second all-time (behind Jack Nicklaus's 18) in professional Majors. Of these 11, two were U.S. Opens (1914 and 1919) while four were Open Championships (1922, 1924, 1928, and 1929), the latter being a particularly remarkable accomplishment because, despite having no experience whatsoever with links golf, Hagen didn't just become the first American-born player to win the Open but spent a decade dominating it.

Despite his successes in the national Opens, however, Hagen's true forte was match play, as his record five PGA Championship victories aptly demonstrate. Having won the 1921 title at New York's Inwood Country Club, he later launched an unprecedented streak of four consecutive victories from 1924 to 1927, a run of 20 straight matches that would leave his career PGA record at an incomparable 35-3. Throw in a 7-1-1 Ryder Cup ledger (as the playing captain of the first five American teams) and a 12 and 11 thumping of Bobby Jones in the 1926s 72-hole "Battle of the Century" and we can fairly conclude—his subsequent pasting by Compston notwithstanding—that Walter Hagen ranks among the greatest match-play golfers who ever lived.

And one final point: Beyond his Major titles, Hagen won the event universally hailed as the Golden Age's fourth biggest, the Western Open, on five occasions (1916, 1921, 1926, 1927, and 1932). This becomes especially relevant when we recall that Hagen never played in the U.S. or British Amateurs (where Jones claimed six of his 13 Major titles), and that his competitive years fell prior to the creation of the Masters, effectively giving him only a three-event Grand Slam to shoot for each season instead of our modern standard of four. In this context, a reasonable argument can be made to count Hagen's five Western Opens as Majors, a move which would raise his career total to 16, just two behind Nicklaus and a stout seven ahead of those next in line, Ben Hogan and Gary Player. With Major championships remaining our most consistent historical measuring stick, it is, I think, an important argument to consider.

In writing of a character the magnitude of Walter Hagen, it is no easy task to summarize his life, personality, and style in a traditionally brief closing paragraph. Thus I shall instead pass the baton back to Gene Sarazen who (with the help of Herbert Warren Wind) told the following story regarding the 1924 Open Championship at Hoylake:

"Hagen had barely been able to qualify for this tournament. His first qualifying round was an 83 that would have crushed a less gallant spirit. After breakfast the next day, a group of us discovered that a large crowd had gathered outside the Adelphia Hotel. They were waiting for a glimpse of the Lord Mayor togged out in his colorful robes of office, but Hagen assumed that they had congregated to see Walter Hagen. He mounted a small platform and waved appreciatively at the gathering—this, after an 83. But who won that tournament? Walter Hagen."

Read on!

Daniel Wexler

THE
Walter Hagen
STORY

BY The Haig, Himself

as told to Margaret Seaton Heck

SMG
SPORTS
MEDIA
GROUP

All inquiries should be addressed to:
Sports Media Group
An imprint of Ann Arbor Media Group LLC
2500 S. State Street
Ann Arbor, MI 48104

Originally published in 1956 by Simon and Schuster, Inc.
Original printing Library of Congress Catalog
Card Number 56-7487.

Printed and bound at Edwards Brothers, Inc.,
Lillington, North Carolina, USA

08 07 06 05 04 1 2 3 4 5

ISBN 1-58726-131-6

For

My son, Walter Hagen, Jr.

My grandson, Walter Hagen the Third

And for

My golf pals all over the world

The life of every man is a diary in which he means to write one story, and writes another; and his humblest hour is when he compares the volume as it is with what he vowed to make it.

—James M. Barrie

Table of Contents

PART ONE: The Tee
            INTRODUCTION by H. G. Salsinger   2
CHAPTER I   The Book   3
        II The Caddie   9
        III The Professional   16
        IV Brookline, 1913   25
        V   Champion, 1914   34
        VI War, 1917   43
        VII Brae Burn, 1919   52
        VIII British Open, 1920   64
        IX French Open, 1920   72
        X   Wind, 1921   77
        XI High Finance   86

PART TWO: The Fairway
            INTRODUCTION by Bill Cunningham   96
        XII British Open, 1922   98
        XIII Joe Kirkwood Tour   109
        XIV Florida Boom   117
        XV British Open, 1924   126
        XVI L. A. Young, 1925   139
        XVII Mr. Jones vs. W. Hagen, 1926   146
        XVIII Early and Late   161
        XIX PGA Champion, 1925   173
        XX Defeat: 18 and 17   183
        XXI British Open, 1928   195
        XXII Ryder Cup Teams   205
        XXIII Four-Time Winner, 1929   212
        XXIV Caddies . . .   226
        XXV . . . and Kings   237

PART THREE: The Green
          INTRODUCTION by Grantland Rice   254
XXVI Hook and Slice   256
XXVII Competitors   265
XXVIII Gasparilla Open, 1935   277
XXIX Pitch and Run   286
XXX World Tour   296
XXXI Safari   307
XXXII The Nineteenth Hole   319

An Afterword by Margaret Seaton Heck   325

Walter Hagen's Record   329

Golf Glossary   332

Acknowledgments   334

Index   335

What They Said about The Haig

H. G. SALSINGER	2
BOB HARLOW	3
GENE SARAZEN	9
BEN HOGAN	16
HERBERT WARREN WIND	25
GRANTLAND RICE	34
TOMMY ARMOUR	43
JACK O'BRIAN	52
GRANTLAND RICE	64
A. C. M. CROOME	72
TOMMY ARMOUR	77
HARRY MOLTER	86
BILL CUNNINGHAM	96
WALTER HAGEN, JR.	98
PERCY HUGGINS	109
TOMMY ARMOUR	117
R. E. (BOB) HOWARD	126
HENRY COTTON	139
HERBERT WARREN WIND	146
BILLY SIXTY	161
A. T. PACKARD	173
BEN HOGAN	183
GENE SARAZEN	195
GEORGE TREVOR	205
HORTON SMITH	212
W. K. MONTAGUE	226
ROKUZO ASAMI	237
GRANTLAND RICE	254
INNIS BROWN	256
SAM SNEAD	265
ARTHUR DALEY	277
LESTER RICE	286
H. I. PHILLIPS	290
BOBBY LOCKE	296
BOB HARLOW	307
WALTER HAGEN	319
ARTHUR DALEY	325

Illustrations

FIRST SECTION *follows page 54*

SECOND SECTION *follows page 86*

THIRD SECTION *follows page 150*

PART ONE: The Tee

INTRODUCTION

WALTER HAGEN made himself the leading player of golf and led his fellow professionals out of bondage. He won more than seventy-five championships and over a million dollars. He gave his victory medals and cups to his friends as souvenirs and spent his winnings on their entertainment. He kept the Prince of Wales waiting at the first tee on one occasion and the Japanese Ambassador on another. He introduced democracy into golf in the British Isles. He spread the gospel of golf in every state in the Union and carried it to England, Scotland, Ireland and Wales (where they thought they did not need his help, having done a lot of gospel spreading before he was born), and to France, Germany, Switzerland, the Hawaiian Islands, New Zealand, Australia, the Philippine Islands, China and Japan (where they greatly appreciated what he did for the game).

He has met more people and is known to more people than any other man who ever hooked a tee shot or dubbed a niblick. He has swaggered through palaces, calling kings by their family nicknames, showing princes how to cure a slice.

There is not a golf course in a distorted world where the name of Walter Hagen is not recognized.

Chick Evans once said of him: "He's in golf to live—not to make a living."

That explains the golfer and the man, his success and his improvidence. He has lived for golf.

—H. G. SALSINGER, *The Detroit News*
[1947]

CHAPTER I: The Book

> So this is the story of Walter Hagen, who, with a
> broad grin on his expansive features, looked at the
> world through the hole in the doughnut, but who
> kept his hands on the dough.
> —BOB HARLOW, *Golf World*
> [1952]

GOLF AND I met when I was five years old, in the little town of
Brighton, New York. A Scotsman named Sandy, professional at
the Country Club of Rochester, first put a club into my hands
and let me knock a ball around in our living room.

Through the fabulous years that were to follow I played golf
in almost every country on the globe. Golf earned me a million
dollars which I enjoyed spending. Golf brought me into contact with more than a million people. Golf made my every move
and statement a news headline anywhere I chanced to be.

Some of those headline stories were true, but a great many
were conjured up in the imaginations of the sports writers who
followed the game. Most of them made good reading and I read
them along with the rest of the public and enjoyed them. I
never bothered to say if they were true or false, because every
story drew more hundreds of people into the galleries following
me around golf courses. After all a ticket was the same price for
anyone, no matter why he came to see me.

While I was playing competitive golf I was too busy living to
think about writing a book. And when I stopped playing com-

3

petitive golf I was just as busy relaxing. Now, for the first time, I'm going to tell my story. It has been a long time in the making and, being the relaxed guy I am, the story will require some time in the telling.

I have been known through the years as a man who likes parties and spreads hospitality. So a party for members of the press, radio and television sports commentators was set up on Wednesday, May 7, 1952 at the Detroit Athletic Club. The invitations caused no lifted eyebrows and everyone who received a bid showed up. I did not invite all my friends in the Detroit area, for as Bob Murphy wrote in his column in the Detroit *Times,* I'd have had to hire Briggs Stadium to hold them.

About an hour after the party had begun, with all the boys thoroughly relaxed and mellow, I climbed on top of a table and signaled for attention. When the room was quiet I told them about my book. Once again I was calling a shot before I'd made it. And it reminded me of a similar circumstance in England in 1926.

I was playing in the British Open at Royal Lytham and St. Anne's and I was trying to catch Bobby Jones at the last and deciding hole. Bobby had finished with a total of 291 and was watching from the balcony of the club house. My drive from the eighteenth tee was as good as I could hope for, but it still left me with an approach shot of 150 yards to the green. I might hole out with a perfect shot and a lot of luck. It had been done. And to tie Jones I would need an eagle 2.

I walked some steps away from my ball to examine the lie of the land. Then I asked the official scorer if he would go down and hold the flag. I spoke quietly and he did not understand. I asked him again, and this time a few people around me heard the request, which I had not intended. The official went on down the fairway, but he remained on a mound short of the green.

Now I had to walk half the distance and tell him again to

4

take the flag. By yelling, "I want you to hold the flag," I found myself informing the ten thousand in the gallery (as well as Bobby Jones and J. H. Taylor on the balcony) just what I intended to do.

However, I then realized that by concentrating the attention of the gallery on the official, standing 150 yards from my ball, I had eased my own tension. With their eyes on him, not me, and with their thoughts concerned with "the blooming ass down there holding the flag" I could concentrate completely on playing the shot. Should I miss he would be the goat for taking the flag at such a distance.

Now that I had everything set, I returned to my ball, carefully took my stance and played. The shot was better than I dared hope for. I saw the ball head straight for the pin, land just on the edge of the green, and roll toward the hole. It had one chance in a thousand of finding the cup. But I had hit it a bit too hard. It jumped over the hole—it would have hit the flag—and dropped into the shallow scooped-out sand trap at the back of the green. The warming part about the episode was that I got almost as much applause as if my ball had holed.

Bobby told me later, "I turned my back on you, Walter, because a guy with that much confidence would be fool lucky enough to make it."

Actually I believe I set up that situation to give the gallery a thrill, but I got just as much of a thrill myself for I thought I *might* make it.

And so it is with this book. Before I ever started to write a line I announced my intention to a gallery, the writers and commentators; I set up my shot. I would answer all the questions that have been asked me over the years—about golf, about the people I've met and played with, about me, personally. Once again I planned to give the gallery, all my friends and acquaintances, a thrill—the chance to drive with me off the first tee and to watch my final putt in competitive golf holed.

5

Fired with enthusiasm and determination and armed with scrapbooks and typewriters, I retired to Cadillac, Michigan, to begin work. Why Cadillac? For a fellow who has followed the sun around the world all his life it may seem queer to choose a northern Michigan town blanketed with snow almost eight months of the year. Actually I had chosen the location very carefully. In the first place this resort of fourteen lodges called Pilgrim's Village on Lake Mitchell near Cadillac, had plenty of accommodation space for everybody—including the many literary kibitzers we knew would be around. And second, it was two hundred miles from Detroit, my permanent residence. That was important.

I like sharing my hospitality with friends, that's for sure. If I had taken a place on any lake near Detroit, or at any resort area where I've lived or played golf, people would just happen to be nearby and *drop in*. But Cadillac is two hundred miles from Detroit. If they came there to toast my labors they wouldn't be dropping in, they'd have to *aim* at it to get there.

"Let's not be in a hurry to start this book," I suggested the day we arrived. "There's plenty of time."

So my pals and I enjoyed the lake breezes on board my yacht, which was the first purchase made after we unpacked. Yacht? Well, not exactly, but at least it was a twenty-foot boat with a lively motor.

And the days passed. With pencil sharpened, fresh ribbons in the typewriters, minds alert and scrapbook pages ready to be turned, we relaxed to take in excellent dinners at famous restaurants close by, play an occasional game of darts or shuffleboard, or maybe do a bit of fishing from the dock. Since our arrival I had added a twelve-by-twelve-foot platform to the dock. I equipped it with plenty of comfortable chairs so that we might discuss the book while enjoying the fresh air and cool breezes, and surrounded it with a latticed fence painted with aluminum

6

phosphorous paint. This made it luminous at night and guarded against our losing anybody.

We had plenty of visitors and we had a wonderful time talking the book. We lived up about $40,000 but I was as far from shooting the volume to a publisher as I had been from holing that shot at Royal Lytham and St. Anne's.

However, it was a good year, for the weather was unusually mild. I learned to plod around on snow shoes and to take a few ungraceful slaloms on skis. I liked having my friends and literary kibitzers around soaking up hospitality and sunshine and I felt thoroughly rested after all that relaxation. Now I knew it was time to get myself a writer and get down to the real business at hand.

I found out that writing a book isn't easy. You sit down and you tell what happened. It's pretty hard to remember all the events you want to remember—just when and where and how they happened. And it's just as hard to put down some of the incidents you'd like to forget. In writing this book I knew I had to tell both the plus and the minus sides . . . take the total and let it stand.

For instance, I can remember with much pleasure the golf I've played with Babe Ruth, President Warren G. Harding, Gene Tunney, Ring Lardner, the Duke of Windsor and the many other notables in all fields—sports, literature, politics, movies and the stage. I can get a big thrill from remembering all the tournaments and the championships I've won and the names of the great golfers of the world I had to beat to win them. I like remembering the applause and the admiration of the galleries, the congratulations and the toasts from my friends all over the world.

On the minus side, there was the terrific defeat I suffered at the hands of Britain's Archie Compston when he beat me 18 up and 17 to play in a challenge match in 1928. There was the near-fatal illness of malaria fever which struck me when I was big game hunting in India. I can still feel the disappointment and disgust over my showing in my first British Open in 1920, when I finished fifty-third in a field of fifty-four.

Yet somehow when I put the plus and minus things together, the minus seems to make the plus better and more worth winning . . . seems to make the victories sweeter.

CHAPTER II

The Caddie

HAGEN was at home with all classes of society, far more than Dempsey or Ruth, the other great champions of the twenties, whom he resembled in the blackness of his hair, his amazing magnetism, his love of admiring crowds, and his rise from humble beginnings.

—GENE SARAZEN, *Thirty Years of Championship Golf*
[1950]

SPORTS WRITERS have written thousands of words and figures about the money I made playing golf. For the record, most of them are correct. I got the highest fee ever paid a golfer in those days in England, when I won a 72-hole match over Abe Mitchell for a stake of £500 (then $2500) at Wentworth and St. George's Hill in 1926. Just two years later I received the same high fee and took the worst trimming of my career from Archie Compston at Moor Park, 18 up and 17 to play.

For that much publicized match with Bobby Jones in Florida in 1926 I received $7600 and that was the highest take ever won by a golfer for a 72-hole match in America. And I gave Bobby the most humiliating defeat of his golfing life.

The truth is I went into the game in the beginning for money—ten cents an hour plus a nickel tip which members of the Country Club of Rochester, New York, paid their novice caddie, Walter, back in 1900.

From our house in Corbett's Glen near Brighton, I could cross Allen's Creek to the top of the hill, look over beyond East Avenue and watch the members of the club on the golf course.

9

I was seven and a half when I persuaded my father to ask his friend, Bill Lambert, the caddie master, if he would give me a job. I got the job. Right then that ten cents an hour looked bigger to me than the $7600 check ever did.

My father, William, and my mother, Louise, were both of thrifty German stock so our family got along fine on the eighteen dollars a week that Father made as a blacksmith in the car shops of East Rochester. That was good pay in the early part of the century. I was the second child, the only boy, in a family which had four girls. Lottie was the oldest. I came along December 21, 1892; then came Freda, Cora and Mabel. We were all healthy and strong. We worked hard and we paid our bills. We had a simple comfortable home and good plain food but there wasn't much left over for extras. That caddie job meant the extras for me.

I tried to give my mother part of my first week's pay but she wouldn't take it. I was taught to save in a coin bank and each week I deposited some silver in the local branch of the East Side Savings Bank of Rochester. In time the green stuff meant more to me than the change, so I would trade ninety-five cents and a golf ball I'd found to another caddie for a one-dollar bill. But that, too, went into the bank. Like any kid I wasn't above snitching from my penny bank now and then. I'd pry the teeth in the slot apart and shake out enough for ice cream. And eventually enough for my first suit with long pants, a sort of wild bluish-green in color. In my teens I even saved enough in my account to blow $380 on a piano for a birthday present for my oldest sister, Lottie.

My first day as a caddie was almost my last. I drew Mr. Erickson Perkins, a prominent broker in Rochester, for my first job. I proudly lugged his slender bag of seven clubs—a full kit in those days—and it was quite a load for me. I got along fine until the tenth hole. It featured an odd trap, in which an island with heavy rough lay in a small desert of sand.

10

He plunked his drive into a tall tree growing out of the grass island. I tried hard to keep my eye on the ball, but I couldn't tell whether it went through, bounced back into the rough, or hit the sand trap. Mr. Perkins didn't know either. We searched, he and I, along with the casual help of several other players and their caddies. But they soon tired of it and went on. Mr. Perkins turned to me and his voice sounded like the end of golf for me.

"Here, boy," he said gruffly, "give me the bag. I'll go down the fairway and you stay here and find the ball. You'd better find it, too, or don't come back."

I was pretty desperate as he strode away from me with that precious bag bobbing on his shoulder. I scurried around rabbit fashion, one eye on the ground and the other on his rapidly disappearing back. But no ball did I see. Finally inspired by terror alone, I lay down and rolled over and over across the rough grass, hoping that my body would locate what my eyes couldn't. I found the ball.

I raced after Mr. Perkins and gave it to him. He lifted the bag from his shoulder and gave it to me. After the round he told me to clean his clubs. I had them cleaned and shining like new when he came from the locker room. He added a nickel tip to the ten cents he owed me. I thanked him and said I was sorry about losing the ball and delaying his game.

"It's all right," he told me. "You're a good boy. You'll learn."

I learned quickly, because I spent every free hour after school caddying, and I sure liked having that money I made. Sunday golf was frowned on, so we kids played baseball. I had decided that baseball was my game. In the caddie pen we'd putt for old balls we found on the course, and whenever I won, I'd take them down to La Bourie's Sporting Goods Store in Rochester and get credit on a baseball, or a first baseman's mitt.

While I was caddying I thought I might as well learn to play

11

golf. Walter Will could drive farther than any other player at the club so it was his swing that I copied. Because caddies were not allowed to play the club course I fashioned my own course on a nearby cow pasture. I knew nothing about course architecture, so I followed the shape of the pasture which vaguely resembled the outline of the state of Florida. I laid out a four-hole affair. For instance, I teed off at Jacksonville, the first green was on the outskirts of Pensacola, then across to the second hole at Gainesville. From there I went down to the third green at Miami and then back to the fourth green in the Jacksonville area again. I must have had a feeling about Florida even then. Many years later I made $1800 to $2000 a day down there, giving lessons for $200 an hour, playing exhibitions and taking on golfing friends for $500 Nassaus.

I learned quickly how to beg golf clubs from members, too. When I'd take the members' bags to the door of the locker room I could see some of their old clubs growing dusty in the lockers. When I was eight I got up enough nerve to ask Mr. John Palmer for one. He gave me two, a midiron and a spoon.

Polo was making inroads on golf the following summer, and all of us caddies had to lead the ponies to and from the stables. We invented a polo game on bicycles. From this fooling around I devised a new grip for my putter that resembled the handle of a mallet. I was convinced that the secret to putting lay in the last two fingers of the left hand. I believe it to this day.

I was growing pretty fast, getting much taller and heavier, and my baseball ability was improving right along. I had a pretty good curve with my right hand, and a clever change of pace with my left. My ambition was to make the big leagues as a pitcher. I was firmly convinced that if I were to make a lot of money, it would have to be in baseball. And if I were to make a success in baseball I would need to have some skill that others didn't have. So I worked hard to improve my speed and control in pitching.

12

Late in the spring when I was twelve years old, I was in the seventh grade and sitting looking out the window, feeling the nice warm air and the sunshine on my face. I could see the golfers out on the course at the Country Club of Rochester. Suddenly I couldn't take it any longer. When Mrs. Cullen, the teacher, wasn't looking I jumped out the window. I never went back to school regularly again.

Throughout that summer I spent every weekday caddying, and on Sundays I played baseball. I was a good caddie, conscientious about my job, and soon members of the Thistle Club asked me to caddie for them. This was a big step up for me. The Thistle Club, composed of charter members of the club which had preceded the Country Club of Rochester, was a sort of inner group whose word carried a lot of weight. I picked up a lot of pointers on the game and played around on my own cowpasture course when I had the free time.

That fall when golfing was over I decided to learn a trade to support myself until I was ready for the big leagues. It seemed natural that anything I'd learn to do would involve skill with my hands. I came from that kind of family. My father was not a large man physically—he stood about five feet eight inches—but he had big powerful hands, perfect for a blacksmith. I was built more like my mother and, like her, I soon towered a good three inches over my dad. Sports writers have often written about *my big hands* but actually my hands are about average for a man of my size. I wear a size nine and a half glove. However, my fingers, even when I was a youngster, were unusually long and tapering.

Harry's Garage in Rochester was taking apprentices in car repairing for a fee of twenty-seven dollars a month. In order to make the payments, I got a part-time job with the Foster-Armstrong Piano Company as a wood finisher. I also went to school three nights a week taking a course supplementary to the car repair work. As a sideline, I enrolled in a correspondence course in taxidermy. A little later, with the piano company job as background experience, I landed a job as a paid apprentice to a mandolin maker. These two jobs gave me a good basic knowledge of woods and woodworking as well as appreciation of fine grains and finishing. When I became a professional golfer my clubs were always bright and polished. As a fellow pro once remarked, "You can shave in Hagen's clubs."

I continued to caddie at the Country Club of Rochester through the summer and the Thistle Club members fixed it so I could play the club course. By the time I was fifteen Andrew Christy, the club pro, needed an assistant and it had to be me.

My pal George Christ and I had been saving our caddie fees for some time and we got the idea we'd be smart and buy motorcycles. He found a secondhand Harley-Davidson and I bought a bright red Indian in a similar need-of-repair condition. We finally got them in running shape and there wasn't a foot of road around Rochester that we didn't cover. We hadn't thought it wise to tell our folks we'd spent all our savings on the machines and I'll never forget shutting off the motor at the top of the hill near home and coasting down. Then I hid the motorcycle in a clump of trees.

The deception didn't last long, however, for I confessed to my mother and asked her to come out and see me ride it. Instead of scolding me, she said, "I've been wishing you could have one of those things. Now you and George can have a lot of fun."

I was playing the Country Club of Rochester course with Mr. Christy when I broke 80. He played with me quite often when we were through work in the pro shop at the end of the day. But we played *with* each other, not *against*. In my own mind, though, I always played him a match on the q.t.

One day, with forced nonchalance, I said, "It's a fine evening, Mr. Christy, and all the members are in. I'll just take you on for nine holes."

14

His answer set me back on my heels. His eyes covered me slowly for a few seconds, then he said, "Young man, when I want to play golf, *I'll* ask *you.*" Then he turned and walked away.

Was my face red! What a lesson he taught me. I never forgot that. Afterwards when I wanted to play with him I was always careful to ask politely, "Would you play a few holes with me, Mr. Christy, and give me some pointers on my game?"

I could beat him and he knew it, too. But he had carried that incident off big. He made himself and his position important and dignified. Win or lose, he let me know he was still the pro, the big guy. I was just a kid and I could beat him, but he still looked and acted the role of the champion on that course. In later years I took some clobbering defeats and wore many a championship crown, yet it was the lesson he taught me that kept me in the groove through all walks of life.

CHAPTER III: The Professional

> In using the word *rhythm* I am not speaking of the swing. The rhythm I have reference to here could also be described as the *order of procedure*. Walter Hagen was probably the greatest exponent of the kind of rhythm I have in mind ever to play golf.
>
> —BEN HOGAN, *Power Golf*
> [1948]

GOLF CHAMPIONS are made, not born. I would be the first to admit that one must have a flair for the game, but only constant practice and concentration on every type of shot will produce the real champion. By the time I was fifteen I had played more golf and practiced more shots than most young golfers of twenty-one today. One reason, of course, is that today youngsters must be fourteen years old before they can start carrying a bag.

I think I was lucky in being born where and when I was, and in being thrown into contact with golf at the Country Club of Rochester. The members of that club were of wealthy, conservative, socially established old families. Their interest in golf was a sporting one. They used the game entirely for recreation with small bets on the side to up the competition. They were just as interested in tennis, polo, ice skating, hunting and fishing. As a kid I, too, engaged in these sports and got to be pretty sharp in a few.

Competition was the factor which drew me. I had a sort of

tireless energy, a compulsion to be doing something, to be on the move. Not a nervous energy, but an inspired physical reaction which gave me so much confidence in my own ability that I was always thoroughly relaxed in any game. I played to win, whether it was pool, marbles, baseball, shooting or golf. I liked the feel of a golf club in my hand and I was forever swinging a club.

When I was fourteen I thought I was capable of taking on anybody within five years of my age. Of course, I'd never been out of Rochester, but I knew I could beat anybody I'd met so far.

When I first began caddying I drew the duffer type players; the better golfers already had their own favorite caddies. But even the duffers helped me. I used to kid around the caddie pen giving imitations of the grotesque swings employed by some of the members. Years later I returned to the Country Club of Rochester many times to play exhibitions and the high point of my visits, to the members, was a repeat performance of my imitations in the grill over a few hoots.

But in those caddie days I'd try to swing in reverse to the duffer style. I was trying to develop a style of my own. I developed a style all right, not exactly orthodox but one that served me well enough through the next few years. I got results and that's what counted.

As I became more experienced and the better players took me on, I caddied regularly for men who unconsciously influenced my life in later years. I caddied often for Walter and John Powers, who owned the Powers Block and the Powers Hotel in Rochester; for Mr. George Eastman of Eastman Kodak Company, whose friendship I treasured throughout his lifetime. There was Beekman Little, not overly free with his tips, but as chairman of the greens committee, he was to give me a much desired push upward. And Harry Strong of the Stromberg Carburetor Company—at his suggestion, the team of five caddies I captained challenged the caddies of Oak Hill Club, located on the west side of Rochester. We won two out of the three matches and he rewarded us with trophies—a cup for each of our members. That was the first and only trophy I ever won as an amateur!

I was tremendously impressed by the conversations and discussions of these men regarding their vacations in Florida and other famous resort spots both here and abroad; about big game hunting in Africa and India. I admired the ease with which they spoke of huge money deals and I certainly eyed wishfully their fancy golfing outfits—tweed jackets, colorful argyles and knickers.

Working with Andrew Christy in the pro shop from the winter I was fourteen through the next five years gave me invaluable knowledge about clubs, their design and construction. The iron heads were mostly shipped over from England and Scotland, but the woods we made right from the block. I learned how to weight the wood heads. I learned to plane the shafts from hickory, scrape them down, polish them to a fine sheen and attach them to the heads. I could wind a grip with the skill of the old-time club makers.

I finally assembled a fairly good-looking set for myself. Although golf writers have often referred to that first set of mine as a "collection of odds and ends," I carried them through 1920. With these so-called "strange weapons" I won two American Opens, the Panama Exposition Open, the French Open—and finished fifty-third in the British Open!

That first set included an old-fashioned spliced driver (known as Ted Ray's Own), steel-faced with a bolt that went right through the face of the club; a brassie of about the same vintage; a spoon; a driving iron, equivalent to a number one-iron; a midiron; a mashie iron, a deep-faced club which I made to fit in between the midiron and the mashie; a mashie; a mashie niblick; a niblick and a putter of the old gooseneck type.

In 1940 the United States Golfing Association asked for one of those clubs in my original set to put in their Hall of Fame. I had them all, except my favorite, the mashie iron. I was in Detroit in July that year for the Red Cross Ryder Cup matches at Oakland Hills Golf Club, where I had once been pro. Sitting around the locker room between matches I mentioned to Midge Murray, my long-time friend and former assistant, that I was unable to locate the mashie iron.

Midge grinned at me. "I've got that club, Walter. I'll bring it to you tomorrow."

Sure enough he turned up with it and carried it all over the course until he found me and presented it to me. I took a couple of swings with it, and it was like meeting a treasured old number.

"I was starting the last nine at Brae Burn in 1919," I explained to Midge, "and I was told I needed a 34 to win the Open or a 35 to tie for the title with Mike Brady. When I reached the eighteenth tee I tried for an extra long drive so I could play my favorite mashie iron to the green. This mashie iron didn't let me down for I got a beautiful shot only fifteen feet from the hole."

That club is now in the Golf House in New York, beside Bobby Jones's famous putter, Calamity Jane.

I played a lot of golf during those five years I was assistant to Andrew Christy at the Country Club of Rochester, but I also played a lot of baseball. I worked out in every position but I liked pitching best. George Christ and I were both pitching for the Rochester Ramblers, a sort of semipro team, pro in that the pitcher got paid a dollar and a half a game. I usually started the game and George relieved me at about the halfway mark. Then I finished out the rest of the game in some other position, so I could get all the experience possible. I have always had unusually keen eyes and I was a pretty fair hitter. While I was with the Ramblers we won the city championship three times.

Andrew Christy, Alf Campbell who was pro at the Oak Hill Club in Rochester, and I went to Buffalo for a few practice rounds prior to the National Open held there in 1912. I got in one round, a 73, much lower than either of the other two could manage. When time for the Open rolled around, however, Andy decided I should stay home and look after the pro shop while he played in the Open. I could understand his point. My practice round was better than his and he didn't want to be embarrassed. It certainly wouldn't look good for his kid assistant to finish ahead of him. Or maybe even win the Open championship. At least, that's the way I had it figured out in my own mind. He did promise me then as a reward for staying home and working that I could go to Toronto and play in the Canadian Open which was scheduled after Buffalo.

However, I was in Buffalo long enough to carry away one big impression: how a real professional golfer must dress. For it was there I saw Tom Anderson, Jr., a brother to Willie, winner of the American Open Championship in 1901, 1903, 1904 and 1905. Right then, I was far more impressed with Tom's clothes than I was with Willie's record. Tom had class! His outfit just about knocked my eyes out. His shirt was pure white silk with bright red, blue, yellow and black stripes. His immaculate white flannel pants had the cuffs turned up just once. If he'd rolled 'em twice, he'd have been a hick. He wore a red bandanna knotted casually around his neck and a loud plaid cap on his head. In my small-town life he was the most tremendous personality I'd ever seen! His white buckskin shoes had thick red rubber soles and sported the widest white laces any two shoes could carry. I decided right then to copy that outfit from white buckskins to bandanna.

I had saved enough money to cover my expenses for the Open at Buffalo, but now I'd need to use that for the Canadian Open. The only item I could afford just then was the bandanna. The

MacFarlin Clothing Company did not have any in stock, but they ordered a supply for me.

When Andy Christy returned from Buffalo (he didn't come close to winning), he helped me get lined up for Toronto. He contacted his friend George Cummings, a former Canadian Open champion and asked him to make arrangements for me to enter. Cummings had played an exhibition match with Christy in my early days at the Country Club of Rochester and I had caddied for him. He remembered me. His protégé, Karl Keffer, winner of the Canadian Open in 1909 was to play at Toronto and would show me around. I took the boat at Charlotte, right near home, for Toronto. That was the longest trip I'd ever made and only the second time I'd been on a boat. I had once gone under Niagara Falls on the *Maid of the Mist*. I felt pretty big taking a boat all the way across Lake Ontario.

Karl Keffer met me at the dock and we went out to the Rosedale Golf Club where he introduced me around. I thought it mighty friendly of a former champion to take so much trouble for an unknown like me and I certainly appreciated it.

I didn't win. George Sargent was the new champion and J. M. Barnes the runner-up. The course was strange and new and different. At least that's what Karl Keffer said to me. But I knew I had placed eleventh because my game wasn't good enough to put me in the champion's shoes. There was one bright spot in that tournament for me. I finished one stroke ahead of Alex Smith, the grand old Scotsman who had won the National Open in 1906 with a score of 295 for 72 holes, breaking 300 for the first time in the history of golf in the United States. He'd won again in 1910.

I went back to the Country Club of Rochester and to my job as Christy's assistant. No one made any big noise about my playing in the Canadian Open. For one reason, I went on my vacation time and not too many people knew I was playing in a

21

tournament. And for another, who knew me? The members of the club had little interest in the game of golf outside their own competitions in their own area.

Their interest right then centered in a series of tournaments which had been set up by the Central League of New York, which included the amateurs of the leading clubs of such cities as Rochester, Syracuse, Elmira, Binghampton and Auburn. Since Owasco Country Club at Auburn had no regular pro, they asked me to come there and act as pro for the league tournament they had scheduled. Christy consented to let me go and I took with me one hundred clubs he and I had made up during the previous winter months. We set a price of $2.75 each on them.

For two hectic weeks at Auburn I was not only the pro, but the club manager, the bartender, the greens-keeper, the instructor and busy as all get out in the pro shop. I rose at four o'clock every morning and I kept going until late each night. I sold ninety-nine of the clubs we'd made and the hundredth I presented to a very beautiful young lady who admired my golf game and who became my dancing partner at a nearby lake pavilion on the few evenings I had an opportunity to indulge in any recreation. I made a hit with the members of the Owasco Country Club, too, for they insisted I stay on as their pro.

I think I might have taken their offer if, upon my return to Rochester, I hadn't been given a more interesting bit of news. Andrew Christy was leaving the Country Club of Rochester to accept the head pro job at the Equinox Club in Manchester, Vermont. Beekman Little, chairman of the greens committee and Thistle Club member, had the final decision on who would take over and he made my appointment definite.

So in 1912 I became pro and I asked George Christ, my former fellow caddie and baseball pal, to be my assistant. I gave my dad a job as greens-keeper, too. Here I was—nineteen years old, a real pro with an assistant, a salary of approximately $1200 for eight months of the year and a chance to make extra cash by giving lessons at two dollars an hour. I also collected a fee of $1.50 a month per set for keeping 200 sets of clubs clean during the season. Also through the winter we'd make clubs in the pro shop for sale during the summer. I really felt important. I'd come a long way from that job as a caddie in 1900 at ten cents an hour.

I was big and strong—almost six feet tall and around 175 in weight—and plenty healthy. I didn't smoke and I'd never taken a drink. In fact I never smoked a cigarette or took a drink until after I was twenty-six years old and had left Rochester.

I was a pro with a good job. Members of the club liked to play with me and treated me as a friend, but I still did not feel that I could walk in the front door of the club house to hoist a post-round glass or to enjoy a steak dinner. Rochester, like all other places where the game was popular, considered the pro, the paid golfer, as someone outside the social sphere.

I had broken that rule once, with the help of a member, Mr. Harry Strong. I was about nine at the time and had caddied many rounds of golf for him. He reached the finals in a tournament and was in a play-off with Mr. J. C. Powers. He hired me again, but for an unusual job. He took another caddie along with him when he teed off and sent me *inside* the club house to Herman, the bartender. I was to meet the two players at the second hole with a shaker of cocktails. That first shaker the two shared equally. I scurried back to Herman for a refill. At the fourth green I hid flat on my tummy in a nearby ditch waiting for them to arrive. This time, after their green shots and putts, Mr. Strong generously insisted that his opponent imbibe most of the liquid refreshment.

I followed this procedure for the entire match—dashing to the club-house bar for a refill in the shaker, then scuttling back to meet the players on alternate holes. In spite of my efforts and Mr. Strong's hospitality Mr. Powers won the match. By the time they had reached the last two holes they were both spraying their shots all over the course.

However, the play-off was most important to me because it gave me the unusual opportunity of seeing the inside of the beautiful and exclusive club house of the Country Club of Rochester. No other caddie had been able to wangle that!

CHAPTER IV

Brookline, 1913

> Great as he was as a golfer, Hagen was even greater
> as a personality—an artist with a sense of timing so
> infallible that he could make the tying of his shoe-
> laces more dramatic than the other guy's hole in
> one.
>
> —HERBERT WARREN WIND,
> *The Story of American Golf*
> [1948]

MY BOSSES at the Country Club of Rochester thought I was
out beyond my depth when I asked for a few days off to play in
the United States Open at Brookline in September of 1913. But
they gave me permission to go. I guess I was pretty cocky expecting to get anywhere in competition with the "big boys" of
golf. And there were plenty of them, both foreign and American
—for the British veterans, Harry Vardon and Ted Ray, chose
that particular year to make their invasion. I figured if I were
ever going to make a name for myself I'd better be getting
started. After all, I was twenty years old.

Actually when I sent in my entry that summer I believe I was
more concerned about the clothes I planned to wear than I was
about the kind of game I'd have to play. The outfit had cost
me plenty of money, ten dollars for the shoes alone! But I had
managed to copy Tom Anderson's get-up as closely as it could
be done. My pure silk striped shirt sported as many bright colors
as Tom's and I had that red bandanna knotted so casually
around my neck. My white buckskin shoes with thick red rubber soles were laced with the widest white laces I had been able
to find. And the white flannels . . . Well, I had the cuffs

25

turned up just once—perfect for the well-dressed golfer or any active sportsman.

Nine years later, when I returned to Florida after winning my first British Open, I had another experience with white flannels that was a far cry from that first pair I worked so hard to get. For in 1922 I was getting into the big money. I was giving lessons, playing maybe two exhibitions a day and a round each afternoon with a few friends. In Florida that winter I had made friends with a number of millionaires—Mr. Replogle, the steel magnate; Mr. Drake, the hotel tycoon; Mr. Henry Flagler, famous for the building and promotion of Florida real estate. They had a standing wager, in our daily foursome, of $5000 on the match. And on each hole I played the best ball of the three of them for a $500 Nassau on the side. On top of that, the one who took the licking paid me $200 for a lesson the following morning or just prior to our afternoon rounds. But all this golf meant I was changing white flannels at least twice a day to maintain the immaculate appearance I liked. It cost me $6 a pair to get them cleaned.

One day I happened to drop into a store along the Boardwalk where white flannels were selling for $5 a pair and I picked up a few pair on the spot and ordered a load more of them. From then on I used the soiled ones to tip and to get special favors from the bellhops at the Royal Poinciana in Palm Beach where I was living. I gave any boy an extra pair if he got me the name and pertinent information on any good-looking number, either widowed, divorced, or single, who'd checked into the hotel. I used this data very conveniently at five o'clock in the Cocoanut Grove Cocktail Lounge. I was all set up; and the best of the deal—I saved two dollars a day on cleaning bills, plus several hundred dollars on tips for the season.

However, I'd scratched hard to buy that first pair of white flannels and I rode the day coach to Boston in September of 1913. I checked in at the Copley Plaza, for I was determined to live "first class" in keeping with the outfit I planned to wear on the golf course. The manager gave me directions for reaching THE Country Club (as the golf club in Brookline was known) and I lost no time in getting out there.

In the locker room a small fellow was pulling on a bright sweater. I recognized him immediately, for he was the defending champion and I'd read plenty about him.

"You're Johnny McDermott, aren't you?" I asked. "Well, I'm glad to know you. I'm W. C. Hagen from Rochester and I've come over to help you boys take care of Vardon and Ray."

That brought some laughter, of course, and a lot of kidding from the pros who were listening, but I didn't mind. I was meeting and seeing the great of the game. I met Vardon and Ray, who'd both won the British Open Championship and Vardon was touted as the best player in the world. As I expected to become the best I decided to keep my eye on him. In fact, I stood around and gawked at him like any other greenhorn from the pastures.

Harry Vardon was a big man with huge hands. My own was practically lost in his handshake. He was reserved, quiet, with almost nothing to say. But I learned plenty from watching him swing a golf club. He had a much more compact and precise swing than I'd ever seen. He had it in a groove and I tried it out in practice and it worked for me too. I did not dare shift into the Vardon swing right then, but I did use it late in the tournament, when I had gone four over par for the first three holes in the final round.

I heard a little about Francis Ouimet in the locker room. The pros were not permitted in the club house proper, which must have made Vardon and Ray feel right at home. But Ouimet, who had won amateur tournaments around the state, was admitted and welcomed to the club house. He was a popular young fellow of nineteen and had a big following. However, since he was so young and an ex-caddie like me, few figured he

27

could beat the top pros in either the American or the foreign group.

Nobody gave me a tumble. I had no background other than my entry in the Canadian Open of the year before and that rated me no consideration as a contender. But in the end Francis Ouimet and I carried the fight for America and he won. Other contenders were Louis Tellier from France; Wilfred Reid of Budwell, Notts, England; Jim Barnes from Cornwall, England; MacDonald Smith, the Scotsman from Carnoustie. Barnes and Smith were then American professionals at Tacoma and Wykagyl respectively.

Francis Ouimet made golfing history that day and became a national sports hero. He put golf on the front pages of the newspapers . . . and in the roar of the crowds for the great golf he played in the Open that year all sidelights were forgotten. But I was in that championship tournament, too, and while I failed I was in there right up to the fourteenth hole of the final round. Through the thirteenth hole I was tied with Vardon and Ray, who were playing a few holes in front. I had a twelve-foot putt for a birdie 3 on the thirteenth green to go a stroke in front of the two Englishmen, but my ball rimmed the cup. My par 4 kept me even with them. To be honest I was not thinking about Ouimet who was playing behind me, for I was engaged in a chase after the big shots from over the seas.

I've rarely seen worse weather for a Championship. It rained and rained and continued raining . . . and the air was chilling and cold. On the final day of the play the fairways were a soggy mess. My handsome golfing outfit, wet and soiled, clung to me limply. But that had become unimportant.

By the end of the third round I was only two strokes behind Vardon and Ray, and a few people had begun to notice the kid from Rochester, among them that great golf writer H. B. (Dickie) Martin, my pal through all these years.

Perhaps I was nervous when I drove off in the final round

and pushed the ball to the right of the polo field. I couldn't get home in 2, made a weak chip and three-putted for a 6. Then I put my second shot over the green into a bunker at the second hole and took 5 . . . and at the long third my second, a brassie shot, landed on a stump which had slivers of wood like needles pointed upward. My ball was nicely teed up on the stump but in the rough far to the left of the fairway. However, I was in no mood to take penalty strokes after that 6, 5 start. I played the ball teed up on the stump figuring I might save two strokes, but it fell short into a rotten lie. It was so bad that I just got on the green with my fourth and by then I was really upset for I three-putted again.

I'm not easily rattled, but I certainly felt that way while I was making a 7 at the third hole in that final round of the National Open and watching my chances fade away. I wondered what they'd think of me back home. I was really discouraged but I couldn't give up, for here I was in the biggest event of my life to date and I had to continue to give it all I had.

Walking over to the fourth tee I began thinking about Harry Vardon's stance and swing. I needed a miracle. At the tee I took what I thought was the correct Vardon posture, and after three practice swings I hit a beautifully straight drive. But this fourth hole at THE Country Club provides a blind second shot. It only requires a five-iron off a good drive to get home, but the green is concealed by a hillock. I remember walking up to take an observation of the ground. That was really optimistic for a guy who had blown wide open on the last three holes.

I looked the ground over and happened to see a boy running out of the woods behind the green. I went back, took my five-iron and hit what I figured was a fine shot. I was sure it landed on the green and was wondering if I were close enough to hole a putt for a birdie.

When I walked to where I could see the green, however, my ball was not in sight. I had a hunch that boy I'd seen running

29

out of the woods had picked it up. I yelled at him, far down the fairway, and sent my caddie after him with orders to search him. Meantime I went hunting through the rough. Then my playing partner thought to look in the hole . . . and there was my ball nestled real snuglike. I had scored a deuce. I figured right then the two would take care of the seven on the previous hole.

After the deuce came a birdie 3 at the fifth. My Vardon drive was good to see. My second, a brassie, carried a row of sand traps in front of the green on the upper side of the slanting surface, rolled, stopped an inch short, directly in front of the cup. I figured that birdie took care of the 6 on the first hole. I was only one stroke over par. Lady Luck was falling for me in a big way.

At the next hole, a drive and a pitch, my drive was perfect. The second I hit a bit too firmly and the ball hit the flag at the top of the pole. But it caught in the folds of the flag and dropped down beside the cup. Another 3! I had lost four strokes to par in the first three holes and recovered them in the next three. Now I was back in the running again. At the short seventh my midiron shot left me twelve feet from the hole, putting for a birdie 2 . . . which I missed. I still was even with par, however.

The eighth, a par 4 hole, I managed to mess up by taking a 5. Coming to the ninth, a long par 5, I finally got on the green in 3, but I was putting badly and I wound up taking three putts. My chin dropped a bit and I felt sick. When I reached the tenth tee a few people who had heard of my run of 2, 3, 3, 3 from the fourth through the seventh wanted to know what I'd gone out in. I told them somewhat gruffly, wondering what difference it made now, "I'm out in 40."

My small gallery began buzzing, and one fellow said, "That's fine!"

"Fine," I thought disgustedly to myself. Then I asked the

30

man who'd made the remark, "What's fine about it?" He informed me that Vardon and Ray had both gone out in 42, which made me even with them and nine holes yet to play. The word got around and I began to pick up my first sizable gallery.

Spectators kept me informed about Vardon and Ray and when I reached the thirteenth green, I barely missed a twelve-foot putt that would have given me a one-stroke lead. Lady Luck left me at that hole and probably went over to take care of Francis Ouimet, who I've heard needed her badly about that time.

It's been forty-one years since that National Open at Brookline but every shot is as vivid in my mind as though it were yesterday. The penetrating drizzle of rain . . . the wet grass . . . my red-rubber-soled shoes slipping precariously on the soggy turf . . . my desperate shift into the Vardon swing . . . that fatal fourteenth hole.

My drive over the quarry with a boundary at the left was good enough, but I needed a long second shot to reach the green. Messengers brought back word that Vardon and Ray had each scored 4's—one under par at this hole. I felt I could not afford to drop a stroke behind, so I used a brassie and went all out for those great Britishers. I don't know if I used the Vardon swing or the Hagen swing. I just know I gave it everything I had. I topped the ball. It did not get off the grass . . . just skidded along throwing water in its wake.

I've seen it time and again in my dreams—that miserable sight—my ball sloughing through the water-soaked grass, spinning like an old water wheel. Now I really had to go for the green—this time with an iron. I wheeled on it so hard and fast I hooked it over to the wall on the left. It hit the wall and settled in the long grass between the wall and the fairway. I now had a niblick over a bunker to the green, and my ball was in very heavy wet grass.

31

My shot hit just at the top of the bunker, not two inches
from the clearing. But it hit in a place where black, pasty soil
used for the green had seeped along the edge of the bunker.
Then I watched the ball hit this muck and roll slowly back
into the trap. Fortunately the hunk of mud attached to the ball
was not on the side where I had to hit it. It still was a tough
shot. I figured the mud would detach itself when I played the
shot. I hit the ball to within fifteen inches of the hole, but the
mud had stuck tight. It was now on the very spot which my
putter would contact. Ordinarily that would have been an easy
putting distance.

Later I realized I should have used a mashie niblick to get
that ball into the hole. But I tried my putter, thinking if I hit
the ball hard enough it would flatten the attached mud and the
ball would hole. It didn't. The ball veered sharply to the right.
I took a 7 and rolled myself right out of the championship.

I played the last four holes in the same figures as Vardon and
Ray and finished with a 307, three strokes behind them . . .
the three strokes I lost on the fourteenth hole. I tied for second
place with MacDonald Smith, Jim Barnes and Louis Tellier.
Ouimet came in later to tie Vardon and Ray, and the three of
them played off a first-place tie the following day and finished
up in that order. A little luck on that fourteenth hole and I
would have been in that play-off.

Back in the locker room I got my gear together and after
assuring the fellows I'd see them next year, I went into Boston
and took the train for Rochester. I was disappointed I had
made such a mess of that crucial hole. I should have been right
up there at the top. But I wasn't.

However, after I reached home I wondered why I hadn't
stayed at Brookline and followed Vardon around the next day.
I could have learned plenty more from him. But I didn't think
about that until after I got home.

I finished out the rest of the golf season at the Country Club of Rochester, then grabbed the opportunity to take my clubs to Florida and play in some of the scheduled events down there. At Tarpon Springs I was the house guest of Mr. George Clemson of the Hacksaw Manufacturing Company, at Middletown, New York. Tarpon Springs was also the training site for the Philadelphia Nationals. Mr. Clemson, his son Dick and I daily met the baseball players shooting some golf after their training workout. Many were fairly good players—Chief Bender, Grover Cleveland Alexander, Gavvy Cravath, Pat Moran are among those I met and played with. Pat was the manager of the Phillies and he thought I had possibilities as a ball player. He told me to come and work out with the team.

He put me in right field in the practice games despite the fact that I insisted "outfield was no place for a pitcher." When I prepared to leave for Rochester in the early spring he invited me to join the Phillies' training camp the following winter. To me this appeared to be the turning point in my career. I promised him I'd be there.

If I could wangle a contract with the Phillies I'd be headed for the big time in baseball. After all, that had been my original ambition. Golf had just sidetracked me temporarily. Now I was back in the groove again.

> Golf is a game which can start a mental flurry in a second, but Hagen has won so many championships because in addition to fine physical skill . . . he has built up a philosophy which Fate can't overthrow. . . . It takes an avalanche of accidents to make him sore. An earthquake would hardly leave him grouchy. He seems to be happiest when there's a hard battle ahead and he must come from behind to win.
>
> —GRANTLAND RICE, *Collier's*
> [1925]

FATE has a strange way of stepping in and taking over just when a fellow thinks he's pretty well lined up with life. In my case Fate and newspaper men have sort of teamed together to give me splendid publicity or a push in the right direction at the opportune time. And it happened first in July of 1914.

Dutch Leonard and I were sitting in the pro shop at the Country Club of Rochester and I was bragging how I'd murder big-league pitching when I made good in the tryout with the Phillies. When winter training started I intended to be right there and ready.

While we were talking I saw Mr. Ernest Willard, editor of the Rochester *Democrat and Chronicle,* get out of his "glass house" electric and head for the shop. I knew he'd come to pick up his golf clubs for his vacation at Loon Lake, so I walked across the shop to get them for him.

"Aren't you going to enter the National Open at Chicago?" Dutch called to me.

"I'm not thinking of it," I said. "I'm going to work harder in baseball and let up on golf."

Mr. Willard overheard me and he repeated Dutch's question. I explained that I believed I could make the grade with the Phillies' team if I tried hard enough.

"Haven't you plenty of time for the Open and baseball?" he asked. "You did so well at Brookline last year, I think you should try again this year."

I told him I was sort of discouraged, that I'd begun to believe that golf was not my game.

"Rochester was mighty proud of you, Walter. You're the first pro we've ever had who has been able to qualify for the Open, let alone finish in a tie for second like you did. I'd like you to go to Chicago and win it."

He waited a few seconds, then said, "If you'll go, Walter, I'll pay all your expenses." He turned to Dutch. "And you, young fellow, if you can make the trip with Walter, I'll pay your expenses, too. Well, what do you say, boys?"

"I appreciate your offer, Mr. Willard, and I'll send in my entry to the National Open right away," I told him.

Yes, that did it. I thought I'd put all future golf competition out of my mind. I thought I was headed straight for the major leagues and baseball's Hall of Fame. But let a man express confidence in my ability as a golfer and I was right back in competition again. Then I remembered I'd told those fellows at Brookline I'd be back next year. Next year was here . . . and I had just three weeks to get ready for the Open in Chicago.

I worked harder than I'd ever worked in my life during the time which was left me, trying to perfect my game for another shot at the "big boys." I got my fancy golf outfit cleaned and ready with only one change, the white buckskin shoes with the red rubber soles. I'd slid all over the course at Brookline in the wet weather. Funny thing was that I'd only played golf in good, sunny weather until I went to Brookline. Now I bought a pair of hobnailed shoes for the 1914 Open. And I played in hobnailed shoes from that time on.

Dutch and I took the day coach to Chicago. We stopped at the old Great Northern Hotel. I'd never been out of the East before so just making the trip was quite an adventure. The night before the tournament started we blew ourselves to dinner at the best restaurant we could find. I forget the name, but the display window housed a huge red lobster. I'd never tasted lobster, so that's what we ordered, lobster and oysters. We ate plenty of lobster and oysters. Then we took in a movie. Before the picture was over my stomach pains began. By the time we reached the hotel I was howling in agony.

Dutch called the house physician about midnight and he gave me some pills. I continued to hold my head, rub my stomach and howl. He called the doctor again in the early morning and still I had no relief. I continued to be nauseated and retching with stomach pains. By dawn I was so weak I could scarcely stand. I told Dutch I didn't see how I was going to play a round of golf for a week, much less compete in a Championship tournament that day. He finally persuaded me to ride out to the club and see how I felt by starting time.

"For after all, Walter," he said, "Mr. Willard and your friends back home might have a little difficulty believing that lobster story."

The hotel doctor came once more, gave me some milk toast and aspirin and told me to take two more aspirin before I began to play . . . *if* I felt well enough to start.

Dutch and I rode the old South Shore Railroad out to Blue Island to the Midlothian Country Club. The day was sweltering hot and the heat plus the coal soot and cinders blowing in on me from the wide open screenless windows added to my discomfort. I felt terrible and kept wondering if I had the strength even to walk around the course.

In the locker room I changed to my fancy outfit and staggered out to the practice field to hit some shots. It hurt me to take a full swing. Both my head and my stomach were throbbing with pain and my body was sore all over. I hit a hundred or more balls and took two more aspirin. Funny thing, but my headache was gone. I told Dutch.

"Then you can start," he said cheerfully.

"I can start," I told him, "but I'm so sore I can scarcely swing a club."

I've never been famous as a golfer who was always down the middle of the fairway with his drives. But that day I was wilder than ever before or since. I was all over the course. After every drive I was in the rough. Yet on the recovery shots I was deadlier than the ptomaine from which I was suffering.

The first hole is over a pond. I took a painful full swing knowing I must carry this pond. I carried it all right. I carried it so far the pond was never in my line of flight. I was in the rough, but my recovery was on the green and two putts gave me a par 4. After that I rarely took more than one putt. The rest of the round gave me lots of practice where my day was spent . . . in the rough. But I finished in an unbelievable 68 and the gallery was buzzing with excitement because I had set a new course record. That round was a miraculous cure for my illness. I even decided against returning to that lobster restaurant to tell the proprietor what I thought of his joint.

I changed to street clothes and went out in front of the club house to look at the scoreboard. Listening to the gallery, hearing them talk about my breaking the course record, led me to believe I was strokes ahead of anyone else. I was sure my 68 would stick up like a mountain peak over all the others. I just wanted to give myself the satisfaction of seeing how far ahead I was. I felt wonderful. At least I did until I looked at the scoreboard. For breathing down my neck with a 69 was Francis Ouimet, defending champion since his sensational victory over Vardon and Ray at Brookline. And he was getting most of the attention from the gallery at Midlothian. And I stood looking at the scoreboard and thinking, "I haven't done anything." One stroke is nothing at the start of a National Championship.

I stuck to regular food like steak and potatoes for the rest of the tournament. And my game stayed hot. I was never headed; I led all the way. Ouimet kept the pressure on, but after my final round I had posted a score of 290. That 290 equaled the lowest score ever made up to that year in the United States Open history. George Sargent, a wonderful golfer, had shot that score in 1909, playing the Open at the Englewood Country Club.

But I needed that 290. For after I had completed my final round news came into the locker room that Chick Evans had a chance. When he reached the seventy-second hole, I joined the crowd watching him on the green. He needed to hole a chip shot to tie me. And just one half hour earlier I had been in the rough to the left of that green short of a trap and had exploded out on the green twenty feet from the hole. I sank the curving putt. Now, as Chick was trying to hole his chip shot I thought how lucky I had been to get that putt down. He made a gallant effort but missed by fifteen inches. I beat him out of the championship by that one putt. It hadn't appeared too important at the time, but now it was the biggest and best shot I'd made.

The morning after my record-breaking 68, the sports pages of the Chicago dailies carried a boxed announcement headlining my name: *W. C. Hagen!* My first taste of publicity and how I loved it! The papers spelled my name correctly that year and ever afterwards. In Boston the year before I had been mentioned briefly as W. C. *Hagin.*

Bob MacDonald, the great old-time Scottish pro from Dornoch, Scotland, and then pro at Buffalo, joined Dutch and me on our journey back to New York State via the day coach. All the trip home I held the championship medal clutched tightly in my hand. It was the greatest thing in my life. I hadn't thought to notify anyone when we were arriving in Rochester, so nobody met us. But back at the club house the pro shop was gaily decorated with flags, the club sported holiday bunting and a huge American flag was set up on the eighteenth green.

Considering my win at Midlothian in relation to the showing I had made at Brookline the year before, one fact impressed me. My mind had been so occupied with the pains in my stomach and head I had had no thought of worry about each shot I made. Even after that first day, I was so spent from physical weakness that I concerned myself chiefly with getting around the course and just taking my strokes, good or bad, as they came. I decided then that mental and physical relaxation during competition was the most valuable asset any golfer could possess. Concentrate on playing the best you can on each shot . . . if it's a good one, that's fine. If it's bad, forget it. I expected to make so many bad ones anyway. I had to recognize that fact and aim to get the good ones where they counted most.

I wouldn't recommend a dose of ptomaine poisoning as a method of forgetting to worry about a golf score, but it taught me to look at each round as a unit and to take individual bad shots in my stride.

I went back to my job as pro at the Country Club of Rochester. Back to keeping the golf shop, giving lessons and making golf clubs. But what a difference in my outlook. Here I was, twenty-one years old and Open Champion of the United States. I notified Pat Moran of the Phillies that I would *not* be in Florida for a tryout with the team. After all, I'd hit the big time in golf, so why bother with baseball?

Almost immediately the winning of the Open began to widen the horizons for me. I was invited to give exhibitions and to play in tournaments arranged by the various clubs. I even endorsed a few products, and this more than anything else made me realize the importance and the potentials of the title. I was fully aware of the weaknesses in my game. I began right then to study golf. I learned the rules forward and backward. Through the years that knowledge has rewarded me many times over. I also began to improve my form. I believed the public had a right to expect the best I could give. In those early exhibitions I was more nervous than a wagering spectator.

I had never been much concerned with form. I had concentrated on getting the ball where I wanted it. Imitating Vardon's stance and swing at Brookline had made me aware of the value of perfect posture and body rhythm such as he had developed. Also I had something of a sway and a very noticeable movement of my hips and knees . . . first forward, then backward. One writer at the time said I "started my drive with a sway and ended with a lunge." And I guess he was about right.

In modifying movement in my swing I tried first to eliminate the exaggerated swaying as much as possible. I found that if I began the backswing by taking the club away from the ball my hip action and pivot would take care of themselves. In doing this I was getting a semi-sway but at all times keeping my left eye focused on the ball, thus keeping my head still. Then my pivot became automatic. The larger arc I got with this swing enabled me to keep the head of the club on the ball longer during the follow-through.

During those months of practice, also, I tried to pave my swing with guards. What is a guard? Well, a guard is the method of controlling the power a golfer gets from the combined use of arms, hip action and the placement of the hands. Keeping the arms together and pinching the knees together in unison, with complete hand control of the club, allows the player to fade or slice intentionally by letting the left hand be the master. In drawing or hooking a shot the right hand becomes master. Movement plays a very important part throughout the swing. With a fade the hips go forward with the arms, while with a hook one must pivot sooner. Don't exaggerate this action for it's wise to retain enough energy for extra-curricular activity—perhaps for some night work on a fancy tango or a few lively steps of the Charleston.

Guards are necessary throughout the game of golf, particularly when the prevailing wind is on one side or the other—or when trees block the way. This last, over a period of years, was my biggest problem, for I found myself in the woods so continuously I began carrying a hunting license. So I practiced using guards by placing two newspapers at given distances on the fairway, and spent long hours learning to control my hooks and slices.

Needless to say, I did not acquire the rhythm and ease and smoothness I desired within the next few months or even the next few years. But I continued to work on it, polishing, practicing and perfecting . . . gaining in some small measure as the time passed.

Through the years I've been accused of dramatizing shots— of knowing just which club I intended to use, just how I intended to make the shot—then holding up the game or the match by carefully scrutinizing the turf, the sky, my opponent or even the caddie. Of making the difficult shots look easy and the easy shots look difficult. Only that last came naturally, believe me. Well, I always figured the gallery had a show coming to them. I deny I ever held up a game by any such shenanigans, but I don't deny playing for the gallery. I don't deny trying to make my game as interesting and as thrilling to the spectators as it was possible for me to make it.

I had the same feeling for the spectator in those early years, but I will admit my ability to put on a good performance increased through time and experience. I loved the excitement of the tournaments, the admiration of the gallery, the words—complimentary or otherwise—tossed my way by the sports writers and radio commentators. All these helped to build me into the international sports figure I became and to hold me there for thirty years of competitive golf.

Competition was always important to me. I played better golf under pressure, whether from an opponent or the elements or lack of money. When I was short of cash I could always win. When I needed a title to enhance my value in exhibitions, I went out and got it. The healthier my economic situation, the lousier I played. But give me some good stiff competition or a lack of the green stuff and I could usually shoot a winning score.

Back in 1914, with the championship medal from the USGA Open clutched in my fist, I was just starting for the top as a professional golfer. Even in those early days, I was brash enough to wonder where else there was for me to go. Too late now for me to go back to school! The many hours I spent studying myself and my game, learning the fine points of golf, perfecting my swing—those were wonderful and purposeful hours for me. And the amounts of cash dribbling in from endorsements and exhibitions were sauce for my first big thick steaks.

I was twenty-one and the world was my oyster. Only my dad could see no future ahead for me. He considered knocking the little white ball around a pasture a silly way to make a living. Although I always thought the British tough people to convince —you had to win their Open more than once before they acknowledged your game was championship caliber—my dad was tougher. He was seventy years young before he ever saw me play in a Championship.

Making a million—or having the return of his laundry delayed by fiscal factors—nothing bothers Hagen. . . . He could relax sitting on a hot stove.
—TOMMY ARMOUR, *The American Golfer*
[1935]

SYNDICATE GOLF was rather common in those early days of my career. Three or four pros would team together and share their combined winnings evenly, thus assuring at least expense money for each of them, since prizes as a general rule were small. If a pro won several Opens he still did not have too much take-home pay, but he was making a name for himself. Actually that's what some of the boys are doing today when they list how many events they play and how much money they win, instead of how many Championship trophies carry their names. A great number of today's golfers have never won a Championship, but they manage to keep their names in print.

Syndicate golf had a second asset in those days. It guaranteed the appearance of all those in the syndicate for each event. Today there's no syndicate golf, but there is appearance money posted for each individual player, which is security that the needed number of players will be on hand for each scheduled event. Appearance money is insurance for the club or the sponsor.

I never liked syndicate golf, and after several brief experiences I never played it again. On my first trip south in the winter of 1913 I teamed up with Tommy Kerrigan, a young pro from Boston. We tried the winter circuit hoping to cut in and get some of the tail-end money. The bigger prizes were taken by name players like Mike Brady, Gil Nicholls, Alex Smith, Tom McNamara, Johnny McDermott and Jim Barnes. Rookies like Tommy and me were outcasts.

Those big-time pros were very exclusive in the reservations they made for the various events and the only way we could learn their next stop was through the porters at the hotels. At each hotel, we'd tip the porter for information on advance reservations made by the "big boys." A trap, similar to a station wagon, met them upon their arrival in each town. Tommy and I finagled rides with them to the hotels, and since they didn't talk to us, we tried to build up our nuisance value.

"I believe they should take us into their syndicate," I'd say to Tommy in a loud voice.

"Sure, today's the day, Walter," he'd boom back at me.

Our daily conversation bored them, nothing more. But they began to get a bit upset when we cut in and took some of the in-between money.

Later I made it a rule to play for all or nothing. I went into every tournament as a lone wolf and the fierce competition I met made a better and a much more consistent player out of me. After my win of the Open at Midlothian I had numerous opportunities to join forces with groups of the big pros for syndicate golf. Instead I jumped at the invitation to tour the Northwest with Jim Barnes in the winter of 1914-1915. We'd each be on our own and what each made, he'd keep.

We played a number of exhibitions in the larger Western cities, including Jim's home club at Tacoma, Washington, where he had been pro for some years. We entered the Panama Exposition Championship at Ingleside Club in San Francisco in January. The first $1000 prize in the history of American golf was awarded the winner of that championship—*me!* I played the first nine holes for a score of 30 and nobody could catch me after that getaway. I finished with a 66.

I was getting a big kick out of all the traveling golf afforded me. San Francisco is one of the cities I'll never forget. It was a tough place. The Barbary Coast had an international reputation. During the Exposition championship matches Carl Anderson and I took in the sights and wound up in a night club where the entertainment convinced us the operators were paying well for police protection. As we were leaving the joint I was a couple of stairs above Carl when a man dashed up past me and grabbed for the door. A bullet whizzed too close to my neck and the guy dropped on the top step. I hurdled his body rolling down the steps, and neither Bannister nor Landy could have caught Carl and me as we got out of the place and sprinted up the steep hill to safer ground. I read the next day that the murder we witnessed was the twenty-eighth committed in the Barbary Coast area that month.

That thousand-dollar prize money put me financially sound for the rest of the tour, and winning from such top golfers as young Chick Evans, veterans Alex Smith and Jim Barnes, gave me a lot more confidence. I was pretty well satisfied with myself right about then, for on top of the prize money, A. G. Spalding & Bros. made me a good offer to play their golf ball. I was now a "big shot." My name and my use of a product meant profit to the manufacturer and to me. I gathered in a few more prizes during that winter season but none so large as the Panama Exposition prize.

One fact I want to make clear. When I endorsed a product and allowed the manufacturers to use my name, it meant I definitely used that product. There was a period when I played a ball designated by a friend of mine as the "iron ball" while other pros used what we termed the "fast ball." That ball probably cost me many a shot. One time in particular at Oakmont,

Pennsylvania, in a National Open, I had hit a tee shot at the sixth hole which buried itself in the top of a bunker some 200 yards away. Any one of a number of other balls, hit by the identical blow, would have carried the bunker and I would have had an easy shot to the green. As it was I had to hack my ball back into the trap, then out, then onto the green for an ultimate 6.

I never put down the ball of another manufacturer when I was obligated to play a certain ball. However, in Great Britain I was released from the contract and could take my pick of the smaller British makes. During those years the difference in the balls shows that my American years were lean ones compared to those I spent in England, where I won four British Opens.

The 1915 National Open was scheduled for Baltusrol early in June. My game was as well rounded out as I could expect when the date rolled around, but I felt I was not tournament perfect. That's the way I liked to feel about my game at the beginning of a Championship. I have never gone in too much for playing practice rounds on a Championship course. If I got there in time I might play the course a few times. But as most everybody learned as the years passed, I usually arrived with just enough time to swing a club before teeing off.

At Baltusrol I did manage to play some practice rounds but nothing compared to the way Gil Nicholls and Jerry Travers were working out. Gil had been playing top golf to win four events in the South and when time came for the National Open he was hot as blazes. The week before the Championship he played the course every day and his scores were consistently 70 or less. No one else was doing anywhere near that well.

The sports writers, watching him play every day, had naturally set him up as favorite. They didn't overlook me but my practice-round scores were high compared to Nicholls'. Francis Ouimet was another favorite and neither Mike Brady nor Chick Evans, runner-up to me at Chicago, were considered lightly.

46

Alex Smith and Tom McNamara were there, too. The only foreign entry was little Benny Sayers, pro at North Berwick near Muirfield, Scotland. He definitely threatened our top players.

We were all possibilities but amateur Jerry Travers finished with a score of 297 and became the new National Open champion. Jerry was considered a better match than medal player and he surprised both the experts and the gallery. And I was dethroned . . . I tied for tenth place.

The American pros had rated it more or less an accident that Ouimet had beat Vardon and Ray in 1913, but they began to worry when Jerry Travis copped the Open title in 1915. And it didn't end there. For the following year, 1916, amateur Chick Evans took the Open championship at the Minnikahda Club in Minneapolis. I placed seventh.

But if the American pros were worried, the Scots and the British felt worse. Since Johnny McDermott, a homebred American pro had won both in 1911 and 1912, and I had taken it in 1914, that made a total of six years since a foreign pro had come out victorious in the United States Open.

Actually since McDermott's win in 1912 I was the only American pro who won through a period of ten years, for I won both in 1914 and 1919. Jim Barnes, pro but not homebred, won in 1921 and I finished second by nine strokes, tied with my old pal Fred McLeod. That Open was played at Columbia Club, Chevy Chase, Maryland and I holed one of the longest putts of my golfing career. President Warren G. Harding was sitting directly back of the hole, which was on the extreme back edge of the green. I motioned to him with a wave of my hand, aimed at him and holed the putt. He got a big kick out of it. Then in 1922 along came cocky young Gene Sarazen to become the second homebred American pro to win the USGA Open since 1912.

But I did pretty well in 1916. Even though I made no important contribution to golf in the National Open I did win both the Western Open at Blue Mound in Milwaukee and the Metropolitan Open at Garden City, Long Island. These rated second only to the National Open in importance.

World War I had ended golf for the British players and we were beginning to feel the effects over here. H. B. Martin suggested a plan for our golfers to raise money for the Red Cross and the idea was sponsored by the Professional Golfers' Association. Exhibitions were arranged for various clubs in the East and individual golfers with strong drawing power were scheduled to play. Members of the clubs bid at auction for the privilege of caddying for their favorite pro . . . and the balls were also auctioned off at the end of each match. Admission was charged for the matches and all money derived given to the Red Cross. I was invited to play in most of these exhibitions and this helped build my reputation as a golfer. Although these Red Cross exhibitions at first included only the professionals, the schedules were later arranged to bring in outstanding amateurs. During the years the matches were played we raised more than a million and a quarter dollars for war relief. I was proud that $125,000 was the direct result of my own efforts.

Life wasn't all golf for me. For some months in 1916 I had been seeing quite a lot of Margaret Johnson, the attractive daughter of George Johnson, owner of the Clinton Hotel in Rochester. Some of my pals humorously insisted I called for her with a golf club in one hand and an assortment of hard candies in the other . . . and that I spent the time waiting for her to appear by chipping the candy into cuspidors spaced around the lobby. Nevertheless, I was in love. On January 29, 1917, we were married in the rectory of St. Mary's Church by the Reverend Simon FitzSimons. Erickson Perkins owned a bungalow on the grounds of the Country Club of Rochester and he turned it over to us for living quarters.

I was very serious about golf and my wife was strictly social. She liked parties and people. The small cottage was usually filled with guests, particularly over the week ends. None of this activity interested me too much, but it bothered me not at all. I could sleep through a cyclone and relax with a brass band playing in the same room with me.

By the middle of April America was in the war for sure. Despite all the war activities the winter of 1917 was a big year for golf. Margaret and I went to Florida where I was pro at the Palma Ceia Golf Club at Tampa and I played a lot of golf at Belleair, both in pro tournaments and exhibitions. On January 11, 1918 my son Walter, Jr., was born and that event made the year a most important one in my life.

Although the draft board had classified me in Class B because of my wife and young son, I felt I wanted to make a more active contribution. I tried to enlist in the Air Force but was turned down. In fact, the draft board suggested that the money I helped raise through golf had more value than my entry into the armed services.

Those war years brought in more money through golf than we'd ever dreamed could be made. This was in fact the beginning of admission charges to golf championships, both amateur and professional. While all this money went to war relief agencies, it did prove that hundreds of golf spectators would pay just to follow their favorite golfers around the course.

Not until Skokie in 1922 was a regular championship arranged with admission charges for the gallery as an experiment. That first trial was not entirely smooth, but it did forecast the ones to follow when the clubs holding tournaments could make rules and regulations to solve the problems uncovered by the Skokie experiment.

Spectators grew to like the idea of paying admission, of having the matches staged and the crowds controlled. Thus the championships could be planned for better viewing for the gallery and for better and more comfortable playing by the competing golfers. Charging admissions for the big matches gave the clubs the cash to keep the greens and fairways in good playing condition, helped build more and higher prizes for the golfers and kept the Association going strong with deposits in the treasury. The USGA made the plans and the suggestions, while the member clubs organized their rosters into crews to man the ropes, teach the galleries tournament etiquette and collect the gate receipts.

In 1914, just after I won my first Open, I received $75 for playing an exhibition and that was the standard price offered a pro at that time. When I found that I was somewhat in demand I raised my fee to $100 and then to $150, just prior to our exhibitions for the Red Cross. The publicity accorded the Red Cross matches made it much easier for me to ask, and to get, an even higher fee after the war. I raised my charge to $200 and then to $300.

Before the war prizes were made up from contributions of the club members into a kitty to pay the pros and finance the meet. The dollar admission tickets for the Red Cross educated both the gallery and the club to potentials of gate receipts.

Gate receipts opened an entirely new financial setup for the professional golfer. We eventually began to receive increasingly higher fees for our exhibitions, based upon the appeal and power of the individual to bring in the crowds. Why did I play for the galleries? Why did I dramatize my game? Because I was one of the first to realize that golf could pay big if the gallery came to see me . . . win or lose. For as I said earlier, all tickets were the same price regardless of where the fan's sympathies lay. I intended to be a drawing card as long as I stayed in the game. And the way it looked to me, I'd be in there for a good long time.

However, back in 1918, gate receipts for the players had not been inaugurated. We played for the varying amounts of money dribbled into the kitty by the club members and were glad to take what we could.

The kind of life I lived as a pro golfer—playing exhibitions, entering the various scheduled PGA and USGA Championships, following the winter circuit, going any place and every place where the sun was shining and the fairways green—was not conducive to a satisfactory family life. Margaret and I remained together until the early spring of 1921. At that time our marriage was dissolved.

The best that today's bunch can offer in the way of gallery-conning color, at a time when the tournament schedule begs for color, is Demaret's pink hats, yellowish green slacks and lavender shoes. Walter Hagen could put more color than that into merely handing a club back to his caddie. Like the day he hit a $3000 putt and, while the ball was still rolling, regally tossed the putter back to his caddie. Or the day he arrived at a golf course wearing last night's tuxedo and this morning's hangover—and shot a 67. . . . Hagen's [kind of color] played a part in the winning of championships.

—JACK O'BRIAN, *Esquire*
[1954]

I'VE ALWAYS had a yen for cars—the long powerful expensive ones. After I sold the Indian motorcycle I owned a series of secondhand masterpieces, among them an Overland, a Stephens-Duryea, a Chalmers and finally the high point to me—a Chandler painted an eye-socking orange and black checkerboard design. I bought the Chandler just before I won the Open at Midlothian in 1914.

Through the years, as I was able to indulge in this luxury, I've owned some of the best and the most beautiful cars ever to come off the production line. I was the first to own a Madam X sixteen cylinder Cadillac—and it was the first Madam X produced. The way I came to own it gave me a good laugh.

Larry Fisher, of the famous Fisher brothers of Detroit, was

president of Cadillac Motor Company at that time and he invited me up to his Maplewood Lodge on Thousand Islands Lake for some fishing. In the meantime I had played a couple of exhibition matches and I planned to pick up a new car for the drive up there. Larry suggested that I go out to the Cadillac plant, select a car and drive it right off the line.

The plant manager showed me the new touring car which I did not want. Then he showed me the first Madam X and explained, "Mr. Fisher took this first one. But I'll show it to you. If you like it, we'll bring one up to the lodge for you."

I looked at that handsome Madam X, liked it at once and told the fellow, "Bring one up for Mr. Fisher. I need to get up there. He doesn't. He's already there."

He protested that Larry's initials were on the door. "Take 'em off," I said, "and put mine on. I'll wait."

I pulled up into the driveway of the lodge about four o'clock in the afternoon. Some fourteen fellows were lined up at the bar enjoying Larry's special cocktail, an old-fashioned.

"Well," I called to them, "I'm just in time for a little hoot!" But Larry immediately insisted on knowing what style car I'd chosen and led everybody out to look at it. His eyes popped when he saw the Madam X.

"Hey," he said, "that's my car!"

"You told me to pick the one I wanted," I told him casually. "Well, this is it."

"But it has my initials on it," he protested.

"W. C. H.," I read to him slowly. "That's me."

He laughed then and frankly I think he approved of my choice and was complimented I had selected the car he liked best, too.

I got four miles to the gallon with that Madam X and drove it over 75,000 miles playing exhibitions. I was living at the Book-Cadillac Hotel then and the doorman always reserved the choice parking space for me—right smack in front of the hotel.

Actually this liking for cars may have subconsciously influenced the decision I made in the summer of 1918.

I played in the North and South Open at Pinehurst that spring and a fellow, Al Wallace, purchased my ticket in the auction pool for $750, making me the favorite against Jim Barnes, Jock Hutchison, Mike Brady and other big stars of the tournament. Tommy Kerrigan was my playing partner in the final round.

Al Wallace followed me around worrying like mad about his bet, for I was joking and clowning around with Tommy and the gallery . . . really having fun. However, I won for him. He made me a present of $500 from his winnings and asked if I'd ever heard of the Oakland Hills Club near Detroit. I had not.

He explained that the now famous course was just about to open under the sponsorship of Norval Hawkins and Joseph Mack, two of the greatest promoters who ever lived. Hawkins, as head of sales for the entire Ford Motor Company, was reputed to make a dollar on every Ford rolling off the production line. Automotive talk had it that Ford was producing better than 900 cars a day. Mack owned a huge printing company. Al Wallace had joined the Oakland Hills Club as a charter member and was enthusiastic about its future. He asked if I'd come down to Detroit within the next few days and talk to Hawkins and Mack about the pro job.

I drove down there in a smart Lozier sports model and slammed on the brakes at the entrance to the Detroit Athletic Club. I leaped over the side of the car and entered the building that was to become more familiar to me than any other building in the world.

Mr. Hawkins and Mr. Mack were friendly as could be and they offered me every inducement to take the job, except the salary I wanted. I think there was possibly $1500 difference between what I wanted and what they were set to pay. We couldn't settle the deal, so Al Wallace walked back down the

54

Three fellows named Walter Hagen
(see the dedication to this book).

A typical scene showing me at Cadillac, Michigan, in the throes of literary composition. "Let's not be in a hurry to start this book. There's plenty of time."

Harry Vardon was a big man, and my own hand was practically lost in his handshake.

H. B. "Dickie" Martin in 1918—my pal then, and through all the years. He was with me on my first trip to England, in 1920.

I met Ted Ray for the first time at Brookline in 1913, but this was some seven years later.

White flannels with the cuffs turned up just once—perfect for the well-dressed golfer in 1913.

I led all the way at Midlothian in 1914 to win my first United States Open.

On the last hole at Midlothian, I had a birdie-3. That gave me a 292 total for 72 holes, and I needed it, for Chick Evans only finished one stroke behind me. George Easterbrook took this unusual series of shots showing me driving on that final hole, taking my second shot (a short pitch out of the rough), and lining up the 10-foot putt which dropped for the championship.

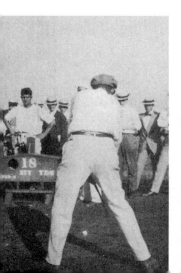

They always said I started my shots with a sway and ended with a lunge, and I guess they were about right.

I've always had a yen for cars—the long, powerful, expensive ones.

corridor with me from the Grill Room where we'd been lunching. They called him back for a moment, then we went on to the men's lobby. I was doing plenty of thinking.

When we reached the street I told Al, "Those are two of the toughest birds I've ever talked to. It's a lousy deal they're offering me, but this is a great town. I know you and I could have plenty of fun here. Maybe I'll come anyway."

Al grinned at me, "Well, let's settle it now. I'll guarantee the amount you asked in full."

I learned later that they'd called Al back to tell him they thought I was right for the job and they didn't want to lose me. That if all other persuasion failed, he was to agree to anything I asked.

Detroit was booming when I hit the town in 1918. The atmosphere was entirely different from Rochester. The few families with established social position were put into the background by the power and money of the automobile men and their wives. The city was rugged, vibrant and growing. Men like Edsel Ford, Larry Fisher and his brothers, Tom Webber, Walter Chrysler and Fred Zeder were piling up their millions and making their own society. They took me in as one of their own. I was a golf champion and a good fellow and that was enough for them. I rated right along with Ty Cobb of the Tigers in the eyes of the great sports fans of Detroit.

The Oakland Hills Golf Club was a popular gathering spot for wealthy and new socially prominent families. And I was as welcome in the club as any member. This was quite a change from my position as a pro in Rochester. In Detroit men were judged on what they had accomplished, not on what their families had set up for them as in the Country Club of Rochester.

The course actually was in the making. The tees and the greens were in the construction period and as yet there was no fairway. One of my jobs was teaching golf. And my instructions from Hawkins and Mack were to line up every pupil as a

55

prospective member, as well as a prospective real estate buyer. I had a queer way of teaching, I guess—the same I've always used. I'd have the pupil take a couple of practice swings, then I'd grab the club from his hand and spend the rest of his paid-for time showing him how it should be done. The guy was darned lucky who managed to get that club from my hand before his time was up.

Although Detroit was wonderful to me, I was very homesick for Rochester those first few months. Detroit was a busy, rushing, bustling city. I missed the quiet slow-moving traffic in the streets of Rochester. I missed the countryside where Margaret and I had lived in our little cottage. I missed the huge trees and the meadows and the little brook that ran through Corbett's Glen. I even missed the telephone poles on the road to the Country Club of Rochester. Detroit was a long jump for me and it took me a while to get over that homesick feeling. But when I did get over it, life in my new home city hit me big!

I played in the Florida events in the winter of 1919 and did exceptionally well. I felt I was in better shape physically and mentally for the try for the Championship than I had ever been. And I particularly wanted to win another National Open, if only to prove that my win at Midlothian in 1914 had not been just a lucky accident. I spoke of this to several friends and they agreed that if I didn't win the Championship that year, I never would again.

I arrived in Boston plenty early, but I didn't get much practice on the Brae Burn course. Missing the practice didn't bother me too much, for practice always took some of the zip out of me. I preferred to be keen, fresh and eager when play actually started. I've been lucky in having the physical stamina which makes this possible no matter what the circumstances. And believe me, I needed that iron-man physique for the Brae Burn course. My friend Al Jolson and his company were in Boston playing *Sinbad* and most of my time was taken up with meeting pals and having parties each night.

Mike Brady had been picked to win and being from Boston he was really popular. However, seventy-two holes found us tied with a score of 301. The eighteen-hole play-off was scheduled for the following morning. A farewell party with Jolson and his troupe had been arranged for the evening and naturally I wanted to be there. The party lasted all night . . . champagne, pretty girls, jokes and laughter . . . no sleep.

In the small hours of the morning I recalled that I had an important date within a few hours. I dashed back to my hotel for a quick shower, a bit of breakfast and fresh clothing. Then I wheeled my big Pierce Arrow out to Brae Burn for the play-off. I found Mike out there. He'd been hitting practice shots for more than an hour.

We tossed for the honor and Mike won. The first hole, a straight par 4 running slightly downhill from the club house, had a brook crossing just in front of the elevated green. I watched Mike taking a couple of swings with his driver. The sun appeared unusually bright on the white ball. And every movement struck me as amusing. While he was still taking practice swings I jogged into the grill to bend a quick elbow. We each made a 4 on that first hole.

Mike was pretty serious about the play-off and had his shirt sleeves rolled high. As he prepared to drive off the second tee, I said, "Mike, if I were you I'd roll down my sleeves."

"Why?" he asked grimly.

"All the gallery will see your muscles quivering," I told him. He did just what I expected—hooked a wild shot deep into the trees on the left. Now he had a 6 for the second and I took a 4.

Those eighteen holes were hard fought all the way. The first rhubarb came on the tenth. I had absent-mindedly picked up a matchbox while looking over a short approach shot. The box was over two club lengths from the ball and well over sixty feet from the hole. Midway on the next hole an official, Fred Hoyt, called me on the twenty-yard-from-the-hole rule which made a two-shot penalty automatic.

A brother professional who was following me volunteered the information to me that Mike had done the same thing on the ninth with a small stone. I stalled off Hoyt. We went on playing the thirteenth, but at the fourteenth tee I called Hoyt over and told him about Mike. He asked Mike about the incident and Mike admitted he had picked up a stone on the ninth but he wasn't aware of the exact location of the stone or its distance from the ball.

The officials suggested we go over and measure both our supposed violations, but I said, "After this hole," for I realized we'd then be closer to the ninth where Mike's incident had happened. That was a little fast thinking on my part. When we'd holed our putts Mike and the officials went over to study his possible violation while I relaxed on a bench and smoked a cigarette. I needed every minute of rest I could grab—this being the morning after the night before!

"Well, what's the verdict?" I asked when they returned.

"Mr. Brady admits a two-shot penalty. Let's look at yours."

"Never mind that," I told Fred Hoyt. "Mike, were you penalized two strokes?"

He admitted he was.

"All right, then," I said, "I'll take two, also."

I was trying to be as unconcerned as possible about the entire deal. But I certainly did not want to win a National Open Championship on penalties.

Going up to the seventeenth I was still two strokes ahead of Mike because of the first two holes and his "quivering muscles." And by this time, too, playing was not my only problem. I was

58

having a darned difficult time just staying awake. The seventeenth is a tricky hole, calling for a draw shot off the tee. I skied my drive and the ball sank in the sandy loam to the right, completely out of sight.

Hoyt would allow only Mike, me and our caddies to hunt for the ball, while he stood watch in hand, ready to call the five-minute rule for a lost ball. Mike and I wandered around sticking our fingers into the sand . . . and here Mike's sportsmanship was displayed. He found the ball and called me over.

I demanded the right to identify the ball. If I played it, taking more than two shots, and it wasn't mine I'd be disqualified. The official protested and I insisted, knowing the rules would back me up. So many different stories have been told about this incident that I'm glad to clear it up. Neither Mike nor any official touched that ball or cleaned it. I picked it up, found it to be my ball, cleaned it off and placed it gently . . . but gently, back in the hole. Now I could see it and hit it. I wasn't worried about what the officials were screaming at me concerning rules, for I had learned them too well in those days in Rochester after my first Open win. I took a 5 on the seventeenth to Mike's 4. We each took a 4 on the last hole and once again I was the USGA Open champion by just one stroke.

That "identification of the ball" rule remained in effect until November 18, 1953. Then the United States Golf Association announced a change becoming effective on January 1, 1954. Now if a ball is covered by sand, fallen leaves or the like the player may "remove as much thereof as will enable him to see the top of the ball." If he plays the wrong ball from a hazard, there is no penalty. But the old rule saved my score in 1919, for I could never have made a decent shot with my ball buried in four inches of sandy loam.

Back again in Detroit with the hearty congratulations of my friends ringing in my ears I decided I was wasting my time as a mere golf pro. I asked Al Wallace one day why I shouldn't come down to his brokerage office and sell all those friends some securities.

My career as a broker was short and far from sensational. One of my shrewder deals concerned an order for 5000 shares of a very prominent automotive stock which had a habit of gyrating wildly in those days. I'd picked up the order as the result of a nineteenth-hole discussion over the previous week-end.

Several days later the cashier in Al's office suggested to me that there'd been no deposit for payment or protection of the shares. I told him not to worry, I'd call my pal who had placed the order and get it straightened up pronto. The following morning when the cashier checked with me again, I really set him back on his heels.

"My pal says there is no use putting up any money," I explained casually, "for he intends to sell it in a couple of days, after he makes a few points profit."

It sounded reasonable to me, but I have the feeling Al Wallace welcomed my departure from the brokerage business. Perhaps that was the idea he had in mind when he financed my first trip to Great Britain to try the British Open in 1920.

I had tentatively decided in Florida the winter before that I'd go to England for their Open, but two factors were against my play: money to finance the trip and ship reservations. Al had now offered to supply the funds and a short time later a friend in New York obtained accommodations on board ship for me. This last was really an accomplishment, for in the first months after the war ocean travel had become so popular steamship companies could scarcely meet the demand of overseas voyagers.

My stock as a golfer was really high right then, for I held not only the National Open championship, but also the Metropolitan Open, the Western Open, the North and South Open and the West Coast of Florida Open—all important events in the golf world.

Another decision I made that year had no precedent in professional golf. As pro at the Oakland Hills Golf Club I found it increasingly difficult to take care of the golf shop responsibilities, give lessons to members and continue to make all exhibitions, the Championships and other such activities as my position in golf demanded. Furthermore, I was getting darned tired waiting for the grass to grow on the fairways.

I decided to give up my job and become a full-time "businessman golfer." I figured I couldn't do justice to a club and follow golf as a business, too. I could concentrate on playing if I left the club. I felt the revenue from exhibitions would be sufficient to compensate for the pro job. This decision of mine caused considerable discussion among both the press and my fellow pros. Most of them were against it, believing I could never make it pay. I suppose my idea originated during the Red Cross exhibitions, when I discovered a great demand for my appearance. Never again did I take on a steady pro job at any club.

H. B. Martin, golf writer for the New York *Globe*, who had booked me for the Red Cross exhibitions, was doing publicity at Belleair, Florida, during the winter months. He was sold on the idea of my going abroad to play in the British Open. I asked him to go along. His paper consented and he was the first American newsman to cover a tournament in Great Britain. I had a special reason for wanting Dickie Martin on this first trip with me. In 1912 Johnny McDermott had received a very bad deal from the British press. I wanted to be sure I had a writer with me who could be on hand to see and to write a true account for the American newspapers. I wasn't taking any chances on having a bad press on my first trip.

Dickie planned not only to write his stories for the *Globe*— he arranged the same sort of service for the Bell Syndicate, a column ghosted for me through fifty newspapers. In a sense I had my own publicity manager, and this, too, was decidedly an innovation in golf. Of course, Bobby Jones had O. B. Keeler, but their arrangement was quite different, born of the newsman's admiration and his enthusiasm for the young golfer and not of Bobby's desire to make money out of golf.

This was the setup we planned, but when Dickie and I arrived in New York to claim our reservations we learned that the little boat on which we were booked to sail had already departed, due to a change of schedule. However, the Cunard Line found space for us on one of their big ships, the *Mauretania*. This was a fortunate break since lovely Constance Talmadge of the famous movie Talmadge sisters was also a passenger.

Dickie and I had concentrated on getting to England and had completely overlooked hotel reservations once we reached London. Connie asked where we intended to stay and when she learned of our predicament, she explained that she had suites at both the Carlton and the Savoy. Since she had decided to stay at the Savoy we were welcome to her suite at the Carlton. Having a glamorous screen star offer me her reservations at one of London's best hotels seemed like a lucky omen for my trip abroad.

At the station in London Dickie and I were met by Bob Howard, golf writer for the *Daily Mail*. He wanted an interview and since we were busy claiming luggage I suggested he meet us for dinner later. So several hours passed before we were seated at a table in a popular restaurant he had named for the meeting.

His first question, over his lobster and beer—a combination of food as silly as his question—was, "What do you think of Deal links, Mr. Hagen?"

I told him what he already knew, that this was my first trip to England and of course I had never seen Deal or any other foreign links. I explained that I had picked up a magazine on board ship which carried a layout of the course at Deal, but owing to the fact the map did not show the undulations I couldn't make a definite statement. However, presuming it to be fairly flat and knowing the bogey of the course to be 78, it would be rated par 72 in our American method.

"Do you like to pitch and run to the green?" he asked.

"Can you play either one?" I asked.

"Yes," he said.

I told him I preferred pitching to the flag.

"How do you like putting . . . a fast or a slow green?" he inquired.

"I prefer a fast green," I explained, "because I happen to be the type of golfer whose best touch is with a putter." No one could outputt me, but I didn't tell him that.

Substantially that was the interview. He left us and we finished dinner and returned to the Carlton. I was looking forward eagerly to making a few practice rounds at Deal the next day. I had high hopes of taking that famous British Open Cup back to the United States with me.

Hagen has shown he can win with a smile and lose
with a smile—that he can be in rare good humor
when his game is working and in rare good humor
when his game is off. If he loses they will never find
him sore or sulking in defeat. And if he starts out
behind they will never find him quitting, for he has
pulled too many forlorn hopes out of the blaze.

—GRANTLAND RICE, *The American Golfer*
[1920]

COCKY DOODLE DOO!
Walter Hagen, boastful American champion, is boyishly con-
fident of winning the British Cup which only once in its history
has ever left British shores. Hagen says that no golfer should
be over 72 around Deal. He intends to show us how to play
the game and he prefers to pitch to the flag so close he doesn't
have to putt. But he is going to putt to prove he can putt.

That headline and those words blared at me the next morning
from the front page of the *Daily Mail* and they carried Bob
Howard's by-line. First I was hurt. Then I was mad. Boiling
mad! My words had been twisted and misquoted into a story
which made me appear an ignorant, smart-aleck young fool.

I had met Lord Northcliffe, editor and owner of the paper
Howard represented when he had made a trip to my home
town of Rochester, New York in 1913. He came to buy shoes
for the British Army. Despite the seriousness of his mission he
found time to play a few rounds of golf at the Country Club

64

of Rochester. Mr. Hepp, manager of the club, had suggested the assistant pro, Walter Hagen, as a playing partner. Lord Northcliffe had been very gracious and complimented me on my game.

"I wouldn't be surprised," he told me, "to hear of you winning the American championship some day. And when you do, come over to England and have a try at our British Open."

The evening Dickie and I had arrived in London, and following the interview and dinner with Bob Howard, I had telephoned Lord Northcliffe. He remembered me and invited us to come down to his country place to play some golf on his private course. So the morning the article appeared in his paper we drove to his estate, North Forelands. His welcome was most hospitable.

During our conversation I asked him if he had seen the morning edition of the *Daily Mail.* He hadn't, but he immediately had a copy brought to him and read the piece Bob Howard had written about me.

"I don't think that's very flattering to me and it certainly is not a true report of the interview," I told my host.

He explained that the British writers have a very different approach to sports reporting from that of the American newsmen.

"You must not feel hurt over anything the English might write about American golfers. Our British Cup is the most treasured sports trophy," he said, "and feeling runs high at the time of the British Open. British readers won't take it the way you have."

"It sounds pretty clear to anyone, the way Howard put it," I said. "American people wouldn't care much for his wording."

Despite the fact that I was disturbed over the article in the *Daily Mail,* I did enjoy the golf on his private course and the time spent at his beautiful estate. However, after we arrived

65

back in London and were having cocktails at his London home, I asked him to contact Howard and have him come to my hotel as soon as possible.

Howard was waiting when we reached the hotel. I never came so close to socking a man in my life. I told him I wanted that article retracted in the next issue . . . and to put the retraction on the *front* page where the original article had appeared. The *Daily Mail* carried the retraction the following morning and Dickie wrote up the incident for our American papers and for the Bell Syndicate. All my plans for getting a good press by bringing Dickie over with me had fallen through the first time I opened my mouth in England. But Dickie got on the beam and our stories of golf abroad were truthfully reported in the United States.

Lord Northcliffe continued through the years to be most cordial to the American golfers and many times he expressed the opinion that international golf was doing a great job in cementing a strong friendship between the two English-speaking countries.

Jim Barnes—an Englishman by birth, an American pro by choice—arrived in England about the same time I did. He wanted to win that British Cup for his adopted homeland, too. Golfing interests in the Isles arranged a four-ball exhibition for Barnes and me against the two outstanding British pros, George Duncan and Abe Mitchell. Everyone expected they would cut Jim and me down to size, but we beat them rather easily.

The gallery at Coombe Hill, where we played the match, was amazed at the American way of putting backspin on the ball. When I did this on one hole in the early part of the match, George Greenwood, an old-time English golf writer, commented that "it was only an accident." Jim explained that he frequently did the same thing . . . and proved it with a shot. But Greenwood refused to be convinced, believing it to be some sort of magic we exercised. A year later Jock Hutchison, the first American-by-choice pro to win the British Open, startled the gallery at St. Andrews by making the ball take a spin and come back a few feet. When he made a hole in one in the 1921 Championship his ball landed on the green a couple of feet past the cup, then came back and dropped into the cup!

No, the British did not understand that art of spinning the ball which Jim Barnes and I were doing so well that day at Coombe Hill, but they did understand a short time afterwards when they barred the ribbed club we were using and hung it on the wall of the great Royal and Ancient St. Andrews. They did the same thing to Walter Travis with the center-shafted putter when he won with it on the tricky greens at Sandwich for the first time in 1904 in the British Amateur.

The British did not consider Jim and me as leading golfers of the day for the reason that they regarded the British Championship as that of the world, not just of Great Britain. Even after our exhibition match with Duncan and Mitchell they didn't invite us to their tournaments to get acquainted with the British links before the 1920 Open was played. Both of us needed practice and we did get some at St. George's Hill, but it was the seaside links like Deal that we were anxious to play. And I was eager to get a look at the British golfers entered in the Open. Great players like Vardon with six wins of the Championship, Braid and Taylor with five each, were the ones I wanted to see. Right now I'm the only living man who has won the British Open four times or more . . . the only man alive and still kicking. Gosh, what an ancient game this golf is!

Braid, Vardon and Taylor, the great British triumvirate, came down to St. George's Hill during the qualifying rounds to watch me play the eighteenth hole. Braid and Taylor commented later that they were a little disappointed in my swing. But Vardon, whom I had met at Brookline, said he would reserve his opinion until he saw more of me. Vardon remarked

67

to a friend in Dickie's hearing that "Hagen seems to have all that is necessary for championship golf since he does the right thing at the right time. I predict he'll win our Championship, not once, but several times."

I was particularly pleased to hear of Vardon's comment, for he was regarded as the world's greatest stylist and his record of six wins proved his game to be substantially solid. So he should have known whether I had a chance or not. And I remembered, too, how shifting to his stance and swing had helped me on those four troublesome holes at Brookline seven years earlier.

I invited Jim Barnes to drive down to Deal in my rented limousine so we could look over the course and get acquainted with the setup. I liked the impression the Austin-Daimler, complete with chauffeur and footman, made as we pulled up in front of the club house. We climbed out of the car and strolled inside. Being early on an off day we couldn't find anyone in the club house, so we looked for the locker rooms. We were dressed for golf, except for changing our shoes. While we were making the change the head locker steward—a little man in a white coat—came hurriedly in our direction.

"Are you Mr. High-gen?" he inquired brusquely.

"I am," I said, "and this is Mr. Barnes."

"Gentlemen," he said importantly, "you're in the wrong place."

"This is Deal?" I asked.

"Oh, yes, indeed," he assured me. "But you gentlemen are professionals. You'll be using Mr. Hunter's golf shop for dressing."

"Well, pardon me," I said and walked out in my golf shoes, giving the other pair to my hired footman to put in the car.

Jim and I went down to the golf shop to pay our respects to Mr. Hunter, the pro, and to look over the facilities. One long spike in the wall had several coats hanging on it and in a far corner many pairs of shoes—the toes turned up like skis—were piled disconsolately. I guess the Oakland Hills Golf Club treatment had spoiled me, made me accustomed to being treated as any golfer, pro or amateur, should be. For I took one look at Jim and he followed me out of the place. I knew we weren't going to use that shop for a dressing room.

"We'll use my car for a dressing room," I told Jim. "We can dress at the tavern in the village, then just change our shoes out here."

I got my two caddies and we started. I used my footman as a fore-caddie to train him for the Championship. I had told the chauffeur to meet us at the eighteenth green with my polo coat and to leave the car parked directly in front of the club.

When we played around to Deal's eighteenth green the club's Mr. Secretary—a small but important little fellow with a waxed mustache—stepped up to greet us. During our walk back to the club house where my car was parked, he apologized for the incident earlier that morning, but explained again that professionals were not allowed in the club house.

I told him I was sorry, too, but we did not know the rules and henceforth we'd use my car. "I'll be living at the nearby pub, so I can easily change my shoes and sweater in the car."

He didn't like the idea of parking my car in front of the club house, either, and of having the chauffeur meet me at the eighteenth green. However, I followed that custom throughout my stay.

Deal is a semi-municipal golf course, the membership proper being shut off from the public by a picket fence which surrounds the club house . . . keeping the sheep from grazing too close to the bay windows. Like St. Andrews and several other British courses, it is kept mowed by sheep. But I didn't intend to let them pull any of the sheeps' wool over my eyes about the manner in which pros should be treated at Deal.

The memory England carried of me from that first attempt

at the British Open was not of my golf, but of my golfing attire. And they wrote much about my clothes in the British papers. The native players, particularly the amateurs, took great pride in frayed tweed jackets, crumpled knickerbockers, and even boots. I appeared on the first tee the starting day dressed in one of the twelve beautifully harmonizing outfits I'd brought over with me. I wore a black sleeveless pullover sweater, white silk shirt with collar and a dark tie, custom-tailored white flannel knickers and black-and-white sports shoes. For a break from the black and white I wore gray golf stockings. Golfers and gallery alike made a special tour around me to take in my sartorial splendor. I had played one practice round at Deal in 72, but when I began to play in the Championship it was another story.

I didn't start until noon and some early scores had already been posted. Nothing sensational yet, however. I had a fair-sized gallery waiting to see me play, mostly Americans who expected to see me in my best form. I played fairly well the first nine holes . . . I had a score of 37. But coming back, well, that was really something. I've never in my life seen such wind. Women were holding umbrellas over them when they passed sand traps to be protected from the grit, sand and pebbles that blew across the fairway. On one tee shot the ball stayed up in the wind so long I turned my back on it to keep from being smacked in the face when the current carried it back toward me. I needed a catcher's mask. That shot didn't even carry the rough in front of the tee. The whipping, blustering wind was a new and puzzling experience for me. I was pressing my shots through the fairway and going for everything on the green, with the sad result that my score mounted to 48, giving me an 85 for a total.

I had decided in the beginning that a 300 would not get me anywhere and I was going all out. But I would gladly have settled for a 75 on each of those first two rounds. When I felt myself slipping, I went for every shot as if it were my last.

When I finished I said to Dickie, "Did you *ever* see me play such terrible golf?"

He admitted he had left me at the end of the first nine holes because he thought he was jinxing my game. He had followed some of the British but hadn't seen anyone playing much good golf. George Duncan was going badly and Abe Mitchell with a 74 led him by several strokes.

Dickie said, "Just keep going and try for second or third, if you can't win."

"I don't want a second. If I can't win I don't care where I finish," I told him. "I won't be any better tomorrow, maybe, but I'm going out to win. I figure I'll either be under 70 or I'll be up over 80."

I was determined to beat the British pros and they were just as determined to take the Americans. We all extended our efforts way beyond the stretching point. I tried to keep fighting. I suppose I should have picked up my ball, as most golfers would. I've never done that and I intended to show the British that I could take a beating and still smile. I took the beating all right. George Duncan won with a not too creditable score of 303. I trailed *fifty-third* in a field of *fifty-four*.

One of the British sports writers reported that finish this way: "Duncan finished but not too triumphantly and made his exit as if he had lost. Yet there was the American, Hagen, finishing with his head up as if he himself had won instead of finishing far down among the also-rans."

But it took Deal's little Mr. Secretary to polish me off. "I'm sorry you didn't do better, 'Eye-gen,'" he gloated, "but golf over here is very difficult. I do hope you'll come back some future year and try again!"

"Don't worry about me," I told him. "You'll see my name on that cup."

He did, too, no fewer than *four* times.

CHAPTER IX: French Open, 1920

I made Hagen's acquaintance immediately after he
arrived on his first visit to this country [England].
. . . It was at once borne in on me that here was a
man who would not fail through excess of modesty.
. . . He makes more bad shots in a single season
than Harry Vardon did during the whole period,
1890-1914, in the course of which he won six Open
Championships. But he beats more immaculate
golfers because "three of those and one of them"
counts 4 and he knows it.

—A. C. M. CROOME, *The American Golfer*
[1926]

I'VE ALWAYS held to the theory that the man who finishes second is soon forgotten. I like to win. I've always gone whole hog or nothing. There's too big a margin between the winner and the runner-up for me to care where I finish if I'm not on top. At least my coming in fifty-third made the whole of England remember me, even though I was far from pleased about the score I'd made.

Another belief of mine—when a tournament is over, forget it. I go into every new one with the idea I'm going to win it. So after Deal I set my sights on the next tournament. The next, as it happened, was the French Open at La Boulie, just outside of Paris.

I had intended making a trip to Paris for some fun after the fiasco at Deal. But during the time I was in London George

72

Duncan, Abe Mitchell and I became very good friends. So we decided the three of us would enter the French Open.

The accommodations for pros at Deal had seemed to me unbelievably bad and inhospitable, but La Boulie was much worse. We were directed to an old and very-much-in-use stable, equipped with several nails for our clothes and a table—for refreshments, we were told. The vile odor and the hundreds of flies swarming about added to the disgust I felt. Duncan and Mitchell had grown up in England and were long accustomed to acceptance of the rigid ruling which barred pros from using, or even entering, the club houses of the famed old British golf courses. But we had a meeting and they agreed with me that it was an impossible situation.

With their concurrence and presence to back me up, I strode into the office of the president, Monsieur Pierre Deschamps, and put it to him bluntly. We were to change and to eat in the club house or else. And that "or else" carried plenty of weight, for Duncan as the current holder of the British Open title, Abe Mitchell as winner of the British "informal" Open in 1919 and runner-up to Duncan in 1920, and I as the American Open title holder were definitely the drawing cards for his French Open. If we three withdrew he was in trouble. Big trouble. The tall French aristocrat knew when he was stymied. He gave in to our demand, but this was the pay-off. He would allow only the three of us to use the club house. None of the other pros were to enjoy the privilege. The shock of winning our point was so great for Mitchell that Duncan and I had to half-push him into the sanctified area of the members and the amateurs. For those two British golfers this was a major revolution we had staged.

The French Championship went on from there with no further arguments. I was confident from the beginning that I could win. The La Boulie course was better suited to my game, since it resembled the American inland courses. And somehow

73

I felt at home the instant I stepped on French soil. Many Americans were in Paris at the time and of course they were eager to see me vindicate myself after the loss at Deal.

I was paired with Abe Mitchell and while my first and second rounds were not sensational I was hitting the ball much better than I had at Deal. Confidence was building with every shot. At the seventeenth of the final round I learned that Eugene LaFitte, the Frenchman, was in with his score. Abe and I were tied going to the last hole; we each needed a 5 to tie LaFitte or a 4 to beat him. I had the honor and drove first.

The eighteenth is a par 4 hole. Abe was an exceptionally long driver and I knew he had the advantage of distance off the tee shot. However, it is always possible to give a drive or an iron shot a little something extra at times and I tried for that extra. I put all I had into my drive and I think I surprised Abe, for his tee shot was not up to mine.

When he came up for his second shot I had already taken my brassie from the bag, showing my intentions. He went for the green with a brassie, and his ball had to carry a row of trees which actually crossed the fairway diagonally. But due to a slight drizzle the shot was not high enough and plunked right into the trees. I knew this would cost him a 6. I quickly returned my brassie to my bag and took a two-iron. I hooked my ball around the trees, pulling up just short of the green. This gave me a run-up shot for my third and a holable size putt to win. However, I missed the putt and got a 5 to tie LaFitte.

After each round during the French Open *Monsieur le Président*, Pierre Deschamps, was host for a spot of tea for Abe, George and me. He was quite a busy fellow, managing the Championship, acting as official during the play and serving as a gracious host in the club house. In short during the five days I was at La Boulie I felt Monsieur Deschamps and I came to know each other quite well.

I have never lost a play-off and I didn't propose to lose this one to LaFitte. I wanted an eighteen-hole play-off because I planned to leave Paris at noon the following day to tour the battle fields. But Monsieur Deschamps informed me most emphatically that we'd play thirty-six holes.

"Eighteen holes may be the system in America, Mr. Haghan, but you are in Paris now."

I covered the thirty-six holes in two and one-half hours with a score of 150, beating the Frenchman by four strokes. A large gallery, mostly French, followed us the entire distance, cheering for their fellow countryman. It's an odd fact, that much as I like a big gallery applauding me, I get a terrific desire to win when I know the gallery is for the other fellow. So, since I knew LaFitte didn't like to play too quickly, I put on extra steam all the way around. On the twelfth tee, for example, which was some 200 feet up an incline, I had the honor. I made the climb and drove off before LaFitte even reached the top. He teed his ball and hit it into the deepest rough right in front of the tee. LaFitte blew any chance he had to win the play-off. With that shot LaFitte went down to defeat.

The French Open was the only Championship title I won in 1920 but in a way it was a big help. For the second consecutive year I had won a national title and I was to win another each year for eleven straight years beginning in 1919 with the American National Open.

The evening following the Championship I dressed in white tie and tails and entertained friends at dinner in the banquet hall of the hotel where I was staying in Paris. There at his regularly reserved table sat *Monsieur le Président* of La Boulie, Pierre Deschamps. I walked over to his table intending to thank him for his many courtesies during the past five days.

He looked up as I reached his table, dropped his monocle but continued to look me over with no sign of recognition in his eyes, although he took in my custom-tailored evening clothes with evident approval.

75

"The French Open——" I began.

But he cut me short as he tapped his forehead quickly with a finger, "Ha-*ghan*, he win the championship."

Immediately I thanked him and went back to my party, not wanting to embarrass him for his lack of recognition. I explained to my friends what had happened and we all had a good laugh out of the situation.

I remember a National Open in the United States when I was appearing to defend my championship title and I had to identify myself to the official at the gate in order to be admitted. I was in street clothes and in my car. He had seen me only in golf clothes. I can understand now how a fellow like *Monsieur le Président*, Pierre Deschamps, couldn't recognize a professional golfer in white tie and tails.

CHAPTER X

Wind, 1921

Walter Hagen's touch is as sensitive as a jeweler's
scale. He can gauge balls from the lightest to the
heaviest, arranging them in order, when there is only
a pennyweight or so difference between half a dozen
balls being judged. If he estimates a club's weight
and the scales don't check with Walter's guess, the
scales are wrong.

—TOMMY ARMOUR, *The American Golfer*
[1925]

MOST PEOPLE are curious about unusual incidents and shots in
golf. Things like the number of times I've made a hole in one.
How many courses I have played. The most thrilling event in
my golfing career, my toughest competitor, and the most sensational shot I've ever made. The gallery watching the play en-
joys the out-of-the-ordinary shots, but to the competitive golfer
. . . well, I'd settle for a deuce or an eagle on a hole any time.
Bobby Jones and Tommy Armour agree with me.

I was playing a practice round at Worcester when the Open
was held there in 1925. Jones, Armour and Joe Kirkwood completed the foursome. A large gallery was following us and we
were kidding around quite a bit. On the fifth hole, playing my
ball from the shallow water of a murmuring brook I had sliced
it wide open. Since it was my last new ball I fumbled around
hunting a used one in my bag as I waited at the sixth tee.
Bobby tossed me a new ball so the match could proceed.

The hole measured about 180 yards. Ordinarily it would
have been a two-iron shot. I took the two-iron from my bag

and was pressing the hickory shaft this way and that with my knee to straighten it. This was a habit of golfers in those days, for the hickory shafts were a bit pliable and often bent out of shape from being carried in our bags. Well, as I pressed the club I heard the hickory shaft click. I couldn't risk putting in a new shaft since the Championship started the next day and a new shaft required a certain amount of practice before I dared trust it. I returned the club to my bag and took out a number-one iron. I opened the face of the club a bit so it would be equal to a two-iron shot. That sixth is a blind hole, but I knew almost immediately it was either in the cup or close from the enthusiastic response of the gallery. It was in the cup.

As it turned out, I had a peculiar combination on this hole in one. It was my first hole in one, the first time the hole had been made in one, the first time the ball had been hit, and it was a number one-iron on the first day of July. Bobby Jones asked why I didn't save that shot for the Championship the next day. Robert Ripley heard about the curious combination and used the incident in his cartoon feature, "Believe It Or Not."

During the actual playing of the 1925 Open I shot a 4 twice on this sixth hole, which I had played in practice rounds in three 2's and an ace. On the last day of the Championship I stood on the eighteenth fairway, a seven-iron shot from the pin to win the championship. If I could have laid the ball on the green close enough for a 3, I'd have tied Jones and Macfarlane, who were tied at 291. But I didn't. So my two 4's on the sixth helped bump me out of that Championship.

I made another hole in one that same year out in Portland, Oregon . . . a really freak ace. It was a short hole and I was playing a five-iron shot to an elevated green. I half-topped the shot, hit short into the rough and with the overspin which always results from half-topping, the ball worked its way up through the grass onto the green and into the cup. Here again

78

it did not count except to win that particular match, for I was playing an exhibition. That was the last ace I ever made.

A hole in one is never the conscious aim of the competitive golfer. He'll try for a deuce or an eagle—and whoop like crazy when he makes either one. Not too many holes in one are made during Championship rounds. I remember Abe Mitchell aced the eighth hole on his first round during the British Open at Deal in 1920. And J. H. Taylor has holed-in-one ten times, his tenth coming on the second hole of his second round in the Open at Prestwick in 1925. Alex Herd, the great British golfer who died in 1944, actually made nineteen holes-in-one, which is the record, so far as I know.

I've seen the worst of hackers make unbelievable holes-in-one! Rex Beach, who wrote far better than he played golf, was my partner in a foursome one day at Sebring, Florida. He was standing on the tee trying to get my advice about which club he should use, when one of our opponents put his ball about four feet from the pin.

I called to Rex, "Now is the time to show what you can do. Save this hole by dropping it in for an ace."

"You know I never made an ace in my life, but if you think I can do it, I'll try." And he holed that ball as pretty as could be.

My toughest competitor? I'll leave him to a later chapter. The number of courses I've played? I can't compute the number accurately, but I imagine in my twenty-six years of competitive golf I've played well over 2500 courses. I do know I played three different courses in one day.

Anyone who knows the coastal links in Kent County, southeast of London, will remember there are three links adjoining each other. Deal, the first, Sandwich directly east, known as the Royal St. George's, then a little south of Sandwich and east lies the Prince's links. While we were in London for the 1920 British Open, Jim Barnes and I started one morning to play the three links as if they were one. After playing eleven holes on the Deal course, we hopped a fence over to Sandwich and played ten holes there, crossed to the Prince's links and completed all the holes there, coming back to the original starting place. We finished the remainder of the holes on the Sandwich and Deal layouts, ending up on the eighteenth at Deal. Scores? I've forgotten. We weren't trying to break any records. We were just lucky to go that far. We did it for fun.

Of the three courses the St. George's impressed me most. The British Open of 1922 was played there, and Walter Travis won his British Amateur championship there. I first met the Prince of Wales there, when he presented me with the British Open trophy in 1928. Contrary to all newspaper stories which have been written about the friendship between us, I did not meet him on my first trip to the British Isles.

When I returned home in July of 1920 I was just the *High-gen* who'd finished fifty-third in the British Open and the *Haghan* who'd captured the French Open . . . with no royalty associations anywhere in my background. However, back here I began signing my name *Walter* Hagen, instead of W. C. Hagen which I'd been using heretofore. That W. C. appeared to have unduly amusing connotations. I heard too many people pronounce it "water closet" over there.

Later that year the British pros invaded American golf Championship matches for the first time since the war. And none of us homebreds were too happy when the great Ted Ray walked off with our National Open title at Inverness. Vardon finished second, tied with Jack Burke, Leo Diegel and Jock Hutchinson. However, this win of Ray's did serve to stimulate fresh interest among the American pros and we organized for another try for the British Open cup in 1921. Our group consisted of Emmet French, Tommy Kerrigan, Jim Barnes, Jock Hutchison and me—along with Joe Kirkwood who came up from Australia to join us.

80

Nineteen-twenty was one of my lean years, for outside of the French Open the only other championship of any consequence I could garner was the Metropolitan Open. I won it for the third consecutive year, by defeating Jim Barnes at the Greenwich Country Club. A young kid, Gene Sarazen, turned up at Inverness that year for the USGA—a fellow I was to meet on many occasions in the future, several times to my discomfiture.

Nineteen-twenty is memorable for another reason. H. B. Martin had been a great help to me on that original trip to England. I realized I needed a manager-press agent and found him in the person of Bob Harlow. He took over that position with me just prior to my embarking for the second attempt to win the British Open, and he was to be my big noise for some eleven years. He knew his business and he grew to know me—my good points and my shortcomings. Through all those years we never had a written contract of any sort. He set up the dates, I played the tournaments and exhibitions. And we carried the greenbacks away in an old suitcase. It was an ideal arrangement, for it allowed me to relax and enjoy my friends and my game. I gave Bob plenty of stuff to keep him fully occupied and worried.

St. Andrews was the scene of the 1921 British Open and here Jock Hutchison, British-born American pro, won their great trophy. For the first time in the history of the British Open the cup traveled across the sea to the United States. Jock tied Roger Wethered at 72 holes and beat the British amateur in the play-off. I finished sixth.

I did learn something at St. Andrews, however. I found out why a golf course has eighteen holes. I was told of an old fellow, one of the charter members of the club board, who liked to sneak a couple of snorts at each tee just to help his game along. The size of his flask permitted him a generous nip for eighteen tees, thus limiting the range of his play. He could have been a pal of mine had he lived that long.

For the second time the British links had defeated me. Here in America we have developed the finest of man-made courses in the world, but the real test of a golfer is a seaside links in the British Isles. Situated close beside the ocean, beset with rolling sand dunes and winds that whip off the channel and the seas, conditions change with the tide. The hazards are far greater than meet the eye. At Deal I had played shots where the wind picked the ball up and almost slapped it back in my face. At St. Andrews I learned that distance was secondary to placing the ball accurately. I learned, also, that in order to be at the top in the golf profession, I must be able to play any course in the world in par.

During the year between Deal and St. Andrews I had tried to gain skill for the British and Scottish links by playing some of our own seaside courses, such as the National on Long Island, Pebble Beach and Cypress Point in California. But there was all the difference in the world between these courses and the rugged wind-swept links of Sandwich, Hoylake, Carnoustie, Prestwick, Troon and Lytham St. Anne's.

I knew the fault lay not with the links but with my game. With the opportunity to play continuously over them Harry Vardon, J. H. Taylor, James Braid and Alex Herd became masters of the skill required to conquer them. Instead of trying for distance they worked on a low ball which would travel hard and sharp against the wind—a ball which they could control. They were experts with the pitch and run shot. They needed to be, for the wind would grab a ball and carry it in any direction.

In the United States we developed the wedge, and it's a fine club where the turf conditions are excellent and the wind is light. We could hit the ball up with action on it. But that same shot on the British seaside links was disastrous. I know because I tried it and once the ball was up in a strong wind the action

82

disappeared and the ball, minus control, would land on a high green and roll over into a trap.

After 1921 I worked on a ball hit quail-high—a ball hit hard enough to resist the pull of that fierce wind and yet not too fast to roll over a lightning-fast green. I tried for short approach shots, keeping contact between me and the ball—giving it enough action to cover the uneven approach surface but not enough to let the wind get under it.

I've repeatedly insisted that I liked competition. Well, I had it from the links in the British Isles. And far from upsetting me, it challenged my skill as a championship golfer so greatly that I was more and more determined to win that British Open cup.

Some of the best shots I've made have escaped the notice of the gallery completely; on others, the spectators have not appreciated how difficult the shots were. On one occasion at Pinehurst in the North and South Open going to the last hole, I had just such a shot.

Quite a gallery was waiting around the green to catch the finish. I was the last one in and I figured I'd show them how a champion finishes. The Championship that year was played on the number three course, where the eighteenth hole was uphill.

I teed up my ball and wheeled on it. But I was a little fast. I got the distance I wanted but the wrong direction. I'd hooked into scrub oak to the left of the fairway. As nonchalantly as possible I strolled over in the direction of its fall and saw an old Negro mammy sitting on a cabin porch peeling potatoes.

"Did you see a ball come over this way?" I asked her.

"No, sir," she answered reprovingly, "I ain't seen no ball. Them golfers don't play over this way, mister. They play over there on the other side of them trees."

My caddie thought it must have landed among the trees and

we searched through them diligently. Finally we came upon a small clearing in the woods and found my ball at the far side nestled up against a cluster of trees. It was teed up on a lot of leaves. A beautiful shot, had I been playing in the opposite direction. It could only be played with a left-handed club.

I was leading by two strokes and although the hole was a par 4, I was thinking I'd settle for a 5 and still have a shot to spare if I could get back on the fairway. Being somewhat ambidextrous I had played some left-handed shots. I'd even occasionally carried a left-handed club for such an emergency. Well, I had come upon the emergency, but I'd left the club I needed in the locker.

I took a seven-iron and turned it upside down, playing it with the nose of the club down, thus making it sort of a left-handed club. I took several swings with it, then held my breath and let one go. The ball went over the trees and made for the green about 150 yeards away. It landed on the green twenty feet from the hole. I received no unusual response from the gallery when I got my par 4. To the huge crowd watching my shot, it looked like routine stuff.

Another time, one of the best shots I ever made turned out the worst for me. At least it cost me three strokes and a championship I wanted to win more than any other for it was my last serious competitive threat. Twenty-one years earlier I had won my first American Open. In 1935 I was trying for my third at the Oakmont Country Club in Oakmont, Pennsylvania. And that's one of the very toughest tests of golf in the United States—one of the finest Championship courses.

Gene Sarazen had completed his rounds and came into the locker room as I was preparing to start my second round. I had played a steady first round and felt I had a pretty good chance of winning the Championship.

"You're going to find the worst weather you've ever played in," he warned me. "There's a storm coming up and the wind is blowing a gale." He slipped his good luck ring off his finger and handed it to me. "You'd better wear this. It could do you some good."

He was right about the weather, but I've never been sure just how his ring affected my game. I had to hit into the sweeping wind on the first tee and took a 4 for the hole. The storm had really broken by that time . . . the wind had cyclonic strength and the rain whipped down in blinding sheets. The reception tent blew down, and crossing the bridge to the second tee I had newspapers blowing wildly over my head.

On the second I took three putts for a 5. I had a 6 on the third, and on the long fourth, the wind was so strong I had to play the ball to the right and let the wind carry it back to the right fairway. I finally holed my ball for a 7. I thought sure I had a fair chance for the championship at the ninth tee. But I hit a wide sweeping hook to ride the wind and it landed on the green, hole high. I had given it just a shade too much and it rolled . . . and rolled . . . and rolled, deep into a sunken trap at the rear of the hole. The wind had actually swept the ball away. It cost me three strokes at least. I was out in 42.

I fought my way around the last nine in a miraculous 34, one under par. I went back to the club house and returned Gene's ring. Luck? Sometimes we have it and sometimes we don't. Not even Gene's ring could bring it to me that day . . . yet I'd played in far worse wind and weather and won. Sam Parks, Jr. won the 1935 USGA Open with a 299.

CHAPTER XI: High Finance

> The term *fabulous* is reserved for an even more se-
> lect group. It is greatness grown into legend. It
> describes the astonishing and incredible. It exudes
> color, magnetic personality and the intangible some-
> thing that attracts crowds and makes news both on
> and off the field. It is as much the manner of victory
> as the triumphs themselves. . . . In golf men like
> Ben Hogan, Byron Nelson, Gene Sarazen and Sammy
> Snead wear the cloak of greatness. Bobby Jones rates
> as perhaps the most brilliant of them all. Walter
> Charles Hagen can be classed as fabulous.
> —HARRY MOLTER, *Famous American Athletes*
> *of Today*
> [1953]

CHAMPIONS in all fields of sport appear with increasing regularity on our television screens, in night clubs both here and
abroad, and in the movies. Some, like Sugar Ray Robinson,
Max Baer and Maxie Rosenbloom, have made some success in
the entertainment field. Jack Dempsey had a try at it, as did
Joe Louis. Dempsey and Baer continue to garner extra green by
occasionally refereeing wrestling matches. Ed Sullivan has featured scores of leading golfers on his "Toast of the Town"
show. I have received invitations from Ed, too, but so far I
haven't had the courage to drive those ping pong balls into the
faces of his theater audiences.

However, Ed's is not the first bid I've had to try for stardom
in the theater. In 1919, just after I won my second American Open, certain vaudeville interests offered me $1500 a week

A few scenes from *Green Grass Widows,* a Hollywood production of the early '20s starring Walter Hagen, Leo Diegel, Marge Beebe, and Andy Clyde.

My dad was seventy years young before
he ever saw me play in a championship.

Jim Barnes won the U. S.
Open in 1921, but I trimmed
him at Inwood to take the
P. G. A. Championship that
year. Here we are with P. G. A.
Chairman Gates.

Returning from England in 1922 with the British Open trophy, after I had won it for the first time on the Royal St. George's Links at Sandwich. With me are Jim Barnes, Joe Kirkwood, and Jock Hutchison.

Gene Sarazen was the P. G. A. Champion in 1922 and I the British Open winner, so we squared off in a match for the informal championship of the world at Oakmont, near Pittsburgh. [WIDE WORLD PHOTO]

Come In Pal

How Willard Mullin, the great sports cartoonist of the New York *World-Telegram and Sun*, flatteringly portrayed my series of actions which helped open the front door of golf to the professional.

for at least one swing around the circuit, made up of approximately forty weeks' time. In those days with no popular radio or television, sponsors with fantastic bankrolls didn't exist, and $1500 a week was big dough.

I was a little puzzled about what sort of an act I'd be expected to present. Certainly no audience would pay to see me demonstrate the correct and incorrect way to swing a golf club. I had no reputation for sure-fire patter . . . I couldn't break into a fast tap dance or give out with "On the Road to Mandalay" in a rollicking baritone. And I definitely was not the matinee idol type who could get the girls swooning with my handsome and virile physique. Or could I? Yet the money certainly looked good and the tour permitted me to take time out for golf Championships and practice. I considered the offer for some time, then turned it down, realizing that my talent lay in the game of golf and not on a stage.

Again, when I was in Los Angeles in 1923, movie producers talked to me about starring in a picture. I lent a willing ear, eager to ink my name on one of those six-figure salary contracts. Golf and social activities occupied me for some weeks and the producers delayed start of work on the film. In the meantime events in the Florida real estate boom necessitated my return there and the movie contract was passed up. My Detroit pal, Al Wallace, got himself talked into making a motion picture, and he in turn twisted my arm with the announcement that Mae West would be the star. Would I take the lead opposite her? I signed at once and took off for Hollywood only to learn that Miss West was ill and a Miss Dumont was replacing her. Titled *The Man Who Cheated,* the film's early shots were made at Truckee, high in the snow-topped mountains of California. We returned to the studio to make the indoor shots but all the cash had been used, so the picture was never completed.

Between tournaments, however, I did manage to star in a

film *Green Grass Widow* opposite the lovely Marge Beebe. Norma Talmadge had originally been scheduled for the lead, but she could not play golf. Marge Beebe's form was as good on the course as off. I don't remember too much about the story, but I do know I didn't win the girl. According to the script, my father was a heel and I was blamed for his misdeeds. The beautiful Miss Beebe kept reminding me of his sinful life by saying, "Like father, like son." I went back to my golf game.

My brief encounters with the theatrical world as a performer never seemed half as fantastic as my experience on Wall Street. I was the most uninformed individual on high finance who ever walked down that famous street. However, in 1921 my friend Fred Pulsifer, head of the Clark-Childs brokerage house, assured me I was just the type to make a huge success in the market. Well, the desire for clinking coins led me easily to his way of thinking. I'm sure his conviction was based on the idea that a golf champion would undoubtedly make a superior stock and bond salesman. I firmly believed that shortly after my entrance into the market Fred and I would be "cutting a melon."

The first step in the venture meant that I must buy a seat on the New York Stock Exchange. As soon as that could be arranged Fred informed me that his firm would provide *my* firm with approximately $2,000,000 clearance daily. I then learned that the current price of a seat was $96,000. To me, the country boy from Rochester, this talk of $96,000 and $2,000,000 was completely staggering. Where would *I* get that kind of dough?

But strange things happen to champions in all fields of sport. A few days after my session with Fred, I was talking to Gabriel Salant who had acquired a huge fortune as an industrial manufacturer and a Wall Street operator. We were finishing a round of golf at Inwood, Long Island, and I told him of Fred Pulsifer's offer. Mr. Salant very generously offered to provide me with $10,000 to get my office started, and to buy me a seat on the Exchange when I was ready to begin operations. I contacted many good golfing friends who had experience in the market and they agreed to teach me the correct methods of procedure.

I walked boldly into Wall Street and rented an office at 10 Broad Street. I had a cashier's cage with a drawer underneath where I could put money. I bought a set of books with red ink on one side and blue ink on the other. I hired a bookkeeper and gave him the books. I hired a cashier and put him in the cage. My office, while not large, was equipped with the usual massive desk and carpeted with the finest of Chinese Orientals. On the door the best sign painter available had blacked in an impressive "WALTER HAGEN, BROKERAGE SALES, INC." I was ready for business. Yet I still had not purchased my seat on the Exchange. I inquired about the price. It had gone up to $100,000. I decided to wait for a few days for the price to drop.

Three days later the price had risen to $106,000. I spent the remainder of that day watching my bookkeeper write nothing in the books and my cashier put no money in the drawer. The following morning Fred Pulsifer called me on the telephone. He asked if I had purchased the seat.

"No," I explained gently, "the price has gone up. I'll wait a few more days."

"Have you made any sales?" he asked.

"No," I told him. "I've been very busy getting my office set up."

"Have you any customers?" he asked.

"No, I haven't a client on the books," I said.

He then advised me to close the office, give my books to the bookkeeper and give my cashier a permanent vacation. He also informed me that the market was now going through a difficult period, such as only those experienced in its intricacies could understand and cope with. I never regretted that week "on the

Street." Thanks to Gabe Salant it had not cost me too much money. Even Fred found the Street difficult. Some time later he committed suicide in his Fifth Avenue apartment.

My trips to Great Britain to play in the British Open were directly responsible for my next Wall Street venture. Those trips were expensive propositions. Getting the cash together each year in time to make a reservation on the Cunard Line and land in England early enough to shoot a few rounds of golf and steady my sea legs meant some financial scurrying on my part. Every pro who ever made the trip went through the same ordeal.

I traveled first class, and that included a suite at the Savoy at five pounds a day, the Chez Paris, cocktail hour at the Ritz, the Daimler car with chauffeur and footman, fine silk shirts custom-tailored by A. J. Izod on Conduct Street just off the Strand. It also included planes chartered for hunting trips over the moors or fishing trips to the northern part of Scotland, and parties at the Savoy Hotel in London where the service was so wonderful. Before I returned home each year I'd somehow managed to spend around $10,000.

Early in 1924 I met Jesse Livermore, better known to the public as the "Wolf of Wall Street." And to Jesse, more than to any other man I've known, I owe my freedom from financial worry during all those many trips I made to play for the British Open trophy. A few weeks after that first meeting, I ran into Jesse again at the fine Westchester-Biltmore Club at Rye, New York, where I was living. We played a few holes of golf. My second marriage, to Edna Strauss, had taken place that spring and Jesse threw a beautiful party in our honor at the club.

Sometime during our many talks he suggested that perhaps he could help finance some of my trips abroad. This statement was certainly a surprise to me and I listened with both ears open. He invited me to come to his office on Wall Street and we'd see what could be arranged. I was greatly flattered and

90

knew that this was an invitation which he did not extend promiscuously. But I was even more astonished when I visited him and saw the tremendous setup he had.

His office occupied an entire floor and his privacy was guarded by a series of secretaries who carefully screened each visitor and allowed very few to penetrate the inner space occupied by Jesse. In all the time I spent with him, not more than half a dozen were ever admitted to that inner office.

Jesse did not attempt to educate me into the complexities of the market. "Walter," he said that first day, "sit down and let me explain a few things to you. I've a couple of rules and suggestions I'd like you to follow. You'll probably never hear my voice other than on one of these four telephones on my desk. Listen to my orders to buy or sell. Follow my operations."

His basic rules were: Buy when he bought; sell when he sold. And most important of all, never let a day end with one single share of stock unsold. I operated on his credit, which he okayed. Where he gave orders in the millions I bought a few hundred shares. I used my own judgment about the amounts I bought and sold. He must have had confidence that I wouldn't go haywire on his credit. It did not take me long to get smart but I was no gambler or plunger.

We sat in the office from ten in the morning until the market closed at three in the afternoon. Our lunch was sent in each day. We spoke very little. When Jesse was not engaged on one of his telephones he was deeply engrossed in a mass of market data. At three we'd leave the office together to join friends for a cocktail or go our separate ways. But his query as we closed the office each day was invariably the same.

"How'd you come out today, Walter?"

"I traded a few shares of this stock or that," I'd tell him, naming the ones he'd been trading in, too.

"You're learning fast," he'd say.

After two weeks that first spring I had enough to cover my

trip to England and I also had that freedom from financial worry which enabled me to relax on the course. Relaxation is a word practically synonymous with the name Walter Hagen. Professional golf is a strenuous game—a demanding grind, both mentally and physically. And only the relaxed golfer can play his best in tournaments . . . firming up on occasion when the going gets rough.

In tournament golf we pros not only pitch for the cup and the title, but also for the ticket home. Sometimes the ticket home means more than the title. Well, after I met Jesse all I had to pitch and putt for was the title. I gave my first British Open Championship check, about $375, to my caddie.

I've known a number of good pros who could not play tournament golf. They got the heebie-jeebies just thinking about it. Every golfer knows that tightening of the muscles, the flicking of the nerves that hits when he finds himself in a tough situation. But only the fellow who can give himself a quick shake mentally and release the physical tension can go on to play championship golf. The champion golfer needs terrific power of concentration. He must keep his mind completely on the shot to be made. And I think the greatest strain on his nerves comes on the putting green.

On the fairway there isn't the crowding-in feeling of the gallery. There's space to move easily, breathe freely and swing the arms about. There isn't the uneasy, anxious silence which surrounds the green. Sometimes the silence sounds louder in one's ears than the cheers and applause which follow after the ball hangs for a brief second on the lip of the cup . . . and then drops in.

Golf is a game, the books say. Well, to the professional golfer, it's a game like big league baseball is a game. And like horse racing is a sport. . . to the jockey in the saddle of a Derby entry. It's a game in which the jockey must bring home a winner, or the batter get the guy in from second, or the golfer get

92

his name on the championship trophy. It's a game in which the pro golfer follows a circuit, just as rigid as the baseball schedule or the traveling from one race track to another for winning mounts. If the pro is on an exhibition tour he may play eighteen to thirty-six holes of golf every day from mid-July to the last day of October, as Harry Vardon and Ted Ray did when they came over here in 1920. Or as I did every year for twenty-six years.

The professional who plays tournament golf must make the courses and clubs where the good prizes are, and that's where the big galleries are, and we're right back to relaxation again. For he can play those tournaments and those exhibitions only if he can handle his game round by round, and hole by hole. He has to concentrate on his game and forget to worry about the ticket home. The pro can play in the British Open, can make the trip across the pond every year, only if he can raise the cash. He can travel as I traveled on the finest ships of the Cunard Line, live in the best hotels, enjoy the social and recreational activities of England and Europe and play the relaxed game of golf I was able to play, only if he is as lucky as I was in having the friendship and the generous financial direction of a man like Jesse Livermore.

Our association continued right up to my last win of the British Open, in 1929. In the spring of that year he telephoned and asked me to visit him at his home in Lake Placid, New York. I found him confined to his bed but the old familiar four telephones were beside him. He was still active in the market. I spent the afternoons teaching his lovely wife and daughters to play golf, and spent the mornings and evenings reliving with Jesse the thrills of my annual ten days' trading splurge on Wall Street.

And I am very sure to this day that Jesse Livermore's name should be engraved alongside of mine on those four British Open cups I carried home to the United States.

PART TWO: The Fairway

THE MAN who makes up his mind to do something and then goes after it with every ounce of power, blasting every barrier with an indomitable will to win, fighting where fighting is necessary, relaxing a bit where he can, gambling like a gasconade where gambling means victory, clamping the pressure on early and bearing down to the positive end—he is the fellow who picks up and goes places.

Such a fellow is Walter the Haig.

He averages over $100,000 a year in prize money, $45,000 a year from his exhibition matches, and his annual salary as the golf expert of the Pasadena Golf and Country Club is just $30,000 a year more.

Babe Ruth, the king pin of baseball, draws $70,000 a year for six days of hard work a week. Hagen gets $90,000 a year for playing golf an average of three times a week and practically all his expenses, tobacco, wearing apparel, golf supplies, automobiles and what not besides.

Golf with him, of course, is a matter of intense business. That's one of the interesting things about him. Here is a pro in the heart of a game that is essentially amateur and of all the professional athletes of all the sporting world, Hagen is the most professional of all.

Hagen has never consciously shot a stroke of golf for nothing, and he probably never will. Other golfers, even other professional golfers, mix considerable chit-chat and persiflage in their play.

Hagen doesn't.

He's as full of foolishness as the next fellow, after a match or even before one, but once he tees off, it's cold-blooded commerce. Watching the grim and almost belligerent manner in which he goes to work on a game, one who has beheld the killer instinct operating in the prize ring can almost imagine a stubble of cocoa-buttered, blue-black whiskers on his jaws and a pair of wine-colored mitts on his hands.

Just as Dempsey used to hurl himself into his fights to punch until something dropped, Hagen strides into his game so savagely that you find yourself wishing to heaven that he'd at least pucker his face with a little window-dressing of joviality, if only to make it seem just the least bit sporting.

That's the way Hagen makes his $90,000 a year. In return he has re-fashioned himself into a colorful personage, like a grand opera tenor, or a movie top-liner. He seldom moves without at least three trunks of clothes. His valet is in constant attendance. He drives only the fastest and flashiest cars. He wears lemon yellow gloves and spats upon occasion.

In England a golf pro has no social standing. He ranks as a sort of boss servant. Hagen has elevated a lowly profession to the heights of a lucrative and decorative art. He has crowned it with dignity, and enriched it with elegance. And for all the scenery he is perhaps the world's foremost competitor. He hasn't subsidized cold skill to anything.

Further power to his slashing blades. May he stick around for many a year.

—BILL CUNNINGHAM, *Detroit News*
[1927]

CHAPTER XII: British Open, 1922

There's nothing he likes better than standing on the
first tee and feeling the bitter lashes of the elements
against him. . . . When most players casually pick
up and others have to be picked up, he draws himself up and stands alone against the wind and the
rain. . . . That's when Dad really fights.

—WALTER HAGEN, JR., *The American Golfer*
[1936]

DESPITE MY FAILURE to win the British Open, 1921 was a great
year for me. I won my first PGA Championship at Inwood,
Long Island when I trimmed Jim Barnes 3 and 2. It was one
of my prize championships. In the morning I scored a 69 yet I
was only 1 up. In the afternoon I fired a 33 on the outgoing
nine to go 4 up. Barnes rallied late, but I was too far ahead for
him to catch me. However, Jim redeemed himself in the USGA
Open at the Columbia Club in Chevy Chase when he won that
Championship. I took it on the chin and became an "also ran,"
for that's just what second place meant to me.

I won the Michigan Open. In the West Coast of Florida
Open I blazed around in 62 to cop the title. That 62 was the
lowest score for eighteen holes in competition ever to be recorded up to that time. In fact that 62 stood for quite a few
years until Byron Nelson equaled it in 1945 at the Broadmoor
Golf Club in Seattle. Since then Lawson Little, Jimmy
Demaret, Jim Ferrier, Herman Keiser and the intrepid Ben
Hogan have also posted 62's in competition. The new record
for eighteen holes was established by Al Brosch in the Texas

98

Open over the Brackenbridge Park Course in February 1951, when he scored 30-30, 60 for his third round. The odd thing about that was he finished fourth in the Championship. Bill Nary tied Brosch's record by scoring a 31-29, 60 in the El Paso Open in February of 1952. But my 62 in the West Coast of Florida Open stood unbroken for twenty-four years.

I won the Western Open at Cleveland in 1921, too, and I hadn't even intended to enter. I was in New York heading back to Detroit when I picked up a newspaper before getting on the train. The first words I read, of course, were on the sports page. Imagine my chagrin when right at the top of the page I saw a small boxed item with my name in it . . . and the reporter stating to the world that I was *through* as a golfer!

"Hagen all through!" I read again. "Where in hell is the next tournament?" I said to anybody who happened to be near. "I'll show that fellow!"

In another column was the announcement of the Western Open at Cleveland. I changed trains at Buffalo early the next morning and headed south. I hadn't planned to enter the Western Open, so that reporter did me a big favor. When the final scores were posted I was right there at the top, the winner by five strokes over Jock Hutchison and Bobby Jones.

As I clipped the results listed in the Cleveland *Plain Dealer* to mail to my doubting friend in New York, I was still muttering to myself, "Hagen all through! The boy's just starting!" And fired up like that I went on to win four other major Championships that year. I was playing sharp golf, and when I crossed the Atlantic for the British Open in 1922 I honestly believed my year for winning that prized cup had finally arrived.

The British Open was played on the Royal St. George's Links at Sandwich, where six years later the Prince of Wales presented the cup to me after my third win. But I was concerned in 1922 with making up for the results of my two

99

previous attempts—the first ending in ignominious defeat and the second, a better but unsatisfactory showing when I finished sixth.

The evening before the Championship a dozen or so of us were engaged in a putting competition on the carpet of the hotel lounge at Ramsgate until well after two in the morning. Someone reminded me of the time and of the fact that most of my opponents had been in bed for hours.

"Maybe they're in bed," I retorted, "but they are *not* sleeping." For no one knew better than I the value of relaxation. And relaxation meant keeping one's mind off the Championship until it came time to drive off the first tee.

The man I feared most among the leaders was Jock Hutchinson who had won the year before. As the last round began Jim Barnes and I were even on the 228 mark and Jock was leading us by two strokes. George Duncan was down the list with 232. I had half a dozen runners out on the course to bring me news of Jock's progress. I learned he had blown up at two holes so my final round of 72, giving me a 300 total, appeared to be safe since Barnes had finished with 301 and Jock Hutchison had come in with a 302. George Duncan was still out. The sports writers jumped the gun and sent in their stories on "How Hagen Won" his first British Open. In fact, some of the evening editions were right then selling on the links!

And then it happened! About half an hour before Duncan finished runners were shouting that he was burning up the course in a frantic effort to tie or beat me. He had gone out in 34, a seemingly impossible score, considering the strong wind which was whipping in from the sea. If he came back in 34, he would tie me. With J. H. Taylor, Harry Vardon, "Andra" Kirkaldy and Arnaud Massy, I joined the huge gallery watching Duncan's dramatic effort at the seventeenth green.

His drive was straight down the eighteenth fairway. He played his second shot wide to the green and to the left, leaving

100

himself an uphill chip shot. I turned to the fellows with me and said, "If he knows that green as well as I do, he'll hit his chip shot firmly, because the ball pulls up fast on that incline. I know it does, because I was short."

Duncan didn't know, however, and played his ball just as I had. He left himself about eight feet short of the hole. He had that putt left to tie me. It was a most difficult, uphill putt, working from right to left.

An English reporter, Fred Pignon, said later that my hands were trembling as I touched his shoulder to get a better view of Duncan as he studied his ball for that tough putt. He missed. I didn't jump for joy when he missed his putt. I felt too weak and too shaky to move. My 300 score had stood up to win me my first British Open but it had been too close for comfort. I did manage to walk onto the green and extend my hand to George Duncan in both sympathy and congratulations for a gallant try. Right then I became the first American-born professional ever to win the British Open.

One hole particularly stands out in my mind with respect to the 1922 British Open—the fifteenth of my final round. I had taken a brassie shot which caught a cross trap short of the green. I knew I'd need to gamble here, for I wanted a 4 badly. With the hole well back, and the lightning-fast green sloping away from right to left, I was blessed with finding my ball resting very cleanly in the sand trap.

I elected to hit the ball with a seven-iron and play up on the slope to the left of the green, hoping to catch the roll and trickle down to the hole. I figured an explosion shot wouldn't leave me close enough to the hole to give me much of a chance for my 4. Played off the contour to the left, if the shot didn't come off, it would cost me no more than a 5 anyway. This was a very delicate shot and I concentrated on hitting the ball cleanly to the left side. I manipulated the shot perfectly and my ball stopped within a foot of the hole. My putt was an easy tap for my 4. I had played a shot very seldom executed for there aren't too many opportunities for trying it on the British seaside links. After that I could do no wrong, so I finished my last three holes confidently with 3-4-4 to give me the winning 300.

I cabled a few of my pals in New York to set up a celebration at the Biltmore Hotel for the night of my arrival back in the United States. Instead, hundreds of cheering golf fans turned out at the pier along with the Seventh Regiment Band and New York's official greeter, Grover Whalen, decorated with his famous boutonniere. A fleet of limousines waited to whisk my party off to City Hall for an official welcome from Mayor Hylan and a ticker tape parade. To the best of my knowledge, that fleet of cars with a dozen motorcycle policemen screeching a path down Broadway was the first ever to be accorded a sports personality.

I passed up the PGA Championship in 1922. Gene Sarazen, the new champion, wanted me to team up with him for an exhibition tour. I felt Gene made a first-class rival, but I had already signed with Joe Kirkwood for a lengthy swing around the golf courses of the country. However, since Gene was the Professional Golf champion and I held the British Open title, we arranged for an international championship match, entirely unofficial, to be played between us. The first 36 holes were scheduled for the Oakmont Country Club near Pittsburgh on October 6, the second 36 the following day at the Westchester-Biltmore at Rye. Three thousand dollars was posted, the winner to receive two thirds.

Over the Oakmont course I was leading by 2 up at the end of the thirty-six holes. That night after the trip up from Pittsburgh some of my fellow pros sat in my room looking over ties I had brought back from England.

One of the fellows picked up a particularly loud number in a red, blue and yellow combination and said, "What do you expect to do with this? How about sending it over to Gene with a cute little note from some girl?"

We wrote:

> *Dear Gene,*
> *You are my ideal golfer and a clever little fellow. I am sending you this beautiful tie and hope you will wear it when you play Walter Hagen. If you do you will win.*

When I walked out on the tee the next morning at the Westchester-Biltmore there stood Gene in a bright new golfing outfit, sporting that red, blue and yellow tie and grinning from ear to ear.

"I'm all ready," he announced. "Let's get going."

"Okay," I said, "but answer one question. Where'd you get that funny tie?"

"Never mind that," he said in his cocky fashion, "you think you've got all the dames on your side, but you haven't. This is my mascot. Just wait and see."

We got under way, Gene starting off the second thirty-six holes 2 down. But it wasn't long before he picked up two holes and we were even. He continued to gain and went 1 ahead and then another. And that was the way we finished, Sarazen 2 up.

After the match, Gene was still wearing the tie, but was laughing about it for he'd learned of the joke. "Well, Walter, so you gave me a tie," he said. "Here it is, I don't need it any more. You can have it back for luck." That was one time a joke boomeranged on me. The darned thing actually did bring him luck.

Gene didn't have the opportunity to celebrate his victory for he was stricken with appendicitis as we walked toward the club house from the eighteenth green and rushed to the hospital in an ambulance. The old gag golfers toss around, "I've never beaten a well man in my life," was actually topped by our match. I had been trimmed by a really sick man.

Five years after our international play-off, Gene and I staged another 72-hole match, to be played over the Miami Biltmore course at Coral Gables, and the course at Sanford. I had never played the Coral Gables course and had promised I'd appear a week early to get in several days' practice. But I knew Gene. I'd always been able to rattle him. I decided not to show up until the morning of the match.

Every day during the week prior to the match Gene inquired from my friends about the time of my arrival. Along about Thursday he was really worried. By Saturday he was frantic with anxiety. In the meantime he practiced every day and was in superb form. When I finally showed up at the first tee on the morning of our match, he came dashing up to me, as excited as a fellow could possibly be.

"Why didn't you get here for at least one or two rounds on a course you've never seen?" he demanded.

"Gene, my boy," I said, "I don't need to see the course to beat you. My caddie will tell me where to shoot."

At the end of the first thirty-six at Coral Gables I had him 5 down. From there we went to Sanford for the second thirty-six and I beat him 8 and 7. He was so disgusted he threw his clubs in the lake.

I really had him that time. My peculiar golf psychology did the trick. Anyway I knew Gene couldn't play the same top form in competition that he'd been playing in his practice rounds. No golfer can.

One more incident with my friend Gene . . . at the USGA Open in 1933. I had played in the St. Paul Open a few days prior to the start of the National Open. I'd come in second and won $1200, and not liking to take the money out of town, I'd been quite busy spending it.

Most of the players for the National Open had arrived some

days before I appeared. When I did reach the North Shore Country Club in Chicago someone showed me an item from a local paper where Sarazen was quoted as saying, "Hagen will need a wheel chair to get around the course."

The North Shore Country Club course had never held any terrors for me. In the third round I had a 78, but on the last I turned in a 66, despite a two stroke out-of-bounds penalty on the seventeenth. That 66 was a record for the course, as well as championship golf, but it was not good enough to win. Neither was Gene's effort since he had to struggle for a poorly played 75 on that last round.

Tommy Armour, Grantland Rice, Spec Hammond and I were sitting in the locker room talking about the finish, and the fellows congratulated me on my final round. Someone said that Gene had just teed off the fifteenth and I remembered his remark about the wheel chair and me. I seldom had an opportunity to retaliate for a remark like that so quickly. I suggested that Spec get a nice comfortable armchair from the club manager and take it out to the seventeenth green.

"Spec," I said, "put the chair down on the green in front of the gallery. Gene'll look over and wonder what it is all about. Then you announce to that faker that Mr. Hagen sent it out with his compliments."

"What an idea!" Grantland Rice said. "I'll cover that for the sports page right away."

Gene took the incident in his stride and following his finish we shook hands and bent an elbow together in the club grill.

Tournament golfers are an unusual breed of players. Yet I've found very few that some form of strategic thinking couldn't reach. With Gene, I'd treat him as a kid, casually remarking that I could beat him any day in the week at any game. Or worry him by not taking a match with him seriously. With some fellows I'd try a different technique, complimenting them highly on the way they were playing or on an especially good shot. I'd

105

insist that when they'd won the Championship, we'd go on tour together. A twenty-year-old youngster came out of Missouri around 1929 and made me live up to my promise. That fellow was Horton Smith, and we made a very successful tour together!

Again, a bit of mild sarcasm . . . trying to impress with my insouciance and skill . . . would sometimes be my way of perhaps throwing a fellow off his game. They tried the same tricks on me. The only advantage I had was the fact that nothing disturbed me too much. I was well accustomed to the razzing and kidding.

In 1924, in the semifinals of the PGA Championship at French Lick, I was paired with Ray Deer. In the grill the night before the match I overheard him telling a few friends at his table how he was "going to take Hagen" the next day.

Going out to the first tee to start the semifinals Ray said, "I only hope you won't beat me too badly. It will look better in the home-town papers if I don't get beat in double figures."

"It's a beating, no matter what the figures show," I said. "If I beat you 3 and 2, you're beat. Actually it's any man's game in the semifinals. You've evidently played pretty good golf or you wouldn't have come this far. We're equal now. You've as good a chance as I have to win this."

I wanted to impress on him that he practically had the championship in his hands. I wanted him to feel overconfident. At the first hole he sank a long putt across the green to go 1 up.

I said, "You see, I'm 1 down already."

Often I've found a man who figures he doesn't have too much chance gets reckless and holes putts from all over the green. Or again the same fellow trying too hard and pressing his shots may miss a few short easy putts. I could see that Ray's idea was to guard that one-hole lead. He wasn't too successful, though, for I won 8 and 7. I took care of Mr. Jim Barnes the following day to win my first of four straight victories of the PGA Championship.

My tendency to stay up late at night . . . or into the wee hours of the morning . . . was another little bit of business that bothered a few of my fellow pros. I usually managed to get eight hours' sleep, but there were times when I stepped up to tee off with an hour or less spent on my cool white pillow. Every athlete needs plenty of sleep and rest during strenuous competition. But few actually get it. This is particularly true of golfers in a championship tournament. I try to get what I require, because I know I'm going to need steady nerves and good physical co-ordination the next day. I never hurry. That goes for both on and off the golf course. People have written that I have no regard for time. I respect time highly and I try always to make the most of it. There is just as much in saving time as there is in spending it properly. It fits the old army gag about "hurry up and wait!" That's been pretty much my idea. I don't hurry, therefore I've never been bothered with waiting.

From the minute I rose in the morning, I kept on an even keel until I reached the first tee. I rose in plenty of time to dress and breakfast leisurely and to arrive at the course just when I was due to play. There's a certain sort of rhythm in such a smoothed-out routine that carried over into my game . . . a rhythm that helped me avoid the jerky, gearshifting movements which characterized the game of many easily upset or nervous golfers.

There were a few times when I stepped up to tee off with not even one hour of sleep. One such incident has been narrated incorrectly so often that I'm going to set it straight. When I was president of the Pasadena Golf and Country Club at St. Petersburg, we made it a point to have exhibition matches over every week end and on holidays to interest the public in the home-site possibilities of the place.

These exhibitions were bread-and-butter promotions for us and the main reason for building the course. This particular exhibition was scheduled for New Year's Day, at ten in the morning. My wife and I had been on a round-robin party New Year's Eve, and ended up at Gene Elliott's home for breakfast. Gene's place was a good half-hour drive from the club. My chauffeur, Jim Randall, came in and reminded me of the exhibition match.

The sun had been up so long I'd no idea of the correct time. Checking my watch, I found I had slightly less than thirty minutes to motor across to Pasadena. I arrived at the first tee wearing my dinner clothes and patent leather pumps. The few hundred people in the gallery thought it great fun as I slid around in all directions trying to tee off in those slippery-soled shoes. After several attempts I got my drive away. I gave the gallery the impression that I intended playing the entire match in those clothes. Then I tossed my club to the caddie, made my excuses and explained that I'd go into the club house and dress properly for the game. Looking over the gallery I remarked that I thought a number of them hadn't been up too long either. They laughed and agreed I had a lot of company.

In the club house I changed to regular golf clothes and spiked shoes. Even then, for the next several holes, I noticed that the fairway was much more slippery than it had ever seemed the dozens of times I'd played it. I managed to keep my footing and balance and went on to win my match with a 68.

CHAPTER XIII: Joe Kirkwood Tour

Is it a coincidence that the world's greatest golfers of the past three decades have been players with five-letter names: *Hagen, Jones, Snead, Locke* and *Hogan?*

—PERCY HUGGINS, *Scottish Field*
[1953]

FOR OVER 400 years golfers had pinched a bit of sand into a suitable tee for their drives. If one did not use sand, he'd hit the earth with his club or kick up a small mound of turf for teeing the ball. There had been no artificial change in the practice since the game's origin.

In 1920 Dr. William Lowell, a New Jersey dentist, a novice golfer with no great respect for the revered traditions of the game, whittled out a little wooden peg on which to mount his ball for the drive. Playing companions ridiculed the idea, but his sons induced the doctor to patent the gadget and put it on the market. The little peg thus manufactured, painted red, was advertised to the golf world as the Reddy Tee. Professional golfers dismissed it as silly and refused to accept the tees as gifts. Amateurs shrugged off their use . . . and even the ladies of the game looked down their pretty noses at Dr. Lowell's little invention. Probably nothing would have come of the tees had not Joe Kirkwood and I decided to use them as a sort of added attraction on our exhibition tour of 1922. That and the fact that the good doctor shelled out $1500 as a persuader.

109

Alex Smith told me some time later, after Joe and I had used the tees in our matches at the Shenecossett Club in New London, Connecticut where he was pro, that he took more than twenty orders for those "silly little tees." He said he put in a stock but felt they were only a passing fad. Joe and I strutted around the courses with the bright red tees stuck behind our ears. At each tee we used them . . . and left them, and the kids scrambled onto the course grabbing them as souvenirs. They became so popular that the club officials found it necessary to rope off the driving tees and the fairways to control the gallery. This was the first time in the history of golf in the United States that the gallery control ropes were used. And it's an interesting fact that the roping incident followed closely upon the heels of the PGA Championship at Skokie where the gallery paid an admission charge for the first time.

My acquaintance with Joe Kirkwood dated back to the North and South Open at Pinehurst in 1921. He came up from Australia as the Australian Open champion and winner of the New Zealand Championship. With Victor East, his manager, he was following the circuit in the States. In his own country he was famous as a great trick shot artist. I decided he and I would make a good drawing pair in exhibitions. Before our tour, I set out to polish Joe up a bit. I took off his suspenders and sleeve garters and started him well on the way to becoming the Beau Brummel of the golfing fraternity.

Golf club officials attending the PGA Championship at Skokie were excited about the tour Joe and I planned and nearly every club in the area wanted to book us. Our price was $500, and if we decided to take the gate receipts instead of a flat fee, our take was frequently doubled.

However, the tour booking in the beginning was one mad mess. We each began scheduling dates—Joe, his manager, Bob Harlow, and I—without consulting one another. On the first Sunday following Skokie we ended up with four separate dates

110

in four different cities, each a night's ride away from Chicago. I had promised we'd be in St. Louis, Joe had booked us for Louisville. Bob Harlow put us in Milwaukee and Joe's manager had scheduled the exhibition for Detroit. We finally took the one made first, St. Louis, and attempted to appease the other three. But that incident taught us a lesson. After that one man carried the book and all dates had to be cleared through him. We had no more conflicts.

We tried to make the jumps around the circuit as easy and as logically planned as possible, because after our arrival in a city we always needed an extra hour or so to drive out to the golf club. Joe was an invaluable partner and the combination of our personalities made a good show everywhere we played. He had a lot of comedy in his act . . . a whole bag of tricks which he sandwiched in between the exhibition rounds we played against opponents picked by the various club officials. I played straight man for his jokes and gags. Our tour of the United States drew crowds through every part of the country, and the success of that first tour undoubtedly suggested the world trips we took some years later.

I never realized how lucky we were, weather-wise, until I met an insurance friend, Ray Balff, whom I had known at Palm Beach and Pinehurst. He was a great booster of golf and always attended the Championships.

Ray said, "Walter, since the fourth of July, you and Joe have played six weeks and haven't had to postpone a match because of rain. This luck can't last forever. Now, I have an idea. Rain insurance will cost you fifty dollars and you'd still get the five hundred, if rain spoiled your playing."

That sounded reasonable to me. "All right, Ray," I told him. "You draw up the contract and make it start tomorrow. We play in Providence with Glenna Collett and her exhibition partner. This exhibition is for the entire gate receipts, and it would certainly be too bad if we got rained out."

The day dawned bright and sunny. A big gallery turned out to follow us. We had passed the tenth hole when a thunderstorm broke loose and chased us off the course. We weren't able to give the crowd the eighteen holes we'd promised but they appeared satisfied with what they'd had and made us promise to sign for a return match. The insurance policy paid us $500 for getting wet, and the gallery receipts amounted to $1200. About a month later we played there again and drew another gate of over $1250. We also played two matches at my old stomping grounds in Rochester, New York, for approximately the same amount on both occasions.

Joe was a quiet sort of fellow and on that tour I used to get a bang out of our interviews. Reporters would ask me a question or two and I liked talking to them and exchanging quips. Joe'd be sitting there listening . . . saying nothing. The newspapermen would turn to him and he somehow got out of saying more than "yes" or "no." Mostly he referred the questioner to me. One thing people always asked: Does luck play as much of a part in golf as in other sports? Of course it does. Just as much depends on getting the breaks in golf as in baseball, football or any other sport. Without the breaks, a golfer is lost. With them, and the good Lord helping, he is unbeatable. He needs every luck break he can draw on to shoot super-golf.

But those trick shots of Joe's were not lucky shots. He had a golf ball trained. He began doing the trick shots to entertain the wounded and crippled Australian veterans of World War I. First he showed those veterans how to hit the ball for varying distances. Then he showed them fancy shots. As Joe said, "It's a matter of keeping your nerve. I don't smoke or drink. I'm in the best physical condition . . . for I must be steady and undisturbed. A fine touch is required, but once obtained, it comes easily the next time."

I've seen him hit a ball as hard and as far with his "pudder"

112

as with his driving iron. He could slice or hook a ball with any club, making it turn from left to right, or from right to left. He'd play a full drive from the crystal of an open-faced watch or from the toe of a spectator's shoe. He would hole six balls all stymied in a row in rapid succession. He'd take a full shot at a ball and without moving from his stance would catch it as it popped up right in front of him. He could turn his face away and hit twelve balls in rapid succession, full shots. He'd play right-hand shots with a left-hand club and vice versa. It was all child's play to him. Every place we toured, Joe's trick shots brought great bursts of applause from the galleries. At every club we used for our tee shots, and left as souvenirs, the "silly" Reddy Tees . . . doing our part to pull the golfers of the world out of the sand buckets. We played more than one hundred and twenty-five matches that summer and the tour was regarded as the greatest golfing crusade for financial gain ever attempted up to 1922.

In 1929 Joe and I met in Los Angeles to get our reservations for the first leg of a six-months tour of Australia and Japan. Joe was always a penurious soul. He kept account of every dime he made and most of the coin stayed close to him.

I had been living pretty well, not participating too much in golf tournaments. Consequently I was short of cash and I put the bite on Joe for a thousand dollars. He let me have it after some argument and with the understanding it would purchase my steamship ticket. My intentions were good. I usually just had a chance to squeeze money for luck, before going out and rounding up another batch. This time was no exception. A beautiful diamond bracelet for a very lovely girl, a bon voyage gift, interfered with my passage reservation. I admitted to Joe that the money was no longer with me and he unbuttoned his pocket once more and paid my way. When the girl proudly showed Joe the sparklers on her arm, his eyes really popped. He got the idea

113

immediately. We steamed on for Honolulu with all our funds in Joe's possession. He kept books and held on to most of the cash for the entire tour!

Following our United States tour in 1922, I returned to the Westchester-Biltmore at Rye around the twenty-first of August to play a 36-hole match with Abe Mitchell. That Mitchell match was one of the most thrilling I've ever played. At the finish of the first eighteen holes, of the morning round, I was 1 up. After the first nine holes in the afternoon, I found myself 4 down with but nine holes to play.

At the first hole of the afternoon round we both got our pars. Then he reeled off a string of birdies and I found myself 4 down at the ninth. He had finished the morning eighteen holes in 76 while I had 75. Going out in the first nine of the afternoon, Abe had a 35 while I had 40. Then the fireworks began. On the tenth hole, the twenty-eighth of the match, I got a 3 to Abe's 4; on the eleventh a 4 to his 5, as a result of his missing a pair of club-length putts. But I was still 2 down and only seven to play.

On the twelfth green I played one of the finest stymies of my entire career. On his second shot Abe's ball was on the extreme back edge of the green. My shot was short and to the left. I played the third shot up and left myself eight feet from the hole. Abe had a thirty-foot putt and he all but holed it, just missing the cup and stopping on the very edge to the right, leaving me a dead stymie, blocking the hole.

Things looked extremely black for me right then—having a dead stymie at eight feet and knowing if I didn't make it I'd be 3 down with only six more holes to play. I could putt around his ball, but I could see no possible chance to hole my ball. I decided to use a seven-iron. I looked the green over . . . back and forth, back and forth. Then I hit my ball just short of Abe's, which lay delicately poised on the very rim of the cup. My ball hit a breath of an inch behind his, jumped it and stayed in the hole! We halved the hole and I was still in business. And that

114

stymie shot of mine disturbed Abe so much he hooked his next tee shot badly, and lost the hole, leaving me only 1 down. I finished the match by winning 2 and 1. That stymie, the greatest shot I ever played, paid off.

Putting has won many a match for me. My penchant for holing the ball has made up for my wildness on the fairway in match after match. Much of the indifferent putting I've seen is due to the shaky, uncertain way a ball is hit. I like to hit a ball firmly. Banging the ball recklessly isn't going to help, of course, because mechanically it is as difficult to hole out from beyond the cup as it is from short of it, distances being equal. But at least you've had one try when you go past the cup.

One of the best putters I've ever known, not a man who figured prominently in tournament play but who won a lot of matches from players who were a stroke better than he from tee to the green, made a special point of hitting every ball at least as *far* as the hole. The way he acquired this practice was to penalize himself every time he failed to give the ball a chance to reach the hole on any green during a round of play.

There is a favorable psychology, as well as logic, working for the player who consistently hits the ball hard enough to reach the hole. I've made it a point to note how often poor putters are short and I've been amazed at how much more frequently the good ones are beyond when they miss.

Experience counts in championship golf. I remember thinking, back in 1914, after I'd won the American Open at Midlothian, that with a few more seasons under my belt I'd be right up on top, consistently beating the best of them. It didn't work that way. Nineteen twenty-one had rolled around before I could coddle a hoot at the nineteenth, count my major championship wins and make them cover all the fingers and thumb on one hand. In 1922 I was undoubtedly the golfer to be reckoned with wherever tournament golf was played. I don't think it's conceited to make that statement. I knew I could win over any other

115

golfer providing the breaks were even . . . and of course, providing I got my necessary minimum one hour of sleep before I teed off for the first round. After all, I needed to have both eyes wide open—I had to keep one eye on my ball and the other on my opponent.

CHAPTER XIV: Florida Boom

He's the most generous of mortals . . . You can
have the shirt off his back, if you can unbutton it
and slide it off while he's slinking back into an easy
chair like a contented and grinning Buddha and
sipping a beverage. Take his shirt. He has a trunk-
ful in the next room.

—TOMMY ARMOUR, *The American Golfer*
[1935]

THE FLORIDA BOOM fitted in perfectly with my design for living . . . sunshine, beautiful scenery, people with time on their
hands for fun, and of course, money. When Gene Elliott, Florida real estate operator in St. Petersburg, wired me in the fall of
1923 to come down and talk business with him, I readily agreed.
I did, however, refuse his expense check for $1000 as I pre-
ferred to feel free to make the deal which would seem best to me.
At the same time, with my alarming financial overhead—a new
bride, a Cadillac limousine and chauffeur—that $1000 looked
awfully big to me.

Edna and I motored down from New York and were guests of
the Elliotts. To afford me a better opportunity to understand
the extent of the area contained in his proposed development,
Elliott took us for a cruise on his yacht. I imagine, too, he
thought a cruise through the beautiful West Coast gulf waters
would serve to soften me up for the deal.

All real estate development operators were basing their promotions strongly on the golf courses they planned to build. This
was extremely important to me, for it led to my receiving the

117

highest salary ever paid a golf professional, when I became president of the Pasadena Golf and Country Club. However, on this particular cruise I wandered up on the bridge to talk with the skipper. I liked fishing and motors, so we had plenty of congenial subjects. While Edna and I were having cocktails with the Elliotts, Gene told me of the plan to build a long bridge from Tampa to the Pinealas Peninsula, where St. Petersburg was situated. The proposed bridge would cut many miles off the distance between the two cities. He asked me where I'd suggest placing the bridge.

So while I was on the bridge with the yacht skipper I asked him where the logical location for such a bridge would be, suggesting, on my own, that it would of necessity be constructed where there was the best channel. He indicated a spot with several channels and I mentally noted it by the trees and shore contour. Later I advised Elliott that the bridge should be erected there. Thus the Gandy Bridge, a four-mile span over water was constructed on the very site I selected. It was the longest water carry I ever made in my life. The laugh was that I had no knowledge of engineering, much less of how or where a bridge should be located. Imagine asking a niblick player about a deal like that!

Following our cruise along the gulf, I told Gene I'd think over his business proposition, since I was in no great rush to arrive at a decision. I might go to Hollywood for a picture, or I might just look around. I covered the waterfront the next few days, looked over Pasadena, met a few of the other pros who were also down playing the circuit and investigating propositions of their own.

I inquired one day about a private railway car on a siding near Pasadena and learned it belonged to Jack Taylor, the big shot of the promotions along the West Coast. He was developing thousands of acres along the Boca Ciega Bay. Across the Bay a narrow strip of land, Pass-A-Grille, faced out on the Gulf of Mexico. Taylor called his parcel, a tract of acreage along the West Coast running from Gulfport along Pass-A-Grille to Pasadena, "Pasadena on the Gulf" but it became generally referred to as the Pasadena Estates.

Not too long after my inquiry about the private car, Edna and I were sitting in that very car enjoying Jack Taylor's hospitality while he talked turkey to me. I explained I'd come down at Elliott's invitation but I was not tied up. I was just looking for a setup that would do the most for me. Taylor wanted me to act as president of the golf club he planned to build, and I would have 300 to 350 acres under my jurisdiction. I consulted with Gene Elliott again and got an offer of $25,000, and then I went back to Taylor. I told him I'd consider the deal closed for $30,000. Taylor protested a bit about the price, until I pointed out that something like one-half of the one per cent commission on sales made by the one hundred and six salesmen under his promotion would pay for my services. And look at the kind of talent he was getting . . . *me*. He called his attorney and we signed a contract for four months at $30,000. I asked for and received one lot, a hot corner, for signing.

We attempted first to choose a good promotion name for the club and the course. Bear Creek ran through the acreage but naturally that name would do nothing for us. Boca Ciega (meaning closed mouth) was used temporarily but we later changed to Pasadena on the Gulf. This was attractive (if a little confusing) because of the famous beautiful city of the same name in California.

My duties at the club were to arrange tournaments and exhibitions for each week end and holiday through the four months of December, January, February and March. The remainder of the year I represented the Pasadena Club at the various tournaments and championships around the country. Also I was supposed to play golf, when the course was completed, with such money prospects as Jack deemed of sufficient importance to al-

119

low them to get into a foursome with the champion. I use the word "play" with some reservations in speaking of these prospects, for I spent most of my time hunting their balls in the palmettos and avoiding rattlesnakes. But during that first season most of my time was spent with Wayne Stiles of Boston, the golf architect, as we planned the design and construction of the championship golf course.

One added arrangement with Taylor gave me one lot for each exhibition match in which I played. I collected ten of them. Although my original contract was for one year, early in 1924 Taylor's lawyer suggested that Jack and I needed each other too much for a one-year contract to be satisfactory. He drew up another for three additional years at the same salary, and we all signed.

Because of the many months of sunshine and fine weather the course was ready for play early in 1924. Mrs. Hagen and I occupied a beautiful Spanish villa in the estates proper and were host to many wonderful parties for the people building homes in the Pasadena development. The fine homes constructed there were landscaped free from a huge nursery Jack Taylor kept supplied with great varieties of flowers and shrubs. Even the golf greens were outlined with gorgeous flame hibiscus bushes, with additional rows of the colorful blooms backing the tees and forming a wide aisle from the greens to the tees. No royal palms had ever been grown in St. Petersburg and many doubted they could survive the comparatively cool climate of that region. I personally went down to Ft. Meyers and brought back ten of them to transplant along the drive from the entrance of the development to the club house. Those royal palms thrived in the northern air and sunshine and are still standing today.

Jack Taylor's Rolyat Hotel was the most magnificent and luxurious hostelry constructed in the booming twenties. The Rolyat today is the Florida Military Academy and its architecture and artistic design continue to be admired.

120

Jack Taylor himself was almost as much a work of art as his Pasadena Estates. Well over six feet tall with an unruly mass of thick curly hair, he wore a green coat which hung to his knees, jodhpurs and boots. He drove about his property in a vari-colored Minerva automobile of extreme design, complete with a chauffeur in eye-catching livery.

While the Pasadena course was under construction I lived at the famous East Coast resort hotel, the Belleair-Biltmore at Belleair. This was a popular spot with many financial wizards. It was also adjacent to Clearwater where the big-league baseball teams trained during the winter months. I played plenty of golf with well-known people who were either vacationing or training there at the time. Between golf games we played rummy and made the time pass very quickly.

Manager Joe McCarthy of the New York Yankees put a ta-boo on golf during the training season but a number of the fel-lows sneaked over for bootleg games. Babe Ruth and I played many rounds together. One thing I noticed peculiar to Babe's game, and to that of most ball players, was that for the length of time an average ball game consumes Babe was a fine golfer. He could concentrate. After the hour and fifty minutes' duration of a ball game, or about the eleventh hole as golf is played, the Babe began to slop his shots away. He usually went out com-fortably under 40. However, returning, he had to struggle to play 15-handicap golf. Years later, in 1936, Billy Burke and I played with Babe in the True Temper Open at Detroit and his game still followed that pattern. Babe Ruth has always been touted as the top-money player among all star athletes and I took a leaf out of his book.

I also played golf with Rube Marquard, Jimmy Foxx, Mickey Cochrane, Cy Perkins and numerous other famous ball players. Among the writers who wintered in Belleair and nearby were the great sports reporter, Grantland Rice, and Dickey Martin, who had accompanied me on that first trip to England. George

Ade, Rex Beach and Ring Lardner were frequently partners of mine. I particularly remember an incident with Rex Beach.

We were playing in a foursome and had arrived at the home hole all even, so that hole meant the match. My second shot overran the green and landed in a very bad spot. Getting out was one thing and getting close to the hole was another. Rex went up to hold the pin and said, "Walter, give it everything you've got!" I went for it and gave the ball enough freedom to reach the pin if I succeeded in clearing the edge of the trap, which I did. From there on Rex took over, coaxing the ball until it ran down and into the hole for a 3.

He ignored the miracle of that shot. He looked at me quite seriously and said, "Walter, I knew you could make it if you just concentrated on it. You know, I'll take you for a partner any time." That shot not only won but with it we collected our bets.

Ring Lardner always insisted that the main purpose of golf was fun. One day we got him into one of the winter tournaments. He qualified in the third flight and was just as happy as if it had been the championship division. He was lined up with an elderly gentleman by the name of Stone, who was completely deaf. We explained to Ring—not about the deafness—but that the old gentleman wanted to play the game in silence, regular Scotch golf. He was just about Ring's match, same speed and so on, and they battled around to come to the eighteenth all even.

Ring played his fourth to the final green, but it sliced into a trap. The old fellow, Stone, had more luck. He reached the green in 5, took the pin and held it while Ring slashed away in the sand trap. After three tries without extricating his ball, he held up his hand in disgust and in a token of surrender.

Thinking the old fellow would understand his breaking the silence now, he said, "I give up. I'm through. It's your match."

Stone continued to hold the pin and gazed fixedly at Ring.

"I'm through," Ring repeated, walking toward him with the ball in his hand. "We're not in Scotland now. I give up."

Stone put a hand to his ear inquiringly.

Ring, talking much louder now, said, "I told you I give up. It's your hole and your match! I have picked up my ball!"

The old gentleman said, "Oh, you don't want to play any more?" He smiled importantly. "Well, in that case I will *claim* the match on you. That is the rule. Good day, my friend."

George Ade, the famed humorist and Chicago reporter, whom I met at Belleair, later built his own course on his farm two miles east of Brook, Indiana. He began by laying out a small pitch-and-putt course. He loved the game so much that he soon built the small links into a full-fledged nine-hole course. Ade's farm became a favorite spot, not only for golf enthusiasts, but also for anyone who owned one of the early automobiles. The test of one of those first cars was whether it would make the trip from the Loop in Chicago to his farm and back without motor trouble.

In later years it was a common event to meet Chick Evans, Gene Sarazen, Jock Hutchison, Joe Kirkwood, Laurie Ayton, Bob MacDonald and many other famous golfers down there. Writer John T. McCutcheon and movie star Tommy Meighan were also frequent visitors. I had promised George many times I'd come down and play his course. So being in Chicago in the thirties, I hired a small plane and headed for the farm. Unfortunately we miscalculated our landing and cut down some of George's prize corn in a nearby field. His remarks to me about the incident made it a lucky thing only the ears of corn and my own could hear him.

He had a strange way of welcoming his guests. He'd let a fellow feast his eyes on a tall mint julep. Then he would hand over a small Flobert rifle loaded with spitfire cartridges and point to a target on a tall tree fifty yards away.

"When you hit the bull's eye," George would say, "a bell will ring. When the bell rings and not before, you'll get the julep."

Fortunately for the guests Ort Wells, a lifelong companion of Ade's, acted as official greeter and he had the happy faculty of being able to hear that bell ring even when the exhausted traveler's trigger finger was noticeably unsteady.

Wealthy visitors to Belleair during those boom days in 1924, 1925 and 1926 with whom I enjoyed golf included Henry Topping, father of Bob and of Dan, who is now co-owner of the New York Yankees; George Hunter of the Coca-Cola Company; George Morse of Rutgers, New Hampshire, and Scotty Probasco, president of the Bank of Chattanooga, Tennessee.

On December 30, 1924 President Walter Hagen of the Pasadena-on-the-Gulf course—salary $30,000 for four months a year —officially opened his office at 77th Street on Central Avenue. Central Avenue was the long connecting highway leading directly into Pasadena from Pass-a-Grille and St. Petersburg. My desk was completely hidden by huge baskets of flowers and the many wires of congratulations kept my beautiful blonde secretary busy with both hands signing for them. This talented secretary also played the ukulele and her greatest effort during her stay as my employee was to compose a song, "Pasadena, Beautiful Pasadena." She'd sit at her desk and keep watch for prospective club members wandering over from the development. Then she would grab the uke from the desk drawer and the two of us would give out loudly with vocal enticement. The fee for membership in the club was $500 and even after relieving the prospect of his cash our singing "always left him smiling."

I saw very little of my office actually. I went in about noon, stayed perhaps forty minutes, then checked out for lunch with some special pals. Business in the minutes at my desk consisted chiefly in lining up the afternoon golf and perhaps a few telephone calls to plan some doings for the evening.

The Pasadena course was formally opened on Saturday, Janu-

ary 10, 1925. In a match played on opening day, Joe Kirkwood and I lost by one hole to Cyril Walker, then Open champion of the United States, and Jim Barnes. The opening was
quite a deal . . . complete with music by the Pasadena band
and attended by the Mayor, Mr. R. S. Pearce, publisher F. F.
Pulver and baseball's Al Lang, Mayor of St. Petersburg, plus the
huge crowds which thronged the course to applaud their
favorite golfers.

The Florida boom paid me off well for three straight years,
then the bubble burst. The fourth year the big real estate tycoons started pulling out, salvaging what little they could. Financially the drop in the property development did not touch
me, for I hadn't sunk any cash into land or construction. The
lots I owned had been given me for promotion of the exhibition
matches. Gene Elliott and Jack Taylor, along with scores of
others, went for broke. The millionaires became paupers.

A few lean years in Florida followed and then conditions returned to normal. Many of the beautiful golf courses created
during the boom remain today . . . some are now municipal
courses. But the West Coast of Florida has never to this day
seen as much big-time golf as during the days when I was president of the Pasadena-on-the-Gulf Club.

CHAPTER XV: British Open, 1924

On Friday morning, the last day of the British Open Championship of 1924, a peculiar phenomenon was observed. There was a distinct halo around the sun, a huge ring of rainbow-like formation. Perhaps it came as a sign and a portent of Walter Hagen's triumph!

—R. E. (Bob) Howard, *Golf Illustrated*
[1924]

I STARTED OFF the 1923 season by winning the North and South Open at Pinehurst and I figured that might be an auspicious note, heralding a year of championship titles, but such was not the case.

On my fourth trip to England to play for the British Open Championship trophy I got another setback, a jolting one. I missed winning by one stroke. Arthur Havers, the popular young British professional, and I were making it an exciting finish for the more than ten thousand gallery spectators crowding the links at Troon. Frankly, I had been more concerned with trying to catch Joe Kirkwood because we were barnstorming. I hadn't been paying too much attention to Arthur Havers. Joe had turned in 72-79-69-78, for a total of 298. I had 76-71-74 for a total of 221 going into the final round. At the fifth hole of that last round Bob Harlow dashed up out of breath to tell me that Joe'd finished the last four holes in 5 over par and I knew I no longer had need to worry about him. He also informed me that Havers had started the last round leading me by two strokes.

"What have I got to do to get Havers?" I asked.

"You'll have to shoot one under par or better," Bob advised me.

Had I known how badly Joe was doing I wouldn't have been so bold on some of those earlier holes where I had gone for a couple of putts and three-putted on the slippery greens.

When I came up to the last hole of the final round Havers had finished and turned in a score of 295. I needed a 3 on that hole to tie Havers. My second shot had carried the ball into a shallow sand trap, hole-high. In fact the ball rolled off the right-hand side of the green, leaving me a not too difficult pitch, with the green sloping away from me. But I had to hole out from that position to get a tie with Havers. I sized up the shot from every possible angle and when I hit the ball, it headed straight for the hole but stopped eighteen inches short of the cup! I holed out with a 296. The huge gallery of Britishers applauded loudly, because England sure needed a win in their Open.

The British Golf Association had stirred up quite a bit of controversy just prior to the championship matches. Their committee had barred the ribbed or "punched" clubs, as they termed them, and that meant discarding or else doing some lengthy hand labor in smoothing out the punches of our clubs in the few remaining hours before the championship began. Besides that bit of annoying business our American boys, stopping at a hotel bordering the golf course, had expected to pick up their daily mail at the "back door" of the club house. However, we were advised that all mail would be sent to the golf shop so we, as the officials stated, "would not find it necessary to go to the club house." This did not set well with us at all.

After my shot missed and Arthur Havers became the new British Open champion, the secretary of the club came out on the green and insisted that I come *into* the club house with Havers for the presentation of the trophy. I walked up the path

127

with them while British bobbies held back the tremendous crowd following us. At the doorway I stopped and turned to the enthusiastic gallery.

"I'm sorry I didn't win," I told them. "I've been asked to come into the club house with Arthur Havers for the presentation." I stopped for a moment and considered my words carefully, then, "At no time have we Americans been admitted to the club house," I continued, "not even to pick up our mail. At this particular time, I'd like to thank you all for the many courtesies you've extended to us. And . . . I'd like to invite all of you to come over to the pub where we've been so welcome, so that all the boys can meet you and thank you personally. If the committee likes, they can present the trophy to the new champion over there."

I turned and walked away with all the thousands in the gallery following me to the pub, leaving only the committee and Arthur Havers at the club house.

Upon my return to the United States I played in the National Open which Bobby Jones won, and I finished seventh. I sent in my entry for the PGA Championship to be played at Pelham Golf Club, Pelham, New York. And there again I ran into trouble, whose name this time was Gene Sarazen.

In the semifinals Gene had defeated Bobby Cruickshank, 1 up, and I had taken George McLean, 12 and 11. This brought Gene and me together in the finals. I'll say right here that Pelham was thickly populated with enthusiastic Italians, and since Gene had come originally from that same district, they were all eager for their little compatriot to win.

Gene says in the chapter of his book headed "Hagen, My Hero, My Rival!" that he played *offensive* golf on the first nine of the last eighteen holes. As far as I am concerned he needn't have limited it to those nine holes. His golf was offensive all the way. One hole in particular I remember—the fourteenth. A water hazard crossed just in front of the green and the percent-

128

age shot was to play your second short, chip over and try for one putt.

We were both playing our second shots as close to the water as possible to leave ourselves easy chip shots. To my surprise Gene played it too strong and I saw a boy in a red sweater run out and stop Gene's ball with his foot. I should have had an easy win, but I managed to halve the hole. After that I kept my eyes open for boys in red sweaters. However, the worst was yet to come! At the end of thirty-six holes of the finals we had a tie.

We went into "sudden death" extra holes. On the thirty-seventh, a long par 4 hole, Gene left himself short about seven feet. I had a sure 4, having put my third up within inches. Gene had to hole his putt to keep the match alive. He putted, the ball hesitated and stopped on the brink. . . . I looked toward him expecting him to walk over and congratulate me . . . when his ball slipped into the cup. Offensive? Well, here's one for the books! On the thirty-eighth Gene had the honor. This hole is bordered on the left by a dead-end street with houses thick as flies paralleling the first three fourths of the fairway. Then it doglegs slightly left around a corner where the dead-end joins a road which runs off to the left. A long tee shot, however, will carry all the houses and give an open shot, a short pitch for the hole.

Gene hooked sharply to the left and the last I heard of the ball it was rattling in between the houses. The officials declared it out of bounds and Gene hit another shot, straight down the fairway. With the two-stroke penalty he had incurred by his out-of-bounds shot, I figured I could win easily if I played safely straight down to the right. I did so and we walked down the fairway. Just then someone called out that Gene's first ball had been found inside the fence. This left him an easier shot for his second to the green. As I walked over to take a look I saw his ball lying in a path where kids had made a huge hole in the mesh

129

fence to sneak through onto the golf course. I've never to this day doubted that such luck *could* happen, but having Gene's ball jump back through the fence and be found teed up could have resulted only from the hand of the good Lord or one of the red-sweatered caddies roaming the course.

Gene played a beautiful shot within a foot of the hole for a sure birdie 3, leaving me a difficult second shot over a sand trap and in a position I never expected to have to face when I'd teed off. I cut it too fine and caught the top of the trap. Suddenly an easy victory for me had turned into defeat. There was nothing left for me to do except to walk over and congratulate Gene.

I won another Championship that year, however, to go along with my North and South Open, when I finished first in the Texas Open at San Antonio. And I was all right financially, for it was my first year with Jack Taylor in the Florida deal and the $30,000 kept me in the champagne and caviar class.

Because of my first ten-day association with Jesse Livermore early in 1924 I was able to make my reservations with the Cunard Line way ahead of time. Mrs. Hagen and I enjoyed the most luxurious accommodations. The British Open was scheduled for June 26 and 27 on the Royal Liverpool links at Hoylake. When we arrived the same old weather prevailed . . . the typical piercing, quick-shifting winds off the sea, cool but not unpleasantly so. As at Troon the year before I barely managed to qualify, but this time I almost lost out before ever posting a score.

Jim Barnes and I were due to qualify on the second day at Formby about forty minutes down from Liverpool, but we arrived ten minutes late. The committee put up quite a fuss. The result of their argument was that they agreed to let me play but to bar Jim. We had a legitimate excuse, a late train; how they arrived at such a crazy decision I'll never know. Of course, we could have put up a tent and camped out on the course the night before in the chilly wind!

130

On my first qualifying round I shot 83, but I made the second in a sizzling 73. Other American pros to qualify included MacDonald Smith, Gil Nicholls and Gene Sarazen. In that second qualifying round I'd been playing the fourth hole, a blind one—British course officials have an attendant ring a bell when the forward players are off the green on these blind holes—and I'd been waiting and waiting for the bell to announce that the pair in front had finished. I told my caddie, "It may take me a long time to ring that bell, too." We finally got the signal and I hit my shot over the direction marker set up to give the players the line to the hole. We then walked down to the green to find my ball in the cup. That eagle right there was the margin which let me qualify. Those two close years of barely scraping by resulted in my taking qualifying a bit more seriously in the years to follow.

I was sincerely pleased when the committee informed me that Mr. John Ball was entering his last British Open and had requested that he be paired with me, Walter *High*gen. I went over immediately to assure him I'd be very honored to play with him. "Uncle John" was a legend in British golf. He had competed in his first Open at the age of fifteen in 1876 and had finished sixth. Between 1888 and 1912 he won the British Amateur title eight times and in 1890 he became the first British amateur ever to win the British Open. Now at the age of sixty-three he was right there shooting for another win. He was playing in his last Championship on the very course where his father's hotel had been located when "Uncle John" began his golfing career. In fact, the course was laid out on the grounds where his father had originally raced fine horses.

My start was not sensational, for I took a 77 for the first round in the championship. But on the second I finished in 73 to stand three strokes back of the leader, Ernie Whitcombe, one of the three famous golfing brothers, and one stroke back of J. H. Taylor. MacDonald Smith and I were tied at 150. On my third round the next day I had a 74 and Ernie Whitcombe and I entered the final round on even terms.

There had certainly been a clearing of the decks from the close play of the previous day. Arthur Havers, the defending champion who had beaten me by one shot in 1923, came to grief with his third round of 80. Abe Mitchell, playing with Arnaud Massy, was spraying his shots wildly and they both gave up on the fourteenth hole and straggled back to the locker room. Mac Smith seemed a good bet to take the lead but his third round of 77 put him three shots back of me. On his final round he finished with a 77 giving him a 304 for a tie with Frank Ball for third. J. H. Taylor, the great warrior who had won five British Championships, soared to 79 on his third round, leaving him four shots behind me going to the final round. His last round of 79 gave him a total of 307.

I went out in the final round in 41, two better than Whitcombe but way over what I'd hoped to shoot. At the twelfth hole Johnny Farrell, who had come over to play in the Open but didn't get the chance because a wasp stung him on the thumb, came out to tell me that Ernie had finished his round and turned in a 301.

"What are you doing?" Johnny asked.

"I've got to finish in par to tie him," I said.

I'd already played my second shot and my third was a difficult niblick shot just over the trap. The hole was hidden behind the trap.

"I'm going to take a chance right here," I told Johnny. "I've got to cut this just right. If it stops right, I can hole it for a 4." It did.

On the thirteenth I thought, since I'd got the twelfth out of the way, the rest shouldn't be too difficult, but the wind had grown to gale strength and there were three long holes ahead of me. The wind was at my back at the thirteenth—a short hole—

but I misjudged the force of it and put my ball right in a trap. However, I made a great recovery shot for a 3.

The fourteenth is a par 5, a dogleg, and here the wind was with me for I got a good tee shot over and across the heavy rough and made my par. At the fifteenth I had to cut straight into the teeth of the wind . . . two long difficult shots to the green. I was now the only one left on the course who had a chance to tie or beat Whitcombe. This was the first time Britain had charged admission, and more than ten thousand paying customers surrounded the green.

I elected to play a driver shot quail-high for my second. This particular driver was a new club. I'd had it made and was crazy about it, but somehow I hadn't been able to make it work for me. As I hesitated for a moment and realized I couldn't reach the green with a brassie, I decided to use a club in which I had little or no confidence. I felt I couldn't expect too much from the driver and perhaps that made me concentrate particularly effectively on making the best possible stroke. Anyhow, the ball stopped fifteen feet from the hole. I missed the putt but was mighty happy with my par 4.

On the par 5 dogleg sixteenth, aided by a favorable wind, I hit my second shot over a huge dike which extends out into the fairway, and which is out of bounds. It was a beautiful brassie shot and let me reach the green in two. But here I lost the one-stroke advantage over par which I seemed to have gained, for I three-putted. This is one of the few times I three-putted.

At the seventeenth—a hole which gave everybody trouble during the Championship, including me—I was straight back against the wind again. Playing this hole right meant placing the tee shot close to the rough on the right side of the fairway, to get a more open shot at the hole. The hole itself was guarded by a series of traps running diagonally in front of the green. It was very treacherous green because you could quite easily hit your second shot too strongly and go through a fence which bounded the back edge of the green. I played a good shot that carried the traps and held the green, stopping eighteen feet from the hole. I hit an almost perfect putt, too, but a bit too hard and the ball hit the cup and jumped out. I got my par 4.

At the eighteenth I was confident I had victory in the palm of my hand, for here was a short par-4 hole with the wind at my back. I got a long tee shot, some 300 yards, leaving me a short seven-iron shot for my second. Again a series of traps crossed the front of the green. However, they didn't seem to be too troublesome considering the shortness of the shot I had to make.

I played my second shot too boldly and went past the flag to the back edge of the green. Here I was on this fast green . . . on the back edge at that . . . and I needed to get down in two. I putted down, sloping away, and left myself five feet short. Had I hit it a tiny bit harder I would have rolled almost to the hole. But a semicircular ridge held my ball and left me with a most difficult putt.

With such a fast green I knew my stroke must be delicate. I looked over both sides of the hole. There was a slim chance of a slight roll as it went down a little incline toward the hole. I studied it carefully once more. I decided there was a double roll down the first two feet of the putt to the right, a slight roll to the left the last two feet. I stood and set myself with one thing uppermost in mind. I must hit the ball delicately. And in a situation like this delicacy is difficult due to the extreme nervous tension one is under. But then I had a second thought which helped greatly in my executing the shot correctly and in not being overanxious to see where the ball was going. Should I miss, I'd only need to stay over another day to beat Whitcombe in the play-off of the British Championship. If I holed, I became the British Open champion.

While ten thousand people held their breath, I stroked the ball . . . gently but firmly; it righted the last turn, straightened out and headed for home! I threw my putter into the air and never saw the ball or the putter again. But I sure saw that British Open trophy!

My wife rushed up and kissed me. London bobbies in their white helmets quickly surrounded us to give what protection they could from the thousands of gallery fans seeking to shake my hand and roaring congratulations into my ears. Some of them lifted Mrs. Hagen and me to their shoulders and carried us off the green.

The committee asked Mrs. Hagen and me to come into the club house for a champagne toast. She was the first woman ever to cross the threshold of the Royal Liverpool links club house. I suggested that MacDonald Smith, who had finished in a tie for third, come along with us and they graciously included him. Mac, on the wagon but sportsmanlike, touched his lips to the rim of the champagne glass but did not drink. I received another great ovation from the gallery when we mounted the platform to receive the trophy and other prizes. The crowd sang "For He's a Jolly Good Fellow," accompanied by a fellow playing a cornet. British golf fans apparently had forgot and forgiven me for a misquoted newspaper statement following the British Open at Troon in 1923.

The news item reported that I'd said, "British golfers are lazy." What I had actually said was that Britain's lack of good pro golfers was due to the very little practice they could get on their home links. Members of the British golf clubs seldom invite their pros to play around the course, while members of the American clubs made quite a point of engaging pros for rounds. Consequently the American pros get a tremendous amount of practice and opportunity to play. I stated that the British golf addicts would do their own games and the pros' games a lot of good by playing more with the pro. If the pro seems lazy about practicing, it's because he must take his rounds alone.

Mrs. Hagen and I were in France on July second where I en-

tered the French Open at Versailles on the La Boulie course.
C. J. H. Tolley, British amateur, won the Championship with a
290; I was three strokes behind him and two ahead of E. La-
Fitte, the Frenchman whom I'd defeated in the French Open of
1920. I won the Belgian Open Championship three days later
at Knocke-sur-Mer, much to the joy of my caddie Jimmy Anderson, whom I'd brought over from England with me. I'd endorsed my prize check from the British Open over to him and
about scared the life out of him when I'd carted him across the
channel to carry my clubs on the Continental courses. After several weeks of fun at the famous resorts and attendance at the
Olympic Games, Mrs. Hagen and I headed for home.

In April before embarking for England I had won the North
and South Open for the third time by two strokes over Cyril
Walker with the record score of 283. Cyril had his revenge
later, however, when he took first place in the National Open at
my old home club, Oakland Hills at Birmingham, Michigan. I
tied for fourth place.

On Sunday before the North and South Open Cyril and I decided to play a few holes over the Pinehurst course. Neither caddies nor the men keeping the course worked on Sunday, so we
had the place to ourselves. We took only three or four clubs and
on the third hole, a par 4, the wind was so strong it was blowing
sand off the green, leaving the surface dry and slick as glass.

I got a good long drive, my ball coming to rest on a slight incline sloping all the way to the green. The gale-like wind sweeping the course made it extremely difficult for me to take a stance.
In order to avoid overshooting the green, I tapped the ball one-
handed with an iron. It started to roll slowly, the wind grabbed
it and I raced down ahead of my ball to the hole. I lifted the
flag and waited for my own shot. I kept talking to my ball,
"Keep coming! Keep coming!" It reminded me of our curling
matches when we'd run along in front trying to sweep a bull's
eye. Believe it or not, that ball followed me directly to the green

136

and dropped gently into the cup. I was my own caddie and beat the ball to the hole for an eagle 2.

In the PGA Championship in mid-September, played on the beautiful courses at French Lick, Indiana, I began a series of wins that has not been equaled since. I had won the PGA first in 1921 and I waited three years to break the dry run I was experiencing in that particular championship. But it was worth the wait. Jim Barnes and I met in the 1924 finals. At the end of the first eighteen holes that morning of September 20, I had a medal score of 71 and the stymies I'd laid Barnes on the seventh and fourteenth greens had aided materially in putting him 4 down at the beginning of the afternoon round.

In the afternoon Jim went out in 34, winning the fourth, seventh and eighth holes to cut my lead to two holes. I shot a 37. We halved the tenth, Jim won the eleventh and I went 2 up again by taking the twelfth. Jim won the thirteenth and we halved the fourteenth. I won again on the fifteenth and when we halved the sixteenth in par 3's I was dormy 2. On the seventeenth I missed a short putt and Jim took the hole.

Playing to the eighteenth, he hooked his drive to the rough in an attempt to lift over an intervening tree, pushed his iron shot, the ball landing to the right of the green. I was on in two, Barnes in three. We started to walk toward the cup when Jim picked up his ball, conceding the hole and the match. We shook hands and I became the new Professional Golf Association champion, a title I was to hold for four consecutive years, through twenty-nine consecutive rounds, the longest run in golfing history. I met good boys in every one of them. One was too good, Leo Diegel, for he ended my string in 1928. However, I cut a path that will be wide open for the boys to follow. I'm hoping I'll be here long enough to read about the fellow who cuts a wider and longer one.

That win at French Lick was a big one. A big "first" in a string of four. But I've had a lot of "firsts" in my life. Some important ones like the PGA Championship titles, others so darn crazy they're difficult to believe.

For instance I believe I was the first golfer to have his knickers pressed with creases down the side, an idea I picked up from riding breeches. I was the first to use the little wood Reddy Tees; the first to own the first Madam X Cadillac to come off the production line. I was the first and the only American golfer to win the British Open four times. I was the first and only golfer to be named on the list of The Ten Best Dressed Men . . . at least, I was the only one until our famous golfing President, Gen. Dwight D. Eisenhower, took that away from me.

CHAPTER XVI

L. A. Young, 1925

> The Haig, as the press called him, loved doing him-
> self well, and I do not think I have met anyone who
> had the capacity and the health to enjoy so much
> what most of us call "a good time."
> —HENRY COTTON, *This Game of Golf*
> [1948]

I HAD some other "firsts" in my competitive golf career which deserve mention. In 1921 at the Inwood Country Club I was trying for my first win in the PGA Championship. I always played the seventeenth hole on that course by driving down the parallel eighteenth fairway. The reason for this was that the hole was opened up to better advantage for my second shot, even though it was a longer one. The green on the seventeenth was trapped on the short and left side, and almost at right angles to the line of play from the seventeenth fairway. If I played over onto the parallel eighteenth, I could open up the hole and come in from the right-hand side with my second shot.

A number of people were familiar with my method of play on the seventeenth hole. I had played it that way on the first day of the championship. That night some joker must have spent more than a thousand dollars to have the late Jack Mackie, the pro, and a landscaper set up a huge weeping willow tree so that it divided the two fairways. They wired it into place just past the lagoon in front of the tee, which lay directly in the line where I'd been playing over to the eighteenth fairway.

Inwood is on the point of the bay and the wind blew in strong. I finished the sixteenth hole and traipsed into the club house to grab a little hyposonica before going over to the seventeenth tee. I had the honor and as I strolled over to take a ball and my driver from the caddie, I thought the gallery seemed unusually excited and noisy. I knew something was happening but I couldn't figure just what. I teed up my ball, looked up and saw that willow tree confronting me. The gallery really laughed now at the surprised look on my face. I hesitated as I picked up my driver, then I took a couple of swings.

"I never saw such fast-growing trees in my life," I remarked to those nearest me. The laughter grew into a roar, but not at my remark. Instead a sudden fierce gust of wind had whipped loose the guy wires holding the tree on the edge of the lagoon . . . and the willow was out of business.

"Well, I timed this about right," I told them. "Now, if I can time my tee shot as well I can be down in my regular spot on the eighteenth fairway."

Some fellow in the gallery said, "You can't beat him!" And no one did that day.

Two other "firsts" are linked with business ventures which oddly enough support me today. Early in 1922 I conceived the idea of manufacturing golf clubs bearing my name. Since 1915 I had been using and exploiting golf equipment for the A. G. Spalding company, and our relationship had been equally satisfactory to both parties. However, I felt that if A. G. Spalding, a baseball player, could parlay the production of sporting supplies into a fortune, I could do the same with golf equipment.

The Spalding group had all been present at the North and South Open at Pinehurst and during a conference following the Championship I told them my idea of getting into business on my own. However, I stated that if they would pay me $20,000 a year for representing them and for officiating in the factory at Chicopee, Massachusetts, I would take the offer. Owing to the fact that they duplicated my prizes at each tournament where I used their equipment I'd already made $9600 that year, but $12,000 was their limit. Harry Curtis was their spokesman and although he used every other kind of persuasion in his power, he would not meet my demand for $20,000. Instead the group told me flatly that I'd be a failure in my own business because I lacked the adequate capital.

They were on the right track, as it turned out, but I said, "I've nothing to lose. If I'm a failure I'll come back to you."

Curtis laughed. "Are you sure?" he asked.

"Yes," I said. "I'm so valuable to you in winning 75 per cent of the Championships, you'd just have to take me, if I wanted to come back."

So with John Ganzil and Joe Tinker, former major league baseball players who lived in Orlando, Florida, I formed the Walter Hagen Golf Products Corporation. The city of Longwood, Florida, erected the building and gave us the property with the idea of booming its population and business. We began the production of golf clubs bearing my name. The first hard fact we learned was that we'd started production in the wrong place. For Longwood and Florida have 11 per cent moisture, the highest moisture percentage of any place in the country. And we were producing hickory-shafted clubs, the only shafts used in those days.

Those early Hagen clubs were beautifully designed, I thought, but the humid climate caused the hickory to swell. While the heads fitted perfectly in the factory, once they arrived in drier temperate zones, like Arizona and states with a similar climate, the iron heads almost rattled off the shafts. When the hickory shafts dried out they gave off slivers of thin wood like porcupine quills which got into a player's hands. We were able to prevent some of this by using a drying kiln, but with the thousands of clubs going through, we couldn't give them all the treatment.

I kept pouring money into the business, and some weeks my big salary from the Pasadena Estates and the exhibitions I played were far from enough to make up the weekly payroll. I lost my partners and wound up carrying the entire burden myself. Finally I telephoned my sister Freda, who was teaching high school in Rockport, New York and asked her to come down and handle the bookkeeping department.

I didn't employ many people, yet my payroll every Friday night amounted to $5000. One or two exhibitions a week, say on Tuesday and Wednesday, allowed me to drag barely enough cash to pay off. In the end it seemed like "fish day" came around more and more often, when another $5000 was due. I sweated it out until 1925 when I was in for over $200,000. I realized if I didn't take some drastic action, I'd be playing golf the rest of my life just to support that factory.

I got in touch with my old friend Al Wallace in Detroit, and he set up a plan for selling the business . . . bailing me out, in other words. This plan brought in L. A. Young, a colorful figure in the high finance bracket in Detroit and owner of the Young Steel and Wire Company, the largest manufacturer of automobile springs in the United States. We wanted L. A. Young to invest in the deal. He surprised us by announcing he would buy the business and move it to Detroit.

A contract with L. A. was drawn up whereby he took over ownership of the Walter Hagen Golf Products Corporation and paid a flat fee of $75,000 for me, just like the bonus paid outstanding young baseball players for signing with a major league. I was made a director of engineering and I was also to receive a commission on the gross sales on each Hagen-designed piece of equipment. My future in the manufacturing business began to take on a more promising and lucrative outlook. Of course, my value to such a company rested on my continued active participation in golf. So the new company proceded to insure my life for a sum of $500,000 to guarantee the investment. That policy, drawn up by Harry P. Trosper, a vice-president of the American Life Insurance Company, was the largest ever taken out on a golfer.

L. A. Young wanted no part of the Florida factory machinery. He transferred the name only. He was quick to discover he had bought a turkey . . . a white elephant . . . but this merely stimulated his uncanny business acumen. He took over actually in 1927 just as the steel shafts were becoming popular. I worked long hours that year designing a more compact blade for my line. This made an instant hit when put on the market and other golf equipment companies were swift to follow my lead.

The theory of the compact blade was that it gave more distance. Through the years we experimented with various types of material for the wooden clubs. Persimmon wood supply was short and manufacturers sought a substitute—a tough yet pliable wood. The end result was the Strata Block, a laminated material composed of scales or layers of hundreds of pieces of veneer so tightly compressed that a hard surface is obtained with light weight. But those experiments took place some years later, following another transfer of the Hagen clubs.

L. A. Young established the original Detroit factory in a first-class building at St. Antoine and East Grand Boulevard. Eventually the business was transferred to Grand Rapids, Michigan. In 1944 the Wilson Company made an offer for the business and L. A. Young sold. It is now the Walter Hagen Division of the Wilson Sporting Goods Company, with Hagen branch offices in twenty-six cities, and the latest catalogue lists some thirty items which are sold through professional golf shops only. That's the way I want it. I feel the professional golfer is entitled to sell golf equipment and knows the needs of players better than anyone else.

The relationship between L. A. Young and me through those years from 1925 to 1944 was an incredible one. He was more

143

interested in me as a sports personality than he was in acquiring a lucrative company bearing my name. He didn't need money, but he liked the contacts with big names in the celebrity field and with important tycoons in the automotive industries. He felt I could get these contacts for him. He'd acquired a lot of experience handling film stars, for he had had financial control of the Tiffany-Stahl Studios in Hollywood for a number of years. He could foresee no difficulty in bringing me into his fold.

I drew no salary after L. A. took over. I never got my hand in the till because I wasn't looking for that kind of small stuff. I preferred his signature on a check. There were sessions between us when he swore he would never sign another check for me, but he paid and paid and paid. He tried to instill in me a reasonable pattern of economy, but I was completely immune to any such foolish suggestions. As long as I kept playing in competition and winning the Championship, I saw no need to cut down in my mode of living. I needed to go "first class." . . . I was the front for the company and L. A. recognized that, although he was also convinced it could be accomplished without the enthusiastic exuberance I devoted to it.

Our business association was one of the wildest financial merry-go-rounds in history. But it resulted in security for me and a profit for L. A. Young. And it came about through another first for me. I was the first golfer to manufacture golf equipment on a production basis.

What with the worry over my factory in 1925, and the official opening of the Pasadena Estates golf course, it's a wonder I got into championship form at all. But I did win the second of my four consecutive championships in the PGA at Olympia Fields in Chicago when I defeated Bill Mehlhorn 6 and 5. I was in at twelve under par in taking that win. I tied for fifth place in the USGA Open, which Willie Macfarlane won over Bobby Jones in the play-off at the Worcester, Massachusetts Country Club.

144

Bobby Jones won the USGA Amateur Championship in 1925 for the second straight year, and I had won my second consecutive championship in the PGA. Since I had won the British Open in 1924, and he had captured our own National Open in 1923, magazine articles and newspaper columns were continually being written comparing my record with his. They tallied up and compared every phase of our games. Here, young as he was, he'd invaded the National Open to compete with us top pros and had routed us all.

Golf addicts, gallery fans and sports writers began yelling for a showdown. They wanted an answer to: "Who's the better golfer, Jones or Hagen?" I'd have felt a lot easier if I could have answered it as smartly as they asked it. And I imagine Bobby would have liked a bit of psychic knowledge in advance, too. At any rate the clamor increased in volume . . . and it added nothing to my peace of mind.

CHAPTER XVII: Mr. Jones vs.
W. Hagen, 1926

> Whenever he entered a tournament, buoyant crowds
> ran out to find him, passing up the pacemakers so
> that they could watch Sir Walter. . . . On his tours
> back and forth across the country, Hagen would
> step, shining and unconcerned, from the limousine
> his chauffeur had moored near the first tee—always
> a little late for his matches. . . . He would stride
> erect down the fairway, his black hair gleaming
> above his weather-beaten face, and not until he had
> holed out on the last green did he relinquish, even
> for a moment, the attention of every person in the
> gallery.
>
> —HERBERT WARREN WIND, *The Story of*
> *American Golf*
> [1948]

BOB HARLOW'S JOB, as my manager during those Florida boom
years, was to arrange exhibition matches which could be
counted on to bring the highest revenue. Despite the big salary I drew, I had no objection to picking up additional green
stuff where I could. And the publicity-minded Jack Taylor
liked the crowds these exhibitions pulled to his Pasadena Estates development.

Since I held the British Open championship in 1924, and
Cyril Walker the National Open title that year, such an exhibi-

146

tion match between us was a natural. It was exploited unofficially as the "world championship match." We played seventy-two holes, the first thirty-six at Hialeah in Miami, where I came away with a lead of eleven holes. Two days later, February 3, 1925 we began the second thirty-six at the Pasadena course. However, the match at my home course resembled the second heavyweight fight between Joe Louis and Max Schmeling . . . a first-round knockout. Spectators who arrived at the Pasadena course for the second round did not get their money's worth, for I had polished Walker off 17 and 16 to play.

Also during these years the first professional golf league was formed with nationally known players representing outstanding resorts and cities. Joe Kirkwood and I represented Pasadena. Other teams were: Jim Barnes and Fred McLeod, Temple Terrace, Tampa; Gene Sarazen and Leo Diegel, Hollywood; Cyril Walker and Eddie Loos, Winter Haven, Lakeland; Johnny Farrell and Bobby Cruickshank, Tampa; Tommy Kerrigan and Dow George, Orlando; Bill Mehlhorn and Tommy Armour, Miami. Seven Open champions were included in this group of fine golfers. Sarazen and Diegel won the league title, after a home and home series for all teams.

There was no winter tour of any importance when the league operated, since the top players were employed by real estate promoters of the Florida Chamber of Commerce. The league was an idea which could have developed into a big organization but the end of the boom also finished off the league. I was president while it existed.

During the fall and winter of 1925 golf writers continued to fan the tide of controversial argument about a match between Bobby Jones and me. Naturally Jack Taylor and the promoters of the Whitefield Estates in Sarasota, where Bob played a lot, were eager for the match. Bobby's loyal fans were loud in their claim that I would be an easy take for him and my followers were just as vociferous in asserting I'd take Bobby like Grant took Richmond. The press generallly favored Bobby, and spent thousands of words explaining just why.

Personally I was not eager for the match for a number of reasons. Inasmuch as the papers said he was the better of the two of us, I'd have everything to gain and nothing to lose. But I was not keen on taking a beating from him. Having won my second PGA title that year, my stock was selling pretty high. I couldn't see how a possible defeat at Jones's hands would increase its value. Besides I was busy having a good time in Florida and I wasn't interested in interrupting the routine. What is more, Bobby, acknowledged the leading medalist in golf, was the Amateur champion of the United States and the public somehow had come to consider the amateurs as the Galahads of golf. While I, rated as the leading match player, was a professional—the natural villain of the game.

I was in Dallas in the fall of 1925 taking a drumming from Harry Cooper in a 72-hole match. He beat me 12 and 11. Bob Harlow came down there to talk to me about setting up the Jones match. Bobby and his advisers had agreed to it and I went along with the plans. One bit of psychology I worked out with Harlow which to me was most important. I wanted to play the first thirty-six holes on Bobby's course at Sarasota. I told my idea to Harlow, who had suggested that they toss a coin to decide where the first rounds would be played.

"Bob, if the crowd at Sarasota wins the toss, act a little disappointed and upset, but agree to play there. But, if you win," I said, "*give in* to playing the first thirty-six on their course, because they were so nice to agree to meet Hagen."

"But why do that, Walter?" Bob Harlow protested. "You'll have a much better chance at Pasadena where you know every blade of grass."

"Here's the point, Bob," I explained. "At Sarasota Bobby's a very popular fellow. He'll have a huge gallery following him

148

around, patting him on the back, shaking his hand . . . and yelling for him. Me? Well, on my side there'll be you, me and my caddie. There'll be nobody and nothing to take my attention off my game. I can concentrate completely on what I'm doing. In a match of this kind I do better with my back against the wall. Do you get the idea?"

"I get it," Bob said, "but I'm not sure you're doing the smart thing."

Harlow returned to Sarasota and made the final arrangements. Harlow was "lucky" enough to lose the coin toss and Bobby elected to play the first thirty-six holes of our challenge match on the Sarasota course on the date set, February 28, 1926.

There is always much more to such a match as Bobby Jones and I were to play than meets the eye or the understanding of the average spectator. Although I was rated a better match than medal player, I had won the British Open twice and the United States Open twice, both medal competitions. Bobby had won the United States Amateur Championship for two consecutive years, match competition. In the last six National Opens in which he and I had both played, he finished ahead of me five times and I finished ahead of him only once. By the score card it appeared that he was the better player. And yet I had lost only four set or challenge matches in the five years prior to 1926, and I had won fourteen major Championships.

Doubtless, galleryites who have followed golf for a considerable time agree that the mental phase of challenge matches or tournament play is a most important one. I don't mean so much the process of reasoning and thinking out what is best to do under any given set of circumstances or conditions in the course of a round. I mean the time the player begins to feel the pressure put on him by tournament strain . . . when he allows himself to worry or fret over things he has no business bothering his mind with at all. He can't be thinking of the dozen de-

149

tails of what he is doing. By the time he gets good enough to win a number of championships, swinging the club correctly and hitting the ball properly should have become almost automatic.

Top quality golf requires concentrated attention on every shot, regardless of what is going on around the player. And right here is where I always have an advantage. A thousand and one things can happen to distract and upset the tournament golfer. Some minor incident, perhaps something he did wrong, sets him worrying and brooding. Why did he do it? How did it happen? Once he sets off on a wild trail of thought like that he might as well give up, unless he can get control of his mind and concentrate on the real job at hand. Luckily for me, I realized long ago that I'm no machine. I'm just human, like the next fellow. And I'm going to make plenty of shots that will make me look like the rankest beginner. But if I let a blunder like that get to me, I'd have kicked away every championship or challenge match I'd ever played.

Bobby Jones always played precision golf . . . every shot had to be perfect. If he could not win, at least his game was so consistent that he finished well up front. To me, finishing well up meant nothing. I played to win. I've always been willing to gamble away a second or third place to try a seemingly impossible shot that would bring me in first.

But the most important quality in my mental approach to golf competition was the fact I could forget the last bad shot and concentrate on the next . . . or the next, if the second shot happened to be as wild as the first. And believe me, that has occurred many, many times in my game.

Winning that challenge match was equally important to both Bobby Jones and to me. And certainly we each went into it determined to give it all we had in skill and experience. Bobby, as an amateur, could not receive any of the gate receipts at the Sarasota course or of the $5000 guarantee which my friend

150

The controversies that raged between Bobby Jones's fans and mine during the '20s, about our respective golfing abilities, will never be settled. As far as I'm concerned, we both did well enough.

[WIDE WORLD PHOTO]

Putting was always my strong point. I once used only seven putts for nine consecutive holes.

Leo Diegel and I had many a tough P. G. A. match against each other.

Tom Webster, England's great humorous cartoonist, rode me almost as hard as Archie Compston did . . .

[THE DAILY MAIL, LONDON]

. . . but I had enough strength left, after taking the worst beating of my life, to shake hands with Archie after our 1928 Moor Park match. [WIDE WORLD PHOTO]

Congratulations went the other way around after I won the British Open that same year, with Archie finishing three strokes back of me.

The Prince of Wales presented the trophy, following my 1928 victory at Sandwich. It was my third British title. [GOLF ILLUSTRATED]

On our return to New York, Mayor Jimmy Walker gave Gene Sarazen (who had finished second) and me the city's official welcome. Johnny Farrell, who is on the Mayor's right, also helped us celebrate.

[WIDE WORLD PHOTO]

New names were cropping up in big-time golf in 1928, and the competition was rougher each year. This shot shows some of the best of the day watching me tee off. From left to right: Paul Runyan, Ed Dudley, Horton Smith, Craig Wood, Billy Burke, Denny Shute, Leo Diegel, Olin Dutra.

"I'm very proud and happy to be the captain of the first American Ryder Cup team to win on *home* soil." (I meant *foreign* soil, but managed to pull off a fast recovery shot!)

A 1929 social match with Sir Philip Sassoon, the Prince of Wales, and Audrey Boomer. The gentleman on the extreme left was the Scotland Yard agent who was assigned to accompany the Prince. [WIDE WORLD PHOTO]

Chill, drenching rains featured the qualifying rounds for the 1929 British Open at Muirfield. [WIDE WORLD PHOTO]

At one point in the championship I had to play a left-handed shot when my ball lodged close to a stone wall.

[WIDE WORLD PHOTO]

But I won that one with a 292 total, six strokes better than the runner-up, for my fourth British Open title and my second in a row. Here I am holing out on the final green at Muirfield. [WIDE WORLD PHOTO]

It was a great thrill, and I still seemed to be enjoying it as I disembarked with the trophy in New York. [WIDE WORLD PHOTO]

Among the caddies I have known . . .

Nagoya, my Japanese caddie

Calcutta caddies, watching the exhibition by Joe Kirkwood and me

Giving the caddies in Salisbury, Rhodesia, a lesson in African golf

Joe Kirkwood's caddie in the Belgian Congo, Africa

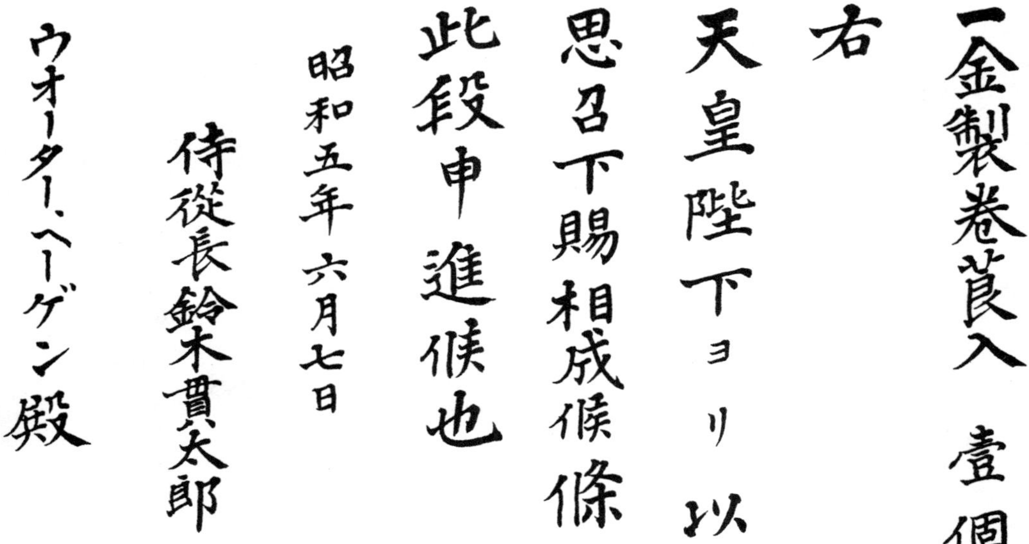

一金製巻莨入　壹個

右

天皇陛下ヨリ以
思召下賜相成候條
此段申進候也

昭和五年六月七日

侍従長鈴木貫太郎

ウォーター、ヘーゲン殿

These documents accompanied the Emperor of Japan's presentation of a gold cigarette case to me.

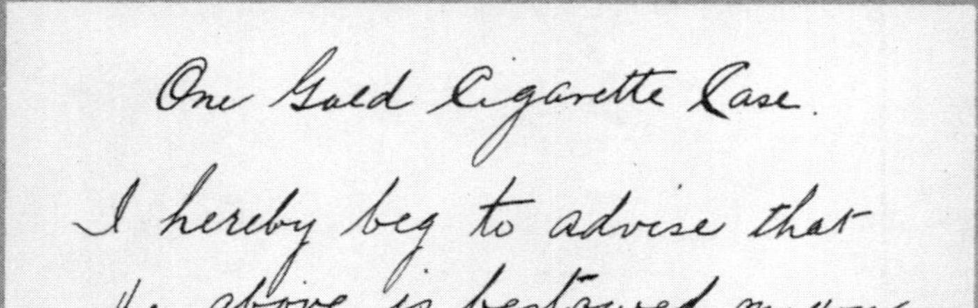

One Gold Cigarette Case.

I hereby beg to advise that the above is bestowed on you by H. I. M. Emperor's gracious will.

Kantaro Suzuki
Lord Chamberlain

June 7th 1930.

To Mr. Walter Hagen.

Playing a left-handed shot in Japan.

Joe Kirkwood and I had pretty fair luck hunting game at Nairobi, Africa.

I don't really remember just where and when this was, but it looks like a fine links, a good crowd when plus-fours were still the rage, and a straight putt that's going to drop.

Where did you get that hat?
The Prince of Wales (in the checked suit) was a keen galleryite when Leo Diegel
and I played a match in 1929.

By 1941 he had become the Duke of Windsor, and he and the Duchess were
gracious hosts at the Red Cross Fund benefit matches in the Bahamas. Tommy
Armour and Bob Jones teamed up against Gene Sarazen and myself.

[STANLEY TOOGOOD, NASSAU]

I always liked this informal shot that my pal, D. Scott Chisholm, took of me along about 1941. Many of the other photos in this book are his work too.

Benjamin Namm of Brooklyn had put up for the match at Pasadena. Tickets sold for $3.30 and while only 750 people paid admission, several hundreds crashed the gate at Sarasota to give their idol Bobby Jones the ardent support he rated. Bob Harlow and I would have been willing to give the money to a charity, but Bobby suggested I take it. I was more than willing to do so when Mr. Namm said that all amounts over the guarantee at Pasadena he would donate to charity.

So that Bobby Jones might become more familiar with the Pasadena course, and to pick up extra dough for the boys, a four-ball match, pairing Jones with Tommy Armour and me with Gil Nicholls, was scheduled for the Sunday prior to our challenge match.

However, for all our plans the match almost didn't come off. Two weeks before the date of the four-ball match, I came down with the flu. The epidemic was quite widespread and I spent the time in bed with a physician in attendance. In fact on the morning of the match I had a temperature of 102 degrees. My doctor flatly refused to approve my playing thirty-six holes of golf.

Doc telephoned Bobby's hotel and asked that he or one of his party come over to my home to verify my condition. Perhaps Bobby suspected this bit of business was some additional skulduggery on my part, some smart trickery designed to upset him. I'd never been ill since that lobster and oyster ptomaine upset in Chicago in 1914. Writers dubbed me "iron-man Hagen" and other such colorful tabs to indicate my ability to resist the common ills of humanity. How could Hagen be sick? I imagine some of those things were in Bobby's mind, for he informed my doctor, "If Hagen isn't on the first tee in an hour, there'll be no match between us. We'll go back home."

I insisted on getting out of bed and playing in the foursome and Doc finally agreed I could start, providing I got no worse as the match progressed.

151

"Doc," I said, "you go around the course with me and take my temperature."

He got me a pith helmet and lined it with huge leaves from a plant in Taylor's nursery. He must have used leaves from a rubber plant for my ball acquired some much needed elasticity and liveliness—a requisite made necessary by the physical weakness with which the flu had left me.

My temperature was still 102 when I stepped up to the first tee. Bobby was openly skeptical, but by the time we reached the eighth hole he realized I was truly a sick man. And then, gentleman that he has always been, he came over and apologized for his earlier attitude. He and Tommy Armour beat Gil Nicholls and me 4 and 3. I shook hands with no one . . . simply turned my back on them all, jumped into my car and headed for home and bed.

The Jones-Hagen match took place two weeks later. By then I was fully recovered from my illness and I was determined to give him the beating of his life. His skepticism had spurred me into a will to win which otherwise might have been much less keen.

I had the honor, stepped up to the first tee, and hooked a long drive to the edge of the woods. Bobby had a nice straight drive down the center aisle. And so, with my good friend George Morse as umpire-referee, the match began.

The number one hole is a par 4. On my second I had a difficult four-iron shot to the elevated horseshoe green and so played conservatively to the short edge. Bobby, perhaps seeing a chance for an early lead, went boldly for the flag with his second shot. His ball went over the green, down the slope into the rough. Being away, I played first and put my shot up within eighteen inches of the cup. This left Bob a very difficult recovery shot, down a sloping green. His shot went past the hole some twenty feet and he missed his putt coming back. I was 1 up.

I had decided early that I would play safely on my opponent's home course, since I was on the defensive and should take care to get pars and keep Bob from building up any kind of a big lead. Because my putting had been so sharp in my practice rounds I felt I could afford to play short and get my pars the safe way.

Two holes stand out in my memory besides that opening hole, which was important because it blocked Jones from gaining the lead and building up too much confidence. I had obtained a lead of 2 up over him in the first nine holes. We halved the tenth and the eleventh, then he got down in one putt to win the twelfth with a birdie to my par 4. This reduced my lead to one hole. That decisive block came on the thirteenth hole. Off that tee, a short hole, Jones hit a fine spoon shot about twenty feet from the hole. I played a number one-iron hole high to the right about ten feet from the flag. Jones missed and I holed a 2 to regain my 2-up lead immediately. I felt a bit easier now. When the morning round of eighteen holes ended I was 3 up due to dropping a ten-foot putt for a birdie on the fifteenth.

The next block occurred on the sixth hole of the afternoon round. Through the first five my lead zigzagged from 3 to 2 and back on each alternate hole, leaving me 3 up at the sixth tee. This sixth is a drive and a pitch. Bobby hit a long ball off the tee, just escaping the bunkers on the left side of the fairway. A single pine tree stands just to the right of this fairway . . . and I drove to a spot which left my ball completely stymied by this tree. I could play a mashie-niblick with a slice or take a chance with a straight-faced iron with the hope the ball would run through the bunker which crossed the entire front of the green. Jones played a good second shot onto the green within possible holing distance. He undoubtedly considered he had an excellent chance of winning this hole. If you had asked me then, I would have had to agree.

I elected to play the mashie-niblick and try to slice it but keep the ball in the air all the way to the green. I half-topped the shot but hit it so hard and gave it such spin that the ball ran and ran, hopped through the bunker, climbed the bank and rolled to a stop a few feet beyond the pin. I holed a 3 and Bobby needed two putts and went 4 down. I'm certain my winning the hole with a shot like that didn't put Bobby or his followers in any comfortable frame of mind. But he won the seventh and I was back to a three-hole lead.

By the twenty-seventh I was still holding that 3 up, with nine holes to play. For the first time I decided to gamble with my lead, owing to the fact that even if Bobby won as many as four holes I'd be only 1 down going back to my home course at Pasadena. I'd become acclimated to the day and the conditions so I felt that some bold moves on my part wouldn't be amiss right then. I followed this decision and it sure paid off, for I played the last nine holes in 32. I picked up five more holes, leaving me 8 up at the finish of the first thirty-six holes.

Despite the fact that I personally felt tremendously elated from that eight-hole lead over Bobby, it did not arouse spectator interest in the final thirty-six holes played at Pasadena. Such a big lead seemed too uneven to make for an exciting day for the gallery.

On March 7, the Sunday following the Sarasota match, we started on my home course. I had a putting streak at Pasadena that surpasses any I've had before or since. At Bobby's home course I'd been sharp in the putting department, too, for I'd used only twenty-seven putts in the first round and twenty-six in the second. Yet Bobby, a fine putter himself, took thirty-one putts in the first and thirty in the second round. He had taken eight more putts than I and perhaps that accounted for his being 8 down. By the end of the Pasadena rounds he had a total of eleven more putts than I and I had won 12 and 11 to play.

As an example of the wonderful putting streak I enjoyed, I recall the second hole in the morning round at Pasadena. We had halved the first in par 4's. Then Bobby was just short of the green on the left; I was on the edge of the green at the right. The hole was cut behind a knob in the green, and I remember I thought if either of us got his long putt even close to the hole, he'd be darned lucky. Bobby played first from sixty feet away, and it looked as if he'd hole his ball. Instead, it stopped less than a foot from the cup for a sure 4. I had a putt of better than fifty feet and for some miraculous reason the ball dropped for a 3 to give me the first win at Pasadena and to put me 9 up in the 72-hole grind. Again at the short fourth, after Bobby had dropped a chip shot for a 2 from just off the back edge of the green, I holed a twenty-foot putt for a half in 2.

By the twenty-fourth hole of the afternoon round I was 12 up with twelve holes to play. This was at the seventh tee. Bobby's second shot was just short of the green and he proceeded to hole a chip shot for a 3. It looked as if this would carry the match for another hole. But once again my boldness paid off, for I had nothing to lose now. My second shot was hole-high and off the fringe at the right side of the green. I elected to take a three-iron instead of my putter, and my little sweet potato went for that hole as if it had eyes. We halved the hole in 3 and that ended the match.

I won the match 12 up with eleven holes to play. For that match I received the biggest fee ever paid a golfer for a seventy-two-hole exhibition or challenge match . . . $7600. I bought a beautiful set of diamond and platinum cuff links for Bobby and cleared $6800. I had shot four strokes under par on both the Sarasota, or Whitfield Estates course, and on my own Pasadena course, both acknowledged as extremely difficult ones to play.

Grantland Rice in his book *The Bobby Jones Story* commented: "Bobby discovered that by playing the card in match competition as well as in medal, he could win matches—and he won nine of them in succession, including two Championships." However, I believe with Grantland Rice and several other writers that he made the fatal mistake of not sticking to his system of play in our match and played me instead of the card.

I always used a lot of strategy and psychology and it often paid off. I used it on them all. I set up shots the way a movie director sets up scenes . . . to pull all the suspense possible from every move. I strutted and I smiled. I hooked and I sliced into the rough off the fairways, but how I clobbered that little white ball when the chips were down, the gallery tense and my opponent either overconfident or sick with apprehension. Sure I grandstanded. But don't get the idea I was merely being amusing and brassy. To me that stuff was all part of my game. It helped fluster my opponent as much as it delighted the gallery . . . and was equally important in releasing the tension from my game.

Bobby Jones and I met again in the British Open that year at Royal Lytham and St. Anne's. He won the British trophy with a 291 and I finished third with 295. He copped the National Open at the Scioto Country Club with a 293 and he was runner-up to George Von Elm at Baltusrol in the United States Amateur. I won the PGA Championship for the fourth time, and for the third consecutive year, at Salisbury when I beat Leo Diegel 5 and 3. I won the Western Open for the third time with a 279. I won the West Coast of Florida Open and I finished high among the leaders in the National Open and the North and South Open. I established a new record for double rounds, shooting thirty-six consecutive holes in 132 when winning the Eastern Open at Wolf Hollow.

Golf fans screamed for a return match between Bobby and me, but the United States Golf Association stepped in and answered for him. "Due to his amateur standing and the fact there was money involved," he couldn't meet me again under similar circumstances. It was all right with me. I considered it wise to leave well enough alone, for Bobby was always a fine player, a dangerous competitor and a wonderful gentleman. In 1930, at the advanced age of twenty-eight, he announced his retirement from competitive golf. He made a movie and released a book on his life and received money for both. Those acts retired him from amateur standing and put him in my class. However, all my wild slashing and clobbering rounds never got me an invitation to join the amateur ranks.

In September of 1929 an article by O. B. Keeler appeared in *The American Golfer*. Keeler, biographer and great admirer of Bobby Jones, compared Jones's and my record from 1920 through 1929 . . . the year I won the British Open for the fourth time. He wrote:

But I remembered the "old Haig" in his younger years had done some pretty good scoring, especially while winning a couple of Open titles. So I checked back over his record and found that in ten consecutive United States Open Championships from 1914 through 1925 inclusive (the war years were out of course) Sir Walter had negotiated some forty consecutive rounds in 2989 strokes, an average of 74.7.

While most of that paragraph was complimentary and factual the phrase, "the old Haig in his younger days" rankled in me quite a bit. I was eating pretty high on the hog in 1929, as far as my game was concerned. I wasn't feeling any pain when I took a full swing and my putting grip was as steady on the club as around a highball glass.

Mr. Keeler set up a table of charts comparing Bobby's and my records during a ten year period of 1920 through 1929, in which Bobby's age bracket roughly equaled mine over the ten opens which were played between 1914 and 1925. The ten

157

years of Mr. Keeler's comparative statistics show that Bobby and I collected the lowest aggregate scores of all the competitors who played during that time in the United States Open Championships. However, although it was a splendid article, I believe the chart would do me more justice if it had shown a more complete coverage of my record, for I played in the Open every year from 1913 through 1936. Here is my record for twenty-two years of consecutive play in the National Open Championship:

ROUNDS

Year	1st	2nd	3rd	4th	Hagen's Score	Won by	Score
1913	73	78	76	80	307	Ouimet	304
1914	68	74	75	73	290	Hagen	290
1915	76	75	76	79	306	Travers	297
1916	73	76	75	71	295	Evans	286
(1917 & 1918 . . . not scheduled . . . war years)							
1919	78	73	75	75	301	Hagen	301
1920	74	73	77	77	301	Ray	295
1921	79	73	72	74	298	Barnes	289
1922	68	78	74	72	291	Sarazen	288
1923	77	75	73	86	311	Jones	296
1924	75	75	76	77	303	Walker	297
1925	72	76	71	74	293	Macfarlane	291
1926	73	77	74	74	298	Jones	293
1927	77	73	76	81	307	Armour	301
1928	75	72	73	76	296	Farrell	294
1929	76	81	74	78	309	Jones	293
1930	72	75	76	80	303	Jones	297
1931	74	74	73	76	297	Burke	292
1932	75	73	79	71	298	Sarazen	286
1933	73	76	77	66	292	Goodman	287
1934	76	79	83	80	318	Dutra	293
1935	77	76	73	76	302	Parks	299
1936	74	72	73	78	297	Manero	282

O. B. Keeler had computed my average for ten years, or forty consecutive rounds, and had come up with 74.7. Well, computing the average for the entire twenty-two years, including the last five when I definitely was past my competitive peak, the figures still show a 75.1 average over a total of eighty-eight consecutive rounds. Bobby's computed average for the ten years of the Keeler chart was 74.2 and that ten years was limited, as was Bobby's golfing career, to his athletic prime. The twenty-two years of my chart covered a span from the age of twenty to forty-one.

As for comparative match play in our respective classes, Bobby Jones in the National Amateur and I in the Professional Golfers Championship, the totals run like this:

Over a period of thirteen years, from 1916 through 1930 (there was no play in 1917 and 1918), Bobby Jones won the National Amateur five times—1924, 1925, 1927, 1928 and 1930. His most noteworthy opponents for these wins were: George Von Elm, Francis Ouimet, Watts Gunn, Chick Evans, Thomas Philip Perkins of Britain, Jess Sweetser, C. Ross Somerville, Harrison Johnston and Eugene Homans.

From 1916 through 1936 I played in the PGA fourteen times and won the Championship five times—in 1921, 1924, 1925, 1926 and 1927. In those years my wins included ones over Jim Barnes, George McLean, Bill Mehlhorn, Leo Diegel, Cyril Walker, Joe Turnesa, Al Watrous, Al Espinosa, Mike Brady, Harry Cooper, Tony Manero, Johnny Farrell and Tommy Armour.

To me, it all boils down to the fact that Bobby Jones and I both did well at a game we loved. We both made Golfdom's Hall of Fame. There's room for both of us there along with other champions of the game, past and future.

What did the one man-to-man match between Bobby and me in 1926 prove? Well, the closest I can come to an answer is that any champion golfer—with his nerves steady, his game at its peak, the weather and course conditions equalized by his skill and luck—can beat any other champion golfer on any given day. I happened to play Bobby on my particular days. And I'm certainly convinced that my putting gave me the big break in that match.

As for putting, as far as I know I'm the only golfer to have had the rather incredible achievement of using only seven putts for nine consecutive holes. I holed long putts on seven holes, and chipped in from off the green at the other two holes. With that record to ponder I believe a break for the nineteenth hole is in order.

CHAPTER XVIII: Early and Late

> From the very first Walter Hagen went in for sartorial elegance. His suits were the wooliest, his cashmeres the fleeciest, his shirts the silkiest and his shoes the finest. He was the fashion plate others copied for years.
>
> —BILLY SIXTY, *The Milwaukee Journal*
> [1954]

SPORTS PERSONALITIES read the newspaper stories of their own activities as avidly as do the fans. And I was certainly no exception. The praise, ironically enough, we accept as our just due, fairly sure that we rate most of it. The criticism, as often right as wrong, we may attempt to shrug away, convinced the man who wrote it is strictly for the birdies.

What about those dreamed-up-out-of-the-blue stories, one tenth fact and nine tenths fiction? Well, we advocates of the brawn and muscle brigade are often as amazed and amused as the sports fans. In fact, to paraphrase the New York *Sun's* Ward O'Malley, "I enjoyed reading some of the stories about me, because I didn't recall living them."

But there were some true stories, amusing to me, which some people missed or didn't get the kick from that I did. One such came about through my acquaintance with that fabulous old gentleman, John D. Rockefeller. I played with him at Ormond Beach, Florida, on one of his customary nine holes of golf. Nine holes was his limit at the time because of his advanced age. Following the round, we shook hands and he thanked me for a fine afternoon . . . while I kept my right hand extended toward him suggestively. He appeared puzzled for a moment, until I said, "But where's my dime?" He smiled and obligingly placed his national trademark, a bright shiny dime, in my palm. He then introduced me to his niece, who had been standing nearby waiting for him.

Upon my arrival back north, I renewed my acquaintance with her and found that she had knitted a very beautiful pair of beige golf stockings for me. I appreciated them tremendously, except for the fact that she had finished off the cuffs by knitting my full name in large dark brown letters. I postponed wearing them because the name was plainly visible below any pair of knickers I owned. However, a few weeks later she told me she'd be out at a Long Island course to see me play in a rather important match. I knew the wearing of those stockings could be postponed no longer.

I managed to buy a pair of chocolate brown knickers cut somewhat longer and fuller than most and strapped them securely below the incriminating letters of my name. All went well until the final hole of the match when I stepped up on the green to sink a putt that would give me a win. I studied my shot, hunched my shoulders a bit and bent slightly to line up my ball. As I prepared to stroke the ball, some joker in the gallery crowding the green directly behind me called out loudly to his companion, "Look at that conceited s.o.b.! He even has his name embroidered on his socks!" My face was really red . . . and my putt shot off at right angles.

When I went to England for my first try in the British Open my clothes elicited more compliments than my game. As the years passed, my taste and choice of golfing attire began to be adopted by both American and foreign golfers, yet the British press and spectators never lost their avid interest in what I'd be wearing each time I came over. When I won their Open for

162

the fourth time in 1929, one paper had a lead for a story on my winning which read:

SYMPHONY IN BLUE

When he appeared on the first tee soon after nine o'clock for his third round, Walter Hagen was a symphony in blue and brown. His over-sweater was a light brown, his under-sweater a vivid blue, while his plus fours and stockings were of two other shades of brown.

I rather questioned the writer's choice of "blue" in the head-line, but I appreciated his interest. I always chose my clothes with extreme care . . . selecting the finest in fabrics and with strict attention to harmonizing colors. After my first appearance at Brookline and Chicago in the wild-striped silk shirt, red rubber-soled shoes, white rolled-cuff pants and an eye-socking plaid cap, I never again went in for loud colors. I liked shades of browns, grays, blues or black and white combinations. Since that plaid cap of 1913, I've never worn or owned a hat.

I did, however, borrow a cap temporarily during the last round of the PGA at Dallas in 1927. I was playing against Tommy Armour, and had him 4 down going to the thirteenth hole. All during the tournament I'd been closely followed by my caddie on one side and a most enthusiastic young boy about twelve years old on the other side. As I squinted at my ball before taking my second shot, I remarked to my caddie, "This is one time I wish I had a cap."

Immediately my young golf fan stepped forward and very politely offered his cap—a baseball type, peanut-size cap with his school insigne on the bill. It was just about big enough to shade my right eye and I wore it cocked precariously when I made my shot on the green. The gallery got a laugh when it almost dropped off onto my ball, but I got the shot away. I then walked over, thanked the youngster and assured him I'd never

163

have made the green without his cap. I won the match from Armour, 5 and 4.

A dozen years later, in 1939, at Pomonok Country Club at Flushing, Long Island, I was playing in the lower half of the PGA Championship against Tony Manero. When I had holed my ball on the home green, a very charming lady stepped over and introduced herself as Byron Nelson's mother. She reminded me of the small boy who had followed me so diligently around the course at Dallas in 1927 and whose cap I had borrowed.

"That youngster was my son, Byron," she told me.

As we talked, Byron had finished his match and was approaching us. "Do you mean this big lug was that polite little boy?" I asked loud enough for him to hear. "Why haven't you told me, Byron, that you helped me win that Championship in 1927?"

He grinned and explained that his mother had written an excuse getting him out of school for the days of the PGA so that he might trail around after me. I hope I gave him some of the inspiration that led to his becoming one of our top ranking golfers. He finished second to the great Henry Picard in that very PGA Championship, he won the Western Open, the North and South Open and the National Open . . . all in that one year, 1939.

I've always changed tie, shirt and sweater after each round of golf. I like the rejuvenated feeling that fresh clothes give, but that constant changing necessitated a large wardrobe. Even on my first trip to England I carried twelve different and complete golf outfits . . . complete even down to the correct shade of cuff links to match the shirt I wore. This tendency to let harmony dominate almost canceled a challenge match at Blackwell in the Midlands.

Fred Pignon, well-known British golf writer, was to pick me up at the Savoy Hotel in London, where I was living, for an early morning train ride north. Although I'd had my customary party for friends the evening before, I was up and almost dressed when Fred arrived at 6 A.M. I intended wearing a pale blue shirt and I had not been able to locate the correct studs. Fred helped me hunt under furniture and in bureau drawers and we finally located them, but barely in time to reach the station and catch our train. I grabbed a hasty breakfast in the railway buffet and managed to arrive spick and span at Midlands just before the golf match began.

My appreciation for fine tailoring led to an incident with the Prince of Wales which resulted in a bit of embarrassment for me. I had expressed admiration of the excellent cut and the exquisite material of his dinner suits on several occasions. He suggested that he make an appointment for me with his draper, so that I might have several tuxedos made. After numerous fittings and consultations the first suit was completed. Well, there's quite a difference in the cut of American custom-tailored suits and those made by the British drapers. I donned the suit expectantly when it was delivered to my hotel. While I was fairly presentable in American clothes, I took on the appearance of a headwaiter crowding the seams in the snug-fitting, trim-cut British tuxedo.

I couldn't immediately figure out an explanation I could give the Prince for not wearing the suit after he had so graciously arranged for me to have it made. I was really embarrassed about the whole deal. However, I did get some satisfaction out of that tuxedo. Following my participation in the British Open I threw a big farewell party before flying to Paris to compete in the European tournaments. The headwaiter looking after my party seemed about my size . . . and he was loud in his appreciation of the gift I presented him—a beautifully tailored dinner jacket, British cut.

Somewhere along the years I picked up the reputation of being a "late arriver." My entry in so many championship tournaments and exhibitions, however, belies that widespread ru-

165

mor. If I had been more than ten minutes late I'd have been disqualified . . . and that never happened. But there have been some circumstances when my delay in arriving, while perfectly logical and understandable to me, puzzled members of the press and perhaps annoyed a few spectators.

An often printed newspaper story insists that I kept President Warren G. Harding waiting at the first tee while I fiddled in the club house selecting a matching pair of socks. Well, here's what actually took place. During President Harding's administration I was many times a guest at the White House. Dining with the Harding family, my regular place at the table was next to the President with his dog Laddie Boy, sitting on the floor between us. On this particular occasion we were at lunch and the President announced he'd duck down and warm up a bit before our golf game. He often followed this procedure and he'd had a practice hole cleared back of the White House—a space between some beautiful stately blue spruce trees. During President Roosevelt's time, Henry Wallace used that green to sharpen his putting, and I have no doubt my good golfing friend, President Ike Eisenhower, is making ample use of it.

When President Harding and Mr. Edward McLean, publisher of the Washington *Post*, ducked down for some practice shots, I remained at the table with Mrs. Harding and their other guests to enjoy our hostess' favorite dessert, fruit cake.

Following the luncheon I went out to the practice tee and arrived just in time to see the President break the head of his favorite driver. The head made more distance than the ball . . . hopping over a blue spruce and over several other trees as well. The ball took a crazy bounce and bopped Mr. McLean on the head as he attempted to retrieve. President Harding was quite upset about his driver, but he had ample time to get a new one from my brother pro, Freddy McLeod, at the Columbia Country Club while I changed clothes in the locker room. Actually his broken driver kept us both waiting, but I'll admit

I didn't break any speed records getting into my golf attire and picking up a spot of reinforcement in the grill.

When we did get started, I was afraid the accident to his driver had ruined his day, for President Harding topped his first drive, as well as his drives on the second and third holes. At the fourth tee he hit one quail-high which went out about 150 yards, hit the edge of a trap and bounced over. We'd had no conversation up to now and I felt he needed encouragement.

"Fine shot!" I remarked. "Fine, very good!"

"Fine, hell!" he retorted. But his tension was eased a bit and our game continued more smoothly.

Golf brought me into contact with many interesting men in all fields, and one of my favorites was the late Edsel Ford. Shortly after the Ford family had received letters threatening the kidnap of young Henry and Benson, Edsel's sons, Edsel and I played a round of golf at the Detroit Golf Club. The two youngsters were romping about the course near us as we played. The day was bright and sunny . . . with a brisk breeze blowing across the fairways. There'd been no rain for some thirty days and while the fairways were hard and dry, the greens had been thoroughly watered by the greens crew.

I suggested that Edsel take the honor at the first tee and he half-topped his drive, hitting a very low skimmer. I hit a very high shot and due to the wind in our faces, I didn't get out as far as I intended. I got no run on the ball so I was left with a number four-wood for my second shot. As we strolled down the fairway, Edsel reached his ball first and took a brassie . . . getting the same type shot as his first. I walked over and played my second. I got an unusually good shot and the ball pulled up and stopped eighteen feet from the hole, due to the wet, soft, spongy greens.

As I approached Edsel he yelled to his caddie, standing some paces away, to bring over his bag. He reached for the bag, unzipped a large pocket, and fumbled around inside it. At that, a .38 automatic pistol dropped to his feet.

I drew back in pretended alarm, "Edsel," I said, "if you want this hole so badly, I'll concede it. You can certainly have it!"

He grinned and explained he was carrying the gun because of the kidnaping threats . . . that actually he'd been getting his glove from the bag. He had neglected to wear the glove when he drove off the first tee, and he believed his hand slipping on the grip of the club had caused his bad shots. Somehow the story of his pulling a gun on me to win a hole got around the locker room and the experts didn't let him forget the incident for a long time.

My tendency to appear just in time to start a match almost got me involved in international relations, but fortunately we smoothed it over without calling in the State Department. In 1935, through the efforts of the PGA and members of the Nippon Club in New York, Japanese professional golfers made the trip to this country to enter some of our tournaments and play exhibitions. This was the second time such Japanese-American matches had been arranged, the first having been in 1934 after the trip Joe Kirkwood and I had made over there in 1930. Of the six who arrived in 1935 "Torchy" Toda, Japanese professional champion, was by far the most colorful. He was rated as the best foreign golfer to visit the United States in many years. Only five feet two inches in height and weighing a slight 110 pounds, he met the big shots of American golf on equal terms. In fact, he was by far the longest driver of any golfer we'd seen in years. With his five companions he teamed up to play some forty matches against PGA teams in all sections of this country.

That first tour of the Japanese golfers provoked no undue incidents. However when "Torchy" and his fellow pro, Chick Chin, returned to the United States in January of 1936, a match was immediately arranged between "Torchy" and me, sched-

168

uled for April 4 in Augusta, Georgia. The Japanese Ambassador made the trip down from Washington to greet his compatriots and wish them luck.

Everybody had assembled at the first tee, the ceremonies were completed and the eager "Torchy" ready to start. Where was The Haig? I was in the club house waiting for starting time, 12:30 P.M., to roll around. Newspapers carried streamer headlines the following day:

WALTER HAGEN KEEPS JAPANESE AMBASSADOR WAITING!

Not so, for when the scheduled hour arrived, so did I. I wasn't late—the Japanese were just fifteen or twenty minutes too early.

In those hectic twenties and thirties I was always booked pretty solid for exhibition matches between the scheduled circuit tournaments and Championships. Exhibitions were my bread and butter and while I could count on at least a half-dozen bookings a week, making them on time often created quite a problem. Meeting me in Chicago one summer during such a series, Bob Harlow arranged an exhibition match in Menominee, a city north of Chicago, for the following Sunday. I was a bit indefinite as to the exact location, so Bob made an X on the map showing the town to be at the southern tip of Michigan, at the boundary of Wisconsin on Green Bay.

I borrowed Al Wallace's car and chauffeur and left Chicago early Saturday evening so I might spend that night with my good friends Mr. and Mrs. Wall. I had often played golf with them and their daughter Bernice, who competed in many of the women's Championships. After an enjoyable visit with them I left for the scheduled match. I turned the map over to the chauffeur and spread myself and the Sunday papers on the back seat of the car. Upon arriving in Menominee we drove directly to the golf club where I presumed the exhibition was to be played. The lack of activity didn't particularly upset me until the manager appeared and expressed quite a lot of sur-

169

prise at my unexpected, yet welcome visit. I explained why I was there.

"Am I early?" I asked.

The manager told me he knew of no exhibition and suggested it might be scheduled for a neighboring club. We drove into town and over lunch I learned another city in Wisconsin existed with a spelling very similar, Menomonie, situated near St. Paul and about two hundred and fifty miles west of where I then was.

I immediately got on the telephone and talked to the president of the club in Wisconsin.

"Where are you?" he inquired anxiously.

"I'm in Menominee, Michigan," I told him.

"Get a plane! Get a plane!" he urged desperately. "We're waiting for you! There are two thousand people here!"

"It's two o'clock now," I said. "Not even a plane, if I could get one, would land me in your town in time to play. If you'll explain my situation to my gallery and to your members, I'll certainly make it up to your club at a later date."

Knowing how my nonappearance would appear to the public and to the waiting gallery in Wisconsin, I realized I needed adequate confirmation of my *Corrigan*. I called the president of the Chamber of Commerce of Menominee, Michigan. He met me at the restaurant and I asked him to have published in the local paper a story to the effect that I had pulled a Corrigan and gone the wrong way—I'd veered right when I should have veered left. I also requested that he send copies of the article both to me and to the president of the golf club in Wisconsin.

Another time I was actually early for a match in Ohio, and this time I hit the right town, too. In fact I beat all the other fellows who had been playing with me in Chicago and also the members of the press. I arrived at the station in Chicago only to have the gates slammed in my face and to hear the derisive shouts and laughter as the rest of the gang boarded the train without me. Imagine their surprise, however, when they walked into the lobby of the hotel in Columbus and caught sight of me relaxing in a big comfortable chair waiting for them. I had been lucky enough to catch a later, fast through train.

I believe my liking for, and interest in, all types of people led me into more close timing incidents than did my own desire to take life leisurely. In London in 1926 I had played a challenge match with Abe Mitchell at Wentworth where I finished 4 down. We were to play a second thirty-six holes the following day at St. George's Hill. The night after the Wentworth match I threw a party in the lounge of the Savoy, where a young American violinist and orchestra leader had entertained us greatly. Talking to him later I learned of his desire to see my match the next day with Abe at St. George's. I invited him to drive out with me, but he insisted on driving me out to the course in his Jaguar, so I instructed my chauffeur to meet us out there after the match.

The young fellow picked me up early the next morning and we began the drive. We drove and drove . . . and about half-way in our trip I began to notice familiar landmarks, familiar to Wentworth where I had played the previous day, not to St. George's Hill. I remarked on the fact and learned he thought I was to play at Wentworth. When we straightened that out and got the correct destination settled, he decided to take a short cut, rather than drive all the way back into London, which was the only route I knew. Wentworth and St. George's were equally distant from London, but in almost opposite directions. My friend cut across country and some miles later we came in at the back of the club premises, and there our car stalled. Bobbies on guard got us to the club house only ten minutes late.

Driving in the back way I could relax and enjoy the fra-

171

grance and beauty of the rhododendron . . . the beautiful bushes lining the driveway . . . blossoming with exquisite rose-purple flowers.

In the club house I changed clothes, exchanged greetings with Abe and with other friends and acquaintances . . . all of which ate up approximately forty minutes. The British papers played up my late arrival and the subsequent delay in the club house as a deliberate effort on my part to make Abe nervous.

Instead I was just preserving my leisurely rhythm and keeping on an even keel. I always tried to arrive at a match with at least a little time to spare, but I could never figure on the number of friends who'd approach and insist on talking for a few minutes, or the number of spectators who'd request autographs. And needless to say, I was the type to enjoy thoroughly those pleasant interruptions on the way to the first tee and the locker room. I never hurried, there was no use worrying—and I always took time to smell the flowers along the way.

CHAPTER XIX: PGA Champion, 1925

Hagen went at the job exactly like a plumber repairing a leak in a drain pipe. Of nervousness or excitement there was not a trace. Apparently gazing at the far horizon, oblivious to the crowding gallery, he went about the business of applying solder in just the right quantity to stop the leak, but not to an extent that would prevent him being called in for another repair job in succeeding years. . . . All he cared for was to do a fairly good job of work that would let him get by with a minimum of labor.

—A. T. PACKARD, *Golfers Magazine*
[1925]

THERE ARE DAYS in competitive golf when every shot is a challenge. In my own game such days would see me hook or slice on every drive. I'd overrun the cup by four feet or more on a simple chip shot. I could miss a sure putt by inches. There were days when I did everything wrong on one hole . . . or two holes . . . yes, even on three consecutive holes. And then on the fourth I could hit a long drive "down the pretty" with a terrific brassie to the far side of the green and chip in for a birdie 3.

Then there were days when I could click my pars off with almost predictable regularity . . . mixing them up for variety with birdies and an eagle. On that kind of day I could break a course record. On that kind of day I shot my 132 for thirty-six consecutive holes of competitive play at Wolf Hollow.

173

I was touted as the "iron man of golf," the imperturbable Hagen. Those rumors and news stories of the nerveless Hagen never fooled me into believing them, or in letting up when I got a golf club in my hand. I had one asset—the uncanny liking for a fight, for tough competition. When the opposition hit me hard enough I developed the ability to play a strong game with my back against the wall and the pressure on. And the chances I took paid off more times than they failed. Undoubtedly this tendency to gamble on making my score the bold way accounted for the tag of "unpredictable" which the press and my fellow pros pinned on me. My game was not built on wizardry or magic. It was based on a naturally good physical coordination, a liking for the game I played . . . and finally on strategy I developed through the years. On knowing what I could afford to take a chance on . . . and where and how to set up a shot. It was also based on a driving urge to win each and every match I played. I don't believe it's conceit to say that I rarely missed in sizing up an opponent or a situation.

This ability to size up a situation, however, didn't cover a couple of incidents with the gals in the game. When I first took the pro job at Oakland Hills in Birmingham a lady called on me to ask if I would permit her husband to join the club.

"Now, he has never played golf and I don't want him to join as a professional but just an ordinary member," she explained.

"I understand," I told her seriously. "But I don't own the club. If your husband wants to join he should send his application to the membership committee."

"I'll see that he does," she assured me. "And now, is there someone here who could show him how to play those green things?"

Another day, when playing a round of golf I passed a woman club member competing in a match for the weekly club trophy.

"How do you stand?" I inquired politely.

"I'm dormy 5," she said.

"That's fine—the match will soon be over, I hope."

She tossed her head indignantly and walked away from me. Later, I met her leaving the club house.

"How much did you win by?" I asked.

"Win!" she exclaimed. "Who said I won? I told you out on the course I was dormy . . . dormy 5 down. And my opponent finished me up at the next hole."

I tried to explain that *dormy* meant as many holes up as there are holes to go. But she was already walking away, not in the least interested.

While working on this book at Cadillac, Michigan, I was approached by a lady who asked if I'd look at her swing. She was to play in a tournament the following day and felt she wasn't getting the full power from her drive.

I gave her a dozen new balls and suggested she go out in front of the big picture window of my writing room and drive a few balls into Lake Mitchell. She was a bit upset—first, because I wanted her to drive *new* balls into the lake and second, because I wanted to sit comfortably at my desk and watch her.

After studying her drive for a while, I changed her grip slightly and suggested she keep the face of the club open. Like most women she had a good form to begin with but she was cramping her arms at the end of her drive and not finishing out her swing. She thanked me and departed. She came back to see me several days later after her match, excited and grateful.

"I hit the ball beautifully," she told me, "and I won my match. I've brought you a gift in appreciation for your help." She unwrapped an appetizingly fresh loaf of homemade bread and gave it to me.

I remembered the days in Florida when I received $200 for thirty minutes' golf instruction and decided I was pretty lucky, for after forty years my instructions were still bringing in the dough!

And that word "dough" brings along another legend about me. Supposedly I never kept track of the time of day, the figure on a check, the amount of a bill . . . or the way of a chiseler.

It's true I've always been called a check grabber. It gives me pleasure to entertain my friends and I expected to foot the bill. Golf and people all over the world have been wonderfully good to me. I tried to return the friendliness, the hospitality and the many good turns I've received by playing the best possible game of golf and by being the hospitable host to my many friends. But I can spot a chiseler . . . I should be able to, for I've seen plenty of them at work and occasionally I've enjoyed watching them operate.

Following an Open Championship I was seated at a table in a Chicago golf club grill with Harry E. Radix, Scotty Fessenden of Chicago and George Murphy of New York when a friend, rather close with a dollar, joined us.

"Well," he remarked, "I see we have four of the fastest check grabbers in America right here."

"They'd have to be with you around," I told him and gave him a choice in the meaning, knowing he'd get the right one.

I may perhaps have helped set up the legend creating the impression that I paid no attention to detail. I learned through the years that people cared only about their own worries, not about mine. They're concerned only with their own financial circumstances; very few cared about my shortage or abundance of cash. I learned early that whatever I got out of life, I'd have to go out and get for myself. And the physical aptitude I possessed gave me the means of beginning. However, I had to create a paying market for that ability to play golf.

Showmanship was needed and happily I possessed a flair for that, too, and I used it. In fact, some fellows sort of believed I invented the kind of showmanship which, in those early days, began to put golf on a big-time money basis. Apparently, too, it pleased the public to think I lived the easy carefree life, the playboy of golf. Frankly, I was happy to support both those illusions, since I was making money out of the showmanship and I was having a grand time living on the money. I've a lot of clippings which seem to prove that I gave rather effective performances in both lines.

Actually throughout my life, I've assumed nothing without proof. Given the opportunity I checked and double-checked everything from the undulations of a putting green to the figures on a check and the curves of a pleasing number. I took nothing for granted for I could not afford that luxury. I was trying to make a living out of a game which had never in its history supplied more than the bare necessities to its professional players, much less allowed them to live in comparative ease. I never wanted to be a millionaire; I just wanted to live like one.

I worked as hard to perfect my golf game as any other fellow would work in his brokerage office, in his job as mechanic in a garage, as a lawyer or as a traveling salesman. My game was my business and as a business it demanded consistent playing in the championship bracket, for a current title was my selling commodity. Willie Macfarlane, who won the National Open at Worcester in 1925, once said to me that a man must be lucky to win the National Open.

"That's right, Willie," I agreed, "if you win it only once."

In 1925 I went to Chicago to try for my third consecutive win of the PGA Championship. The matches were scheduled at Olympia Fields Club, one of the most beautiful in the country. Boasting four championship courses, plus an expansive, low rambling club house, it even had red carpets on the long ramp and throughout the locker room.

I drove up to the entrance to the ramp and my chauffeur, Jim Randall, unloaded the golf bags and luggage. Then, followed by my secretary and the locker-room attendant and Jim, all

177

loaded with my clothes and equipment, I strode down the long carpeted ramp. At the far end I could hear laughter and talking. At closer range I saw Al Watrous, Mike Brady, Leo Diegel, Harry Cooper, Tommy Armour, Willie Klein and Bill Mehlhorn sitting around on the floor leaning back against the lockers. Before them a low bench was plentifully supplied with liquid refreshments. They pretended to ignore me.

"Let me take Hagen this year," Leo pleaded loudly.

"Oh, no!" Al Watrous yelled. "This is my year!"

"I'll get him," Bill Mehlhorn put in. "He's mine!"

The needling went round and round. I walked past the bench, hesitated until they were quiet. Then as though I'd heard nothing they said, I turned and pointed to each one individually.

"I wonder," I said slowly, "which one . . . of you . . . fellows . . . will be . . . second . . . this year!"

Then I followed my coterie around the corner to my own locker. Once there, I dropped my coat and went back to join the fellows and get in on the fun.

I played some of the best golf of my career in that Championship. Amusingly enough in the earlier elimination rounds I took Al Watrous 1 up in the first round, after thirty-nine holes. One hole in my match with him stands out in my mind, the final one. There was a boundary close on the left of the third, or thirty-ninth, so I kept safely on the right side, but my ball landed on a nursery kept up for repairing the greens. Al played his second shot and caught a trap guarding the green. Upon reaching my ball the official suggested I drop it off, in order not to ruin the putting surface which was so well groomed. That certainly gave me a laugh.

"I don't think, with all the acreage you have here," I told him, "that the nursery would mind a tiny bit of a divot out of it . . . particularly when a drop might cost me this match!"

My ball was lying so perfectly that it was easy to put a beautiful shot over the banks of the creek and some neighboring trees and land smack on the green. I got my par and the match was over.

I took Mike Brady 7 and 6 in the second match. Diegel and I met in the third, or quarter-finals. In our match I had trailed Leo all day, and by mid-afternoon even my most loyal fans were ready to concede Leo's victory. However, I was never willing to concede until the last shot was played and with 2 down and 2 to play, I made a last-stretch sprint.

The seventeenth on the Number Three course at Olympia Fields is a two-shot hole with a ditch in front of the green. Leo's second shot went into the ditch. I played a shot, hole-high, to the left of the flag some fifteen feet away. Leo meanwhile had found his ball stuck in the mud where he was able to play without taking a penalty. He got out nicely . . . just on the green, leaving him a forty-foot putt.

I was not paying too much attention for I figured the best he could get was a 5. I was left with a putt I'd be unable to stop near the hole, for the contour of the green was such that it started from nothing and bulged hog-back below my line of putt. Then it slanted upward sharply at the back edge. Mentally considering all these facts I was suddenly aware that Leo had holed his long putt for a par 4.

Leo's 4 didn't alter the picture of my plans for I'd felt from the first that it was impossible for me to lay my ball dead for a 4. I had to hole out for a 3, or my ball would roll past the hole so far that I'd have darn near as long a putt coming back. It was one of the most difficult putts I ever faced, for my ball would gain momentum going down this incline of some ten feet or more. I was 2 down. I was on the green in two. I had to sink that putt to win the hole and I had to win the hole to stay in the running.

I elected to putt away from the hole. I noticed a small leaf at the top of the green and I used it for a target. First, I had to stop the forward and upward progress of my ball at just the right point so that, when stopped, the ball would pick up its own momentum and trickle down the slope to the hole. Second, I had to hit dead center because if I hit at either edge of the hole, the ball would not stay in the cup, with the momentum it was bound to pick up. I took my stance and stroked the ball upward toward my target leaf.

I wondered a bit desperately if my survey had been correct. I backed across the green keeping my eyes on the ball. It reached the leaf, hesitated momentarily, then angled obliquely to roll down the slope and drop dead into the cup. Leo dropped flat on his face when he saw it go in, and honestly, I almost joined him. Winning the seventeenth by means of such a crucial and extremely difficult putt assured me of the win of the eighteenth, for the shock of that putt was entirely too much for Leo.

I had a good drive straight down the fairway on the eighteenth. Leo missed his, and hit a large tree on the right of the fairway. It left him in a bad spot which gave me the hole and tied up the score. The match went into sudden-death extra holes. We were alternating the play between the Number Three and the Number Four courses at Olympia. As I left the thirty-sixth green on Number Three course, my walk of several hundred yards toward the first tee of the alternate course led past the club house. I stopped in for a breather, and your guess is as good as mine as to the extra fortification I picked up.

At the first hole, a par 5, we both played our third shots on the green, and had putts of approximately twenty feet for birdie 4's. At the second, or thirty-eighth, we halved in regulation par 4's.

We both had good tee shots off the thirty-ninth and were on the green in two. But we were each faced with putts of around forty feet. Leo putted from an angle from the back edge, leaving himself about two and one-half feet short, with a curving putt for his 4. I putted past the hole some four feet. As I walked up and looked mine over I saw I had a straight downhill putt. I said a little prayer. If I could only make this putt, I'd be darn happy to halve the hole, even though Leo had a tricky shot from left to right. Before tapping the ball, I decided if I made this one, I'd concede Leo his putt. And believe me, up to this moment we'd conceded absolutely nothing.

The instant I tapped the ball I knew it was going into the cup. I reached over, tossed Leo's ball to him, giving him his putt. This act, combined with the miracle putt I'd holed on the seventeenth, really confused Leo. His evident mystification excited the gallery, too. People surrounded him, wanting to know what had transpired between us, while Leo wondered just what I was up to. Actually, I was so happy to make my putt that I was darn glad just to halve the hole, and hoped that my strategy would pay off on the next.

I was well on my way to the fourth tee before Leo and the gallery had the issue explained to the partial satisfaction of everybody. Having the honor, I was ready to play my tee shot before anybody arrived. I hit a beautiful drive, for me, and Leo was still fussing around trying to regain his composure. He topped his ball off the tee into tall grass a farmer would appreciate as hay. And the long forty-hole match was over. It was certainly a trying and difficult win . . . one of the toughest I ever had throughout the twenty-nine matches I won in taking the PGA Championship five times.

The following day I trimmed Harry Cooper 3 and 1, and came up against Bill Mehlhorn in the finals. I was sure before eighteen of the final thirty-six holes were completed that I'd win. I was really on my stick that day. Bill was 69 in the morning round, 3 under par, and still was 3 down, and starting out in the afternoon round he was out in 35 but stood 5 down at the end of twenty-seven. He was even par on the first four holes of the second nine of the afternoon round when he shook hands with me, beaten 6 and 5.

So I'd finished off in order five of the pros who were sitting in the locker room bragging they'd take me, and I'd found the answer to the question of who would be runner-up in 1925. I was kidding when I called the turn to those fellows . . . but I may have been kidding as Babe Ruth kidded when he pointed over the center-field fence for his famous home run. For I was certainly dead serious about wanting to win and I got a terrific thrill out of being the first three-time winner of the PGA Championship.

I did not have such a difficult time in the PGA Championship of 1926. I cut out the extra hole matches, but I did meet up with Leo Diegel again in the finals. Nineteen twenty-six appeared to be a bad year for champions, and I could easily have been among those clipped. George Von Elm beat Bobby Jones in the Amateur; tennis' Bill Tilden bowed to René Lacoste of France; Helen Wills lost her crown to Mrs. Molla Bjurstedt Mallory. In baseball the long-frustrated St. Louis Cardinals, with Rogers Hornsby in his first year as manager, knocked off the New York Yankees and Miller Huggins. And my pal, Gene Tunney, met Champion Jack Dempsey on September 23 in Philadelphia and took his heavyweight crown in a ten-round decision. A Championship crown was a shaky item of wearing apparel that year and I felt extremely lucky in holding on to mine for the fourth time and for the third consecutive year.

CHAPTER XX: Defeat: 18 and 17

Walter Hagen had the greatest mental approach to golf of any player I ever knew. That is probably why he won the PGA Championship, which is decided by match play, *five* times. . . . Walter always *thought* he was going to miss a certain number of shots a round. . . . Take the attitude that you are going to miss so many shots anyhow and then go ahead and play each hole for all that it is worth.

—BEN HOGAN, *Power Golf*

[1948]

I KNOW full well that a great many of my sports writer friends and my golfing pals as well expected to see me knocked off my perch as PGA champion when I showed up at the Cedar Crest Country Club in Dallas for the 1927 matches. I hadn't planned on being there at all for I'd decided not to compete that year. I was up at my camp in Watersmeet, Michigan, enjoying the fishing and the cool lake breezes. Only two days before the Championship I decided I owed it to my fellow pros to give them a chance to beat me—if they could. I rushed down to my golf factory, picked up a new set of clubs and hopped a train for Dallas. I arrived at four o'clock on the afternoon prior to the start of the matches.

I went out immediately to try the clubs and get in a few practice shots. I probably owe my win to that new set of clubs . . . the only thing rusty was my swing. Having held the title for three consecutive years, I felt the mathematical odds were against my winning again. But once the matches started I had other ideas in mind.

183

I was in the upper half along with Tommy Armour, Johnny Farrell, Tommy Harmon and Bobby Cruickshank. Luck was certainly with me when Tony Manero upset Bobby Cruickshank, and Tommy Armour took Farrell 4 and 3, for there went two great golfers whom I wouldn't have to meet. I played against another Farrell, Jack, of Chicago's North Shore Club, and I came mighty close to being eliminated right at the outset. He had me 4 down at the end of eighteen holes. He shot two birdies, one on the seventeenth and a second on the eighteenth and I certainly wasn't happy over the lead he had on me when we walked into the locker room at noon. I was ready to look for another set of clubs, but fortunately I didn't . . . I sold myself on the idea that any golfer should be able to use any uniform set.

Following my rule of trying to preserve rhythm—what little I apparently had at the time—I ate a hearty and leisurely lunch. I knew Jack thought he had me hooked. When we came back for the afternoon round I could see he was very nervous. Perhaps he felt close to beating me and that put a little more strain on him. However, his nervousness settled me down, and gave me quite a bit more confidence. I knew Jack would play to preserve his lead. I went all out to break it up. When we completed the first nine of the afternoon round I had picked up five holes. I made the turn 1 up . . . when the round ended I beat him 3 and 2.

Tony Manero, a pretty good putter, was my opponent for the next match. Bobby Cruickshank had told me earlier that Tony holed everything against him. But when I got him he was overeager, and his putting streak had completely fizzled. I took him 11 and 10.

Tommy Armour, my next opponent, presented a more dangerous problem. His desire to win was as strong as mine. I figured the only way to get Tommy was to let him beat himself.

184

He was a bit tired, for he had played two hard matches with Johnny Farrell and Tommy Harmon. He made his one big mistake in our match on the fourth green, when he stymied himself and let me win a hole which he should have won or halved. The first thing Tommy knew I had him 3 down and I was on my way. I got birdies on the last two holes of the morning round to go 4 up. I wound up with a score of 71, despite a 6 on the par 4 third, and knocked Tommy out, 5 and 4.

In the quarter-finals Joe Turnesa won over Johnny Golden and I met Al Espinosa. To all the gallery I was beaten when he went 1 up at the thirty-fifth hole. Al had a fine tee shot at the home hole, leaving him twenty-five feet from the green with a short pitch over a sand trap facing him. My tee shot was pushed and faded way to the right in the rough, half buried in sandy loam. This looked like curtains for me.

Apparently all I could expect was to get out short of a trap guarding the green, with my second, and that's all I did do. I was still away and had to play my third shot before Al played his second. It was a beaut, and went just past the hole about two and a half feet. This made Al's shot a bit more difficult. He needed only to pitch over the trap up close . . . but should he go past the hole he might stymie himself. Al had an anxious moment or two right then. He scuffed his shot, or should I say peeked a bit, and just got over the trap. Once again he was afraid of going past the hole on his thirty-foot putt, and left himself three feet short. He missed his putt. I holed mine to square the match and go on to extra holes. I, of course, took a longing glance at the club house as we walked to the thirty-seventh tee but put down the tempting thoughts crowding my mind and decided to polish the match off as quickly as possible. The hyposonica could come later.

On the thirty-seventh we both had good tee shots. Al's second caught a trap to the left of the hole and I played my second

185

within a few feet of the cup. The match was over. I holed that putt and the match had been pulled out of the bag.

In the finals Joe Turnesa gave me a rough time, taking me right down to the thirty-sixth hole, which I won. Once again I had kept possession of the coveted PGA trophy and the championship. Now I'd won twenty consecutive matches, five each year for the past four years. I'd played in six PGA Championships beginning with 1921 and through 1927, and lost only one match out of thirty. In 1922 I had not competed, and in 1923 Gene Sarazen had defeated me on the thirty-eighth green at Pelham.

The Walter Hagen Golf Products, Incorporated, kept me so busy the remainder of that year I had little time for competitive golf. I did finish fourth in the Western Open, but outside of a few tournaments and exhibitions, I stuck pretty close to the manufacturing of golf clubs. And business was beginning to look good . . . we might make a fair profit from it.

I did not make the trip to England in 1927 for the British Open, but Fred Corcoran, in charge of the Ryder Cup Team, did. I gave him a note to a great friend of mine, Karl Hefflin, manager of the Savoy Hotel in London. Corcoran reported to me later that Karl had welcomed him vociferously, thinking I was along, too. When he learned I had not made the trip, Karl heaved a big sigh of relief.

"Well," he said, "I'm not sure we could have weathered another visit from The Haig right now." Then he grinned, "When that boy is around, God bless him, there is never a dull moment. Always something cooking! I do hope he won't disappoint us next year."

And it was that next year, 1928, that Hefflin arranged a publicity stunt to keep the Savoy Hotel's name in the news. I had once boasted I could drive a golf ball off the Savoy roof across the Thames River and hit a coal barge on the far side. So Karl set the stage for the stunt and invited the press and the public to watch me make good. However, he neglected to notify me of the hour set. When he finally located me, it was well past eleven that night.

"You've ruined the stunt for us!" he exclaimed heatedly. "It's too late now."

"It's never too late," I told him. "Let's go up there and try it. At this time of night no one will ever know whether the ball clears the river or not."

He refused to go for that, so we put the stunt on for another day. I made good . . . the ball clearing the river in a most satisfactory driving feat. I was doubtful about actually trying it, but I remembered I had once driven across the Delaware River . . . the carry being about the same distance.

I had gone out to Hollywood early in the year to make a film and actually had not played any golf for a full two months prior to my trip to the British Isles in late April. In fact, we were shooting the picture right up to the day I left California. I went directly from the studio to my house on King's Road, picked up my luggage and dashed for the railway station. On the train, perhaps a few hours en route, I found I was minus a small grip—an important one containing my passport and other valuable papers. I wired my houseboy from Chicago asking that the bag be expressed to me in New York. However, it did not arrive in time to save me the bother of getting a new passport from Washington . . . and that consumed the two days before the sailing date.

Due to the fact that I'd had no practice I thought the challenge match, scheduled with Archie Compston for the day following my arrival in England, should be postponed. Fearing the committee would think I was alibiing, I cabled them after I'd sailed on the *Aquitania* asking for a short postponement.

In a return cable they refused. I presume I made a mistake in sending the cable from on board ship, since they knew full well, if I'd already sailed, I'd arrive in time to play. Whether I

187

was in form evidently interested them not at all. Tommy Armour, Gene Sarazen and Bill Mehlhorn were among the American golfers on board and we did get in a little practice driving several hundred balls into the big pond.

To say that Great Britain was excited about this match between Archie Compston and me would be one of the classic understatements of all time. The stake of £750—about $3750 in our money—was the highest ever paid for a golf match in that country. And more important than that, the British were getting darned tired having their trophy cup taken out of the country. If Compston could handle me, fans and experts alike figured they'd have three possible players—Abe Mitchell, Archie Compston and George Duncan—capable of keeping the big cup home for a while. Since Jock Hutchison had won the British Open in 1921, only one British win had kept the Americans in line . . . Arthur Havers' win over me by one stroke in 1923. But British hopes were riding high in 1928.

So much interest centered on the match with Compston that temporary membership badges were issued for gallery fans at a fee of 15 shillings. Moor Park Golf Club in Herefordshire is a part of the beautiful Moor Park estate, Rickmansworth, and is about thirty minutes by train from Baker Street in London. Train and bus service transported spectators direct to the club entrance.

In the early morning of April 26, the day prior to the match, I docked at Southampton, some one hundred miles from London. Upon our arrival at the hotel in London, Bob Harlow produced a Scotland Yard detective who was to be my shadow for the following two days. Since my late arrival at the Abe Mitchell match in 1926 had created so much unfavorable publicity, Bob had determined I'd be on time for the Compston deal. That fellow Bob hired was just the sort of detective I'd always pictured from English fiction. An enormous man, standing about six feet three inches, he was heavy and muscular and

188

adorned with a fierce, bristling mustache. He balked, however, when Bob asked him to wear a Sherlock Holmes type hat. Cartoonists and news cameramen had a field day picturing him following me around.

Tom Webster, Europe's foremost sports cartoonist, did a series on us. One of them depicted me deep in the luxurious softness of a Savoy Hotel bed, my head wrapped in a towel, an alarm clock perched on top the towel ringing out in ear-splitting blasts. He drew the detective waiting patiently outside the door . . . hoping for my appearance. The *Evening Express* featured the story with headlines reading:

HAGEN'S HUMAN ALARM CLOCK! A DETECTIVE TO GET HIM OUT OF BED TOMORROW! ONE DAY'S PRACTICE!

On the afternoon of my arrival in England, Bob Harlow, the detective and I drove out to Moor Park where I got in a few practice shots. Archie was out there working, too. He was an indefatigable golfer. He practiced for that match at Moor Park with the curious determination which consistently characterized his game. A big, homely fellow, the semi-bull type, he gave the impression of a serious battler but actually he was temperamental and highly emotional. He was capable of playing inspired golf. In order to shoot his brand of golf he would practice until he was actually ill. He was suffering at that time from ulcers . . . which again brings up the fact that it seems I've never played against a well man yet, but I've taken beatings from two very fine sick ones . . . Gene Sarazen in 1922 and Archie Compston in 1928.

Our match of seventy-two holes was scheduled thirty-six for Friday, April 27, and the final thirty-six for Saturday, April 28. My pal, the big Scotland Yard detective, got me out of a comfortable bed about six in the morning of the first day. After a leisurely breakfast, the limousine placed us on the first tee shortly before nine. As our Daimler pulled up in front of the club house, out stepped the Scotland Yard giant, followed by Bob Harlow, then me. A crowd of some several thousand people had already gathered and at the sight of our little group they burst into shouts of laughter. The British have a keen sense of the ridiculous.

That first round was an amazing one for me. I found myself swamped by a flood of Compston's superb shots. He started by winning four holes of the first six; we halved two. His every shot was masterful. On those first nine holes he consistently out-drove me by twenty yards. He holed an eight-yard putt on the ninth for a 3, giving him a lead of five holes. He had gone out in 32 and I had taken 38.

On the tenth he holed a putt of ten yards for a 2, going 6 up. We halved the next two and at the thirteenth I finally won my first hole with a 5 to his 6. And please note that he had to take a 6 for me to win. He took the fourteenth, I won the fif-teenth by one stroke. We halved the next two and I won the eighteenth when Compston was short with his tee shot. He failed to negotiate a half-stymie. He became 4 up on me at the end of the morning round.

I've talked a lot about liking to fight when the pressure was on. Believe me, I certainly felt that pressure when I stepped on the first tee for the afternoon round. Having played only practice shots on the Moor Park course, I'd been handicapped during the morning round by not being familiar with the course. And Compston was very careful not to show me a shot. He didn't even resort to my well-publicized strategy of picking the "wrong" club as an indicator for me. Perhaps because I automatically picked the wrong club anyway. Compston just let me get around by the Braille system.

I started a bit more comfortably on the second eighteen holes, but my feeling was short-lived. Compston was not quite as sharp in the afternoon, for he pulled his drive at the fourth and sliced into the rough off the tee. He recovered from this first mistake with a good run-up shot and won the hole, as I three-putted on the green. I got one hole back with a 4 on the fifth. At the turn I was 7 down, a serious but to me certainly not a hopeless situation. I was over the tenth green with my drive. I got a 3 with a pitch and a long putt. But it did me no good, for he came up with a 2.

He got greedier as the round progressed. Outside of the twelfth and the seventeenth, he took every other hole from me. I was suffering from mild discomfort from a blister on my right hand . . . but suffering far more over the fact that at the end of this first day's play I was 14 *down.*

Compston had come home in 30 on the afternoon round to give him a 66 to my 76. Only four wooden club shots were played through the greens in the entire thirty-six holes and all of those on the seventh hole. On each round he had holed the third and tenth in 2. He missed only one putt of four feet or less in the entire thirty-six holes. He had me over the well-known barrel!

My Scotland Yard detective earned his money the next morning, for it took him some twenty minutes to roll me out. I had slept the dreamless sleep of an exhausted kid. The day was beautiful, warm and sunny . . . just like Long Island in July. I enjoyed the drive up from London to Moor Park. I felt like playing golf and I expected to do well. However, I had no brilliant golf in me and Compston kept right on with his remarkable run.

He won first blood in the third round with a 3 at the big hole, the third, where I took three putts—a fault I was guilty of five times the day before and four times on Saturday. By the time we reached the ninth I was 17 to the bad. At least I was being consistent! At the eighteenth green I was faced with a putt of twenty feet or the match was over, for I was then 18 down. It was high noon . . . a balmy day. The drive up to the club house, passing the eighteenth green, was bordered with

191

colorful rhododendrons and busy with cars bringing more fans to see the afternoon round. If I don't make the putt, I thought, I'm beaten 19 and 18 to go. And all those beautiful shillings must be paid back to customers at the gate. As luck would have it, I made the putt and guaranteed at least a start of the afternoon round.

That last round of our match consisted of a single hole. We fought to the end, however. I had to putt from a foot and I made Archie putt from six inches. We halved the hole for him to take the match, 18 and 17 to play. We shook hands and proceeded to play an exhibition match for the remainder of the round. I'd invited some friends out to see the match and they did not arrive until noon . . . just in time to see me get knocked off by an expert. I thought they and the other late arriving spectators deserved to see some golf in return for making the trip up to Moor Park . . . although I may be facetious in terming what I had played in the Compston match *golf*.

Several incidents of the match amused me . . . even while Archie was piling up his lead. The Moor Park officials conceived the idea of having a tall caddie carry a big blackboard around with us, on which they marked the standing of the match, after each hole. Not *once* did my name appear on the board. Another sight that really got me was Compston's caddie toting a large toy black cat . . . Archie's mascot and good-luck piece.

That gallery threw me, too. Never in my long career of competitive golf have I been conscious of getting the *kind* of applause I received at the fifteenth hole when I made a fair recovery shot from a trap. I realized that for the first time in my life I was getting "sympathy applause."

Compston was a great golfer and he'd worked hard at his game. He did everything right. He gave me the worst beating of my career and I had only one statement to make to the British press: "When you are laid out good and flat, you must not squawk!"

One quality sparked Archie Compston's play from the moment we stepped on the first tee on Friday—confidence. He had it right in the beginning and I certainly did nothing to take it from him. His wonderful control and consistent brilliance on every hole, his aggressiveness—all were remarkable. The hope of the British took a definite leap upward in looking forward to their Open, which was to begin on Monday, May 8.

Archie had put in long periods of intensive practice and it paid off. Yet, I've learned through much experience that it's difficult to hold a peak for two events scheduled within such a short time of each other as were our challenge match and the British Open. The Saturday morning London press was jubilant after our initial thirty-six holes on Friday. Interviews with Archie quoted him as saying, "I am as good as any golfer in the world today. And I am going to prove it." Needless to say, I had no comment to make to that. He proved it to me the next day. Sunday morning I woke with a headache. I asked for the morning papers . . . and a bicarbonate with which to digest them. Here are some of the headlines:

HAGEN SUBMERGED!

CONQUERING COMPSTON!

THE ROUT OF WALTER HAGEN!

AMERICAN GETS HIS OWN MEDICINE!

HAGEN'S GHOST IS LAID!

THE ECLIPSE OF HAGEN!

HAGEN TAKES HIS PHYSIC!

Sports pages quoted Archie as saying, "I will play anyone, anywhere, for anything!" The sedate *Morning Post* remarked in an editorial, "Such a signal victory as that accomplished by Archie Compston in his match with Walter Hagen deserves more than passing celebration. It is an event that must be dear and refreshing to a British golfer's heart, which for a long time has been uncheered by any challenge to American ascendancy."

Someone told me that the great castle at Moor Park, used as a club house, had once been a favorite rendezvous of Henry VIII and Anne Boleyn. If so, their memories of it must have been far pleasanter than mine.

The great Tommy Webster ended his series of cartoons on the Compston match with another picture of me in bed at the Savoy. This time the huge Scotland Yard detective was astride my stomach using his massive bulk to restrain me, while I struggled valiantly to rise . . . with my head protruding at one end and my feet at the other. Flashes of lightning zigzagged from the alarm clock. The caption: "Harlow Should Have Paid Scotland Yard £5 to Keep Hagen in Bed. . . . 18 and 17!"

Perhaps I took solace in my defeat by remembering Bobby Jones's comeback after I had trimmed him 12 and 11. Our match in Florida had taken place in February and March of 1926. He'd gone out that same year, after bowing to me in the worst beating he'd ever taken, and had won the British Open at Royal Lytham and St. Anne's and the United States National Open at Scioto.

There was only one play for me to make and I made it. I left the memory of the licking I'd taken right where it belonged . . . on the links at Moor Park. I was no temperamental star . . . I was just a fellow working at golf for a living. Moor Park, of necessity, must be for me just another seventy-two holes.

CHAPTER XXI: Britsh Open, 1928

Golf had never had a showman like him. All the professionals who have a chance to go after the big
money today should say a silent thanks to Walter
Hagen each time they stretch a check between their
fingers. It was Walter who made professional golf
what it is.

—GENE SARAZEN, *Thirty Years of*
Championship Golf
[1954]

THE WEEK FOLLOWING the Compston match, a British daily
paper published two entire pages of advertisements listing the
varied products which supposedly had enabled Archie to
beat me. That fellow had really cashed in. Besides the prize
money from the match he had money from manufacturers of
practically everything he wore, every bit of equipment he
used, and everything he ate, drank, smoked or glanced at in
passing. I thought he was pretty smart. Pro golfers have to grab
coin when they can and I haven't been bashful about taking on
sponsors . . . if their products were directly connected with
golf; and my club factory at Grand Rapids, Michigan, is no
peanut business. I was always in there looking for the loot, too.

The newspapers had a few things to say about me that week,
too . . . after they'd hashed and rehashed the Compston victory. Most writers insisted I was more quiet and a bit more
serious. Well, they were right on part of it. I was serious about
one thing . . . winning the British Open. That defeat by
Compston had been a terrific blow to my pride. I'd had the
smile wiped off my face temporarily, but I hadn't lost my sense

of humor. I had come face to face with the very obvious fact that no trickery or funny stuff was going to win a third British Open for me. This time I'd let the other boys take the risks. I intended to play for safety all the way. I had one week to get some badly needed practice.

On Monday I left London and checked into the Guilford Hotel about seven miles from the golf links at Sandwich, where the Open would begin on Thursday. This famous old resort hotel, standing only one hundred feet from the sea, high on the Dover coast, was an ideal place to follow the routine I'd set for myself. I really went to work.

I played endless rounds of golf, existed on a rigid diet, spent numerous sessions in a Turkish bath, and tried to put the beating I'd taken from Archie completely out of my mind. I locked my little black book in my trunk and even refused the tempting telephone calls. Believe me, the black book and the telephone numbers I'd collected in Great Britain made that last bit of business hard to take. In such a romantic setting I felt somewhat selfish enjoying it alone, particularly since I had, in London the previous week, introduced Doug Fairbanks, Jr. to a very lovely British girl who had been my companion for a number of parties. Young Doug was in London with his dad, who was setting up his new Fairbanks International Company. Doug, Jr. was to star in his dad's productions and both the Fairbankses had assured my beautiful girl friend a chance for a movie career. With such powerful competition my withdrawal from circulation just at that time promised to be catastrophic for my romantic life.

Eight times from 1920 through 1929 I played in the British Open Championship. The first time I finished fifty-third. Then I finished sixth once, third and second once and four times I won it. I'm proud of the whole record, but I know my greatest thrill came from the win at Sandwich. I believe the

British people appreciated that win most, too. I had received tremendous acclaim in 1924 when I won at Hoylake. But there was increased warmth and sincerity to the applause, the cheering, the quick words of congratulations and the eager smiles from the huge galleries following me around when I won in 1928.

At Hoylake I'd had some downright bad streaks followed by good, even brilliant spurts. I played a different brand of golf at Sandwich. My game was more consistent. I did not shoot a 6 on any hole of my four rounds. I made some bad shots, but my recovery shot was always a good one and prevented any serious setback.

In the first round Bill Mehlhorn turned in a 71 and Gene Sarazen was just back of him in 72. I trailed them with a 75, behind the fine little Argentine golfer, José Jurado, who had turned in a 74. George Duncan and Archie Compston also had 75's and Abe Mitchell, one of Britain's chief hopes, wound up with a 76.

After the second round Sarazen and I were tied at 148, for I'd turned in a 73 and Gene had gone up to 76. Compston with a 149 was breathing down our necks, when in came little Jurado with a 71 for 145. He had gone out in 38 and come home in the very low score of 33. His score sent him ahead of Gene and me by three strokes. On the last day the pace began to tell.

José Jurado set the pace . . . and a slow one, for he was undoubtedly the most painstaking and deliberate man on the green that I've ever seen. However, all his care didn't pull him through for he turned in a 76. I reached the turn in 33 but had a 39 coming back. And my 72 put me in front of Jurado. So now with one round to go, I'm 220, Jurado, 221, Sarazen 221 and Compston 222.

Jurado was first to start the final round. I had not been sensational through the first three rounds, but I had been steady. By the time I reached the eleventh tee I began to sense a change in the gallery. This encouraged me. I began to pick up a bigger gallery . . . they came streaming after me, calling out my name and giving me reports on my competitors. I finished the last three holes in par and turned in a 72 for a total of 292.

Compston and Sarazen were at the far end of the course when I finished. Compston needed a 70 to tie me, Gene a 71. Since the wind had now dropped, they certainly had a good chance of making it tough for me. Finally, runners brought me word that Archie had finished with a 295. Gene still had a chance. He had begun the round with six holes in 23 strokes and finished the nine in 36. He needed a 35 on the last nine to tie me. I stood watching him, "the calmest person in the whole crowd," so the papers stated the next day. Standing there watching a fellow trying to knock me off was fully as nerve-wracking as playing against Archie Compston when I was 14 down. But Gene took a 37 on the back nine for a final score of 294 . . . two strokes behind me.

The Prince of Wales, who had been playing a round of golf at Prince's (a neighboring course), followed me most of the last nine to the finish. He then went back to pick up and follow Sarazen and Duncan. Later the Prince presented the British Trophy cup and I was happy I was the recipient.

"We're getting a little jealous about the cup," he said in his short talk, "but we like it going to the best player. We hope the Americans will continue coming over, so that we may have the opportunity eventually of 'putting it over.'"

I thanked him and the gallery for the warmth of their hospitality and expressed my happiness at winning their great trophy again. "I don't want to bore you," I said, "but I am going to keep on coming over."

That was my first meeting with the Prince of Wales but it was not to be my last. We became firm friends and spent many hours together, both on the links and off.

198

The day after the Championship I returned to London with the British trophy once again in my possession. The press was a bit more pleasing to me this time, carrying such streamers as:

HAGEN'S GREAT VICTORY!

PRINCE WATCHES HAGEN!

A BONNIE GOLFER!

THE GOLF BLUE RIBAND!

HAGEN'S FAREWELL!

And the *Daily Mail* commented: "All over the world at this moment golfers are engaged in a simultaneous act of homage. They are taking off their hats with the most generous and courtliest of flourishes to Walter Hagen!"

I asked Bob Harlow to arrange a return match with Archie Compston in America and together we persuaded him it would be a great money maker. He sailed on the same boat with us on our return. Arrangements were made by cable for thirty-six holes at Boston and thirty-six at the Westchester-Biltmore in New York.

Our ship docked in New York on June 8 and the welcome was really tremendous. A wonderful band at the dock kept playing "Among My Souvenirs" and thousands of golf fans and thousands more who didn't know one club from another lined the streets. The late Mayor Jimmy Walker welcomed me at the City Hall following a long motor ride down Fifth Avenue, with police on motorcycles and enthusiastic children waving and yelling to me. At the City Hall Mayor Walker presented me with the key to the City of New York.

We then proceeded to the Biltmore Hotel where the president of the Westchester-Biltmore had the presidential suite packed with all my pals and decorated with huge floral gifts . . . and my two cases of selected bottles of imported "hyposonica" which I had managed to mix in with my many and assorted pieces of luggage. One bit of business at the dock

199

just before we walked down the gangplank . . . I had also brought a magnum of very fine old champagne which I had placed inside the velvet-lined trophy case belonging to the famed British trophy. I asked Mayor Walker to carry the nude trophy ashore for me, while I handed the locked trophy case containing the champagne to my old friend L. A. Young from Detroit. I told him to meet us later at the hotel with the trophy.

L. A. Young was delighted with the task of carrying what he presumed to be the British trophy through Customs. He had some difficulty since he had no key and Customs officials like to see what's being brought into this country. However, he finally made it and arrived, hot and disheveled, about an hour after our party at the Biltmore Hotel was well under way. I complimented him, opened the case with the key from my pocket and poured everybody a taste of the sparkling bubbly. L. A.'s face was really red when he saw what he'd worked so hard to get through Customs for me, particularly since he did not indulge. However, he took the joke gracefully.

The next afternoon Archie Compston and I played an exhibition match at the Westchester-Biltmore against Gene Sarazen and Johnny Farrell.

The American challenge match against Archie provided us both with some laughs. We'd been given a cash guarantee for the thirty-six holes in Boston but in New York we were to get the gate money. We came down from Boston after the first half of our match on the overnight train and motored out to the club in New York early in the morning. I kept arguing with Harlow, for Archie's benefit, about New York being the poorest golf town in the country.

"Why, Archie," I insisted, "there will be present about nine people and a dog. We'll make no money at all."

All he could say, over and over, was, "Well, now, Bob, how about that, sir? How about that?"

At least I knew he was thinking more about the gate than he was about me. I told him I'd suggested that Bob set the second match at Coney Island, for there were many thousands of people who came there daily. And good old Archie agreed with me wholeheartedly.

"I believe you're right, Walter. I've heard of the place. Tons of people at Coney Island, by Jove!"

Compston did pretty well on the cash deal, however, for his take amounted to $1500. I beat him 8 and 7 and my pride was eased a bit, too. It took a wee part of the sting out of that awful whipping he had given me in his homeland a month earlier.

I teamed up with Johnny Farrell for the remainder of the summer for exhibition matches. We did pretty well and when we split up in the fall I returned to my home in Hollywood. My match with Compston had convinced me I definitely needed to play more tournament golf and keep in better shape. I got as far as the semifinals in the PGA at the Five Farms course in Baltimore that fall. Then Leo Diegel trimmed me 3 and 2.

A week later in the annual eighteen-hole tournament over Harold Lloyd's manicured course on his estate in Beverly Hills, I broke the course record with a card of 30-31, 61, knocking out the 62 set by Bill Mehlhorn the previous year. Lloyd's miniature course, with small greens guarded by overhanging trees and numerous water hazards, demanded accurate iron play. I had just the shots for that course.

Another week and I was trailing Horton Smith, twenty-year-old youngster out of Joplin, Missouri, by one stroke in William Wrigley's famous Catalina Island Open. And this despite the fact that I shot birdies on the last three holes and played the last nine holes in 29! I won the Long Beach Open January 3 and 4 over the Long Beach Municipal Course with a 71 and 66. On January 5 we moved over to the Virginia Beach Country

Club for another Open and I scored 70 and 69. I won that Open by five strokes over Johnny Rogers, a long-driving pro from the Denver Country Club.

New names were cropping up in big-time golf that year. In the East Craig Wood was drawing big galleries with his mighty tee shots, and in the Middle West Clarence Gamber of Detroit and Horton Smith of Joplin were drawing gasps from the spectators at the tremendous distance of their drives. On the West Coast, Ed Dudley's booming tee shots drew gallery approval.

All these boys were swatters, powerful hitters. From the precise, accurate type of golf we had been trying to achieve in our game for the past twenty years, came these boys to play the Babe Ruth, "Sultan of Swat" kind of game. Needless to say, spectators all over the country loved the wide open, blasting game. It injected into golf the same miracle Ruth brought to baseball with his home runs and Jack Dempsey brought to boxing with his massive fists and powerful jabs. Bill Tilden, striding onto the tennis court with eight rackets under his arm, had brought the same sensational interest to tennis with his murderous socking of the ball.

Of these new young golfers, Horton Smith impressed me most. In early November he had been comparatively unknown, yet later that month he led the small field of entries in a tournament at Oklahoma City and a month after that he and I met at Catalina. Neither of these tournaments rated much prestige, but competitors were beginning to be impressed with the boy. Early in 1929 he began to hit his real stride. He was runner-up at La Jolla, California in January and at San Diego. He took fourth in the Los Angeles $10,000 Open and was runner-up to Bill Mehlhorn defending his championship in the Texas Open at San Antonio, and again at the South Central Open at Hot Springs, Arkansas. That winter, against the pick of American professional golfers, Horton Smith won all but one of the Open tournaments in which he played. I picked him as the baby member of the Ryder Cup Team, to make the trip to the British Isles with us in April of 1929.

Going back for a moment to William Wrigley's Catalina Island Open where Horton had nosed me out by one stroke—Mr. Wrigley had invited me to shoot wild goats in the high mountainous country nearby. He fixed me up with a safari and off we went into the hills very early on the morning of the tourney. The officials gave me the privilege of starting late, owing to the fact the course was short and would be congested anyway.

So I began my first round shortly before noon. The entire field had finished their first round. I was allotted a rather stout woman for my scorer . . . and I undoubtedly gave her a workout, for I practically ran around the course. I needed to run, for I had to lap the field somehow. As darkness approached, I was climbing the steps up to the sixteenth tee. All the golfers and gallery were out to greet me with gags and laughter. I was told that Horton Smith was the winner so far.

He was among the crowd and he grinned at me, nodding his head to acknowledge his leadership.

"What is your score?" I asked.

Horton told me and said, "You'd better come into the club house. You'll get lost in the dark in one of those barrancas up there."

I figured for a moment. "I have a good chance to tie you," I told him. "I merely have to make the last three holes in six shots." I raised my voice for the gallery to hear. "Horton," I said, "I can make a 3, a 2 and a 1 to tie you."

I hit a long tee shot—long for me at least—and away we went up the hill, followed by the whole gallery. I hit my second shot to a plateau and found my ball about six feet from the hole. I gave it a quick glance, knocked it in and turned to the gallery. "Well, there is my 3. Now for a 2."

I hit a five-iron on the seventeenth about twenty feet from the hole. I could scarcely see the hole, for it was getting quite dark. I looked over the green, gave the ball a rap and to my surprise it holed.

"There you are," I said casually. "Now for a hole in one!"

I ran to the eighteenth tee, pulled out my two-iron, then had to wait while gallery fans were chased off the fairway. The hole was approximately 190 yards. Now about all I could see in the distance was the club house. I aimed for that hoot in the grill. I hit the ball well and a very loud cheer went up. I thought I had made it. Instead I had hit the flag gently and stopped about six inches away. The 2 gave me a second place.

As I walked across the green two avid spectators were arguing over my play. One said, "I can't understand why they didn't take the flag out. He would have made it. Didn't he say at the sixteenth that he would finish 3-2-1?"

CHAPTER XXII: Ryder Cup Teams

A Ryder Cup Team match without Hagen would seem like *Hamlet* without the melancholy Dane to our British cousins. . . . To them Sir Walter personifies the swashbuckling tempo of American golf. They love him for his showmanship and his truculent bravado. . . . Like the Irishman who repudiated his first giraffe, the English won't believe a Hagen who-can't-putt even if they see him foozle the little ones. They've been reared on the creed The Haig can do no wrong on the greens.

—GEORGE TREVOR, *The New York Sun*
[1936]

IF I WERE extremely logical I suppose I'd begin telling about the Ryder Cup Team by explaining how the teams were originated. Instead, the first fact that comes to mind actually concerns 1937, the last year I captained the team . . . and the first time we won in the British Isles. The competition had run rather consistently since its inception in 1927. We won when the matches were played in the United States. England won when we played in the Isles. The fact that we'd finally scored a win on British soil was actually more important to us than the win itself.

Throughout these great matches such a wonderful spirit of competition and sportsmanship had existed, Fred Corcoran and I realized that the acceptance speech I would make when the Prince of Wales presented the cup to me at Southport, would have to be one of extreme tact. I realized I must emphasize this first victory on foreign soil, and that I must make the British people feel our deep appreciation for their kindness and hospitality.

At the eighteenth tee I had been standing by Gene Sarazen's bag as he came up to drive off. I suggested that he use a spoon and play for a safe 4 to insure our win. And following his successful play, I had accompanied the Prince of Wales into the club house for a hoot and to make a few notes on some cards to make certain I'd remember all I intended to say in the speech.

On the terrace in front of the club house a table and loud speaker had been set up. The Prince, J. H. Taylor, captain of the 1937 British team, and I took our places. I placed my cards on the table, convenient for me to push off one at a time for easy reading. Some fifteen thousand enthusiastic British spectators jammed the terrace, cheering and applauding loudly. The Prince stepped forward, presented me with the trophy and congratulated us on our victory. I accepted the cup and placed it on the table just as a swift gust of wind sliced around the loud-speaker and away went my cards.

The huge crowd waited in respectful silence for me to speak. I fumbled vainly in my mind for some memory of those notes. Then, "I'm very proud and happy," I said, "to be the captain of the first American team . . ." I hesitated a moment, then tossed caution to the duffers. "I'm proud and happy to be the captain of the first American team to win on *home soil.*"

The crowd maintained a stunned silence, then a few giggled nervously. Finally a cockney voice called out from the back of the gallery, "I say, *High*-gen, 'tis foreign soil, ye mean. Eh, old chappie?"

The gallery roared with appreciation of his correction. I'd blasted my way out of the rough too many times to let this slip throw me. I raised my hand to ask for silence, then grinned at them.

"Aye," I said. "And you'll forgive me, I'm sure, for feeling so much *at home* over here."

206

There was a roar of applause and my ordeal was over. But I'm sure that was the fastest recovery shot I ever made.

Actually international team matches were not new when the Ryder cup was established, but up to that time the matches were arranged by several individual pros getting together and challenging a team in the country decided upon. As early as 1913 an American pro team made up of Johnny McDermott, Mike Brady, Tom McNamara and Alex Smith played a specially arranged match at Versailles, France, against Arnaud Massy, Louis Tellier, Jean Gassait and Pierre LaFitte. The French won that match.

World War I upset all plans for continuing the idea just then, but in 1921 another American pro team invaded Britain. During the intervening years many of the great British and Scotch golfers traveled over here to try for our Open but there was no concerted effort to plan and arrange a scheduled match until 1926.

That year a group of us decided on another invasion of Great Britain. I picked the team and asked Emmet French to act as captain. Homebreds on the team included French as captain, Bill Mehlhorn, Joe Stein, Al Watrous and Walter Hagen and such foreign-born pros as Jim Barnes, Tommy Armour, Cyril Walker, Joe Kirkwood and Freddie McLeod. The British were too much for us . . . we were defeated thirteen matches to one. Bill Mehlhorn, the only American to win his match, defeated Archie Compston; Emmet French halved his match; the rest of us lost. But that expedition served to point up the need for the American and British professionals to have a cup for international competition on a level with the famous Walker cup of the amateurs.

So Samuel Ryder, wealthy British seed merchant, established the Ryder cup in 1927 and the first international matches were scheduled for Worcester, Massachusetts. However, the stipulation that the United States team must be composed of

207

American-born pros prohibited many of our fine golfers including a number of boys who had been instrumental in getting the cup donated, from playing on the teams. The aim of
every professional golfer became a berth on the PGA's Ryder
Cup Team and thus to represent the United States in the international matches held every two years. The PGA has developed through the years a plan which is fair to all, and which
likewise produces a strong team.

As long as I was playing competitive golf, from 1927 when
the cup was established until 1938, when I voluntarily gave up
the position, I was captain of the American Ryder Cup Teams.
In those early years, I picked my own teams with the consent
and approval of the PGA. I chose fellows whose game I considered peculiarly suited to the type played by the British we
were to meet. My first team consisted of Johnny Farrell, John
Golden, Joe Turnesa, Gene Sarazen, Al Watrous, Leo Diegel,
Bill Mehlhorn and myself, as playing captain. We had no alternates that first year. We competed against British players
Ted Ray, George Duncan, Archie Compston, Arthur Havers,
Aubrey Boomer, C. A. Whitcombe, F. Robson and H. Jolly.
We won nine matches to Great Britain's two, with one match
halved.

Although I was officially named captain of our teams for
eleven straight years, the method of selecting the teams became more systematic. First places on the team went to the
American Open champions of the current and previous years,
and to the American PGA champion. The other places were
awarded to members, based on their competitive records for a
period of two years prior to the meetings. These records were
compiled and recorded by the official statistician for the PGA.

Ryder Cup Team wins zigzagged back and forth after our
win in 1927, for the British took six matches to our four, with
two halved, at Moortown in 1929. We won again in June of
1931 at Scioto in Columbus, Ohio. At Southport in 1933 our

team was composed of Billy Burke, Gene Sarazen, Ed Dudley, Olin Dutra, Craig Wood, Paul Runyan, Denny Shute and me, with Leo Diegel and Horton as alternates. We had our first real chance that year to win the Ryder cup on British soil.

Denny Shute was our last man out on the course, and I was in the club house with my host, the Prince of Wales. We stood at the big front window facing out on the eighteenth green. A wide path had been cleared for the Prince so that we might have a comfortable and unobstructed view from the club house to see each man finish. I was having a fine time . . . laughing and talking with the Prince . . . when Denny came onto the eighteenth green. If he made the putt in 1, we would win the cup; if he got down in 2 we would keep it; if he took 3, we would lose it to Great Britain. Of course, Denny, not knowing how some of our players before him had finished, did not know this. In fact, if Sarazen and I had done better than to tie our match with Percy Alliss and Charles Whitcombe, Denny would not have had to worry.

I was wondering if I shouldn't be down there putting him wise to how things stood. If I were at the green I could whisper in his ear . . . tell him to play safe . . . not to take three putts. I wondered if I were perhaps sacrificing the Ryder cup for the pleasure of being with my friend, the Prince. I knew it would be discourteous to walk out on the future King of England just to whisper in Denny's ear and tell him how to putt.

Denny played it bold and much too strong. His ball rimmed the hole and went three feet past. He missed coming back and three-putted for a 5. There was a terrific silence . . . and then the gallery around the green broke loose from the restraining line the bobbies had formed, and surged forward to congratulate the winning British team. Enclosed in the club house as we were, the Prince and I heard none of the din and the cheering. We could only take in the action—it all happened in a matter of seconds—and then he and I were on our way to the platform where the Ryder cup would be awarded the British team . . . taking it from us 6 to 5 with one match halved.

Some of our fellows were quite upset by Denny's failure to play it safe and keep the cup in our possession. Fortunately, I was able to persuade them to say nothing to Denny about the loss, and two weeks later he and Craig Wood came through for a tie for first place in the British Open at St. Andrews. Denny beat Craig Wood in the play-off, and became British Open champion for the first time in his career.

When Samuel Ryder established the Ryder cup as a trophy for international matches he stated that only homebred pros were eligible for the teams. However, before his death, he saw the injustice done pros of long-standing residence in this country, and let it be known that the original terms of the agreement could be changed. In that way foreign-born pros who had served a certain length of time in the United States or Great Britain would be eligible for their respective teams. PGA politics in America, however, prevented this change.

I've always thought it an unhappy situation that fine players like Tommy Armour, Jim Barnes, MacDonald Smith, Jock Hutchison, Willie Macfarlane, Bobby Cruickshank and Harry Cooper were made ineligible. Harry Cooper came to this country when only five years of age; he learned his golf, and a good game too, in this country, yet birth in Europe prevented his making the Ryder Cup Team.

And yet, there was another side to the argument. Our American homebred pros had a very difficult time in those early days breaking into the top ranks of professional golf, so long dominated by Great Britain and Scotland. To me, it seemed only fair that our homebreds should make up the Ryder Team, particularly since having foreign-born pros declared eligible might have discredited our victories in the eyes of the British.

I captained the first six Ryder Cup Teams and played in five of the meetings. My record shows four wins and one match halved in the foursomes; three wins and one defeat in the singles. I played only in the doubles at Ridgewood, New Jersey in 1935, with Gene Sarazen as my partner. We played against the British Open champion, Alfred Perry, and J. J. Bussom and beat them 7 and 6.

The Prince of Wales was a frequent and most interested spectator at the Ryder cup matches. When it was known he would be present, huge crowds lined the roads and the streets through which his limousine would pass, hoping to get a glimpse of their much-loved "Eddie." On the links the galleries always gave him plenty of space . . . only the American spectators stared at him. The British seemed to respect his desire to be left alone . . . although they occasionally took sidewise glances at him.

After my meeting with Sir Philip Sassoon in 1928, when the Prince and I had played a social match against him and Aubrey Boomer, Sir Philip was gracious enough to ask me to bring our Ryder Cup Teams down to his beautiful estate each year we came over. His hospitality flowed plentifully . . . and American pros are traditionally a thirsty group. Usually the Prince of Wales and his brother, the Duke of Kent, were also among Sir Philip's guests.

During my years as captain of the Ryder Cup Team I insisted that our fellows be fittingly uniformed. Various manufacturers offered knickers and coats free for our use but I turned them down. Instead I ordered, and paid for, beautifully tailored marine-blue jackets and pale gray trousers from the Alfred Nelson Company in New York. I obtained permission from the army to use an official government eagle ensign embossed with crossed golf sticks and the insigne RYDER CUP TEAM for the pockets. Although I consistently picked my teams for their game and not their beauty, I must admit we stacked up pretty well in the Beau Brummel department, too, when we showed up for the Ryder Team matches.

CHAPTER XXIII: Four-Time
Winner, 1929

> I knew Walter Hagen, first, as a legendary figure in golf. Then I caddied for him at the age of fifteen at Joplin, Missouri. After I turned professional, I got to know him, played with and against him, and toured with him. I know him as a man and as a friend. He's my all-time favorite. . . . Though there were times when he endeavored to use psychology and strategy on his opponents, I never knew him to do an unsportsmanlike thing. He was a fine sportsman, a gracious competitor, a gracious person.
> —HORTON SMITH, *Detroit News*
> [1954]

I CROSSED the Atlantic in mid-April of 1929 to play once again in the British Open. This, my eighth attempt, with three previous wins to my credit, I hoped to parlay into a fourth. The great Harry Vardon had won the Open six times. James Braid and J. H. Taylor, the great veteran golfer of the Isles and captain of the Ryder Cup Team that year, each had five wins to their credit. No American had ever come close to their records.

Johnny Farrell, Joe Turnesa, Leo Diegel, Al Espinosa, Ed Dudley, Gene Sarazen, John Golden, Al Watrous and Horton Smith, members of our second great Ryder Cup Team, also played in the qualifying rounds at Gullane and Muirfield. Other Americans who had come over specifically for the Open included Jim Barnes, MacDonald Smith, Tommy Armour and

212

Bobby Cruickshank. In all, twenty-two Americans made the trip.

We had time for about a week of practice on those layouts, and they commanded the respect of every man. During the first qualifying rounds we played through chill, drenching rains over the solidly frozen ground of Britain's early spring. The following day fine American-type sunshine and calm sultry air blessed us . . . only to change when the Open actually began at Muir-field to Scotland's cold, blustering winds which swept the links with challenging wildness. Muirfield is located in the Arctic Circle part of Scotland—the water actually froze in the pails on the tees. Overcoats and heavy warm wool clothes were a necessity walking the wintry stretches of fairway . . . and rough; but we did discard heavier garments and the warm gloves on the greens.

From a field of 242, 95 professionals and 14 amateurs qualified for the first day of pre-tournament play. In the Ryder cup singles I had taken a terrific shellacking from George Duncan, 10 and 8, so British golf writers were playing down my chances of coming through with a repeat win of the Open. Yet on Wednesday, playing into the great gusts of cold bleak wind I shot a 75. The following day, under far better weather conditions, I was lucky enough to break the course record with a 67. The previous record on the course set by J. H. Taylor in 1904 was a 68. I had shot a 68 at St. Anne's in 1926 and Bobby Jones had tied it in 1927 at St. Andrews. So that 67 of mine broke the record by one stroke of any round ever played in the British Open. Although Henry Cotton tied my record in 1934 and Alfred Perry in 1935, it was not broken until 1950, when F. Daly shot a 66 in the Open at Troon.

So on Thursday evening, when the field was further cut to fifty-eight pros and six amateurs, I was still in there. The leaders after Thursday's play were:

213

Leo Diegel 140
Walter Hagen 142
Abe Mitchell 144
Percy Alliss 145
Johnny Farrell 147
B. Cruickshank 147
Gene Sarazen 147
John Golden 147

Leo Diegel was waiting to practice his putting one evening as the greens-keepers were working. They never artificially altered those greens . . . the idea is to play them as nearly in the natural state as possible. So these fellows just ran a close mower over what little grass had dared show its head after the sheep got through and shaved it off pretty clean. Leo watched them disgustedly, noting the slick smooth surface. "Why don't you iron it now?" he asked.

Gene Sarazen was the first man off at 8:30 on Friday morning. Abe Mitchell and Percy Alliss followed at six minutes to nine and I started at eighteen minutes past the hour. The whitecaps topped huge rollers in the Firth of Forth, the wind whipped around us as we struggled to maintain a stance for a shot, and grabbed each ball fiercely as the shot was played. It was simply impossible to hit the ball and feel any assurance it would finish anywhere near the spot you'd aimed for.

When I arrived at the course that morning and found the wind still howling, I decided I might do two 75's, for I believed a 292 might possibly be good enough to win. It had brought me in first over the links at Sandwich the year before. I decided, too, to use the ground route whenever I could, for against the wind my ball was simply held in the air, with no control and no distance at all. The fairways were hard and fast, and a ball hit close to the ground would roll a great distance and

214

would conceivably avoid the wind. I played what was known as a push shot.

Leo Diegel, low scorer on Thursday evening, had to wait some two hours after my start before teeing off for his first round. I knew what he was going through for that wait is when one really sweats it out. I'd been last man out on Wednesday and had shot a 75. On the following day, as one of the first to start, I had shot my sizzling 67 . . . out in 33, back in 34. Oh, what a beautiful morning! As the day grew older the winds got higher, so Leo got the worst of the weather.

Frankly I considered the weather my chief competition. I'd spent plenty of effort and study to conquer that type of weather, since that disastrous finish I'd made in my first British Open in 1920. I elected to use clubs with less loft . . . and to hit my approach shots for a long roll. I played a number of strokes of ordinary mashie-niblick and mashie length with much straighter-faced irons.

I played the same sort of shots all day, especially at the short thirteenth. I literally sneaked up on this one, and even though I was trapped twice in front of that green, I managed to get a 3 and a 4 here. There is no telling where a high shot would have blown with the extremely narrow target the green afforded.

My greatest asset all through the 1929 Championship came from my ability to get the ball down in 2 from any reasonable distance. For some lucky reason I seemed to have just the right touch for the British seaside links, which are always much faster and more undulating than most of ours here in the States. I was playing with Henry Cotton the last two rounds. His game suffered terribly from the wind . . . he was just floundering around the course. His game was young, then, and just coming along. He did not have the finesse around the greens which experience and acquired skill gave to his game in

215

later years. He eventually turned out to be a great champion.

However, I could not count too much on what luck I might have, so I played a careful game all the way. The thousands in the galleries lined the fairways and the greens and formed a blanket for the wind. Many times I walked some hundred yards away from my ball for a few moments' stand on a hillock, so I might better gauge the strength and direction of the wind, and play my shot accordingly. On some of the greens I would draw the putt into the hole, while on others I would cut across the ball and trickle it into the hole allowing for the wind to help it along.

I got my 75 on the first round Friday with a 37 out and a 38 coming home. Checking on my competitors during lunch I learned that the scores turned in were:

Percy Allis	a 76 for	221
Leo Diegel	an 82 for	222
Farrell	a 76 for	223

Gene Sarazen and Bobby Cruickshank and Jim Barnes had posted 81, 78 and 78 respectively. Believe me, I began the afternoon round with a lighter heart, for my 75 gave me a 217!

I was at the eighth in 3 under par and then I ran into trouble. My second shot on the ninth lay close to the wall. I took my putter and played left-handed and ran several yards over the green. My run-up shot left me a six-foot putt which I missed. It cost me a 6. I'd had a 6 on the fourteenth during the morning round and I sure hated to take this second 6 at this time. Particularly after my 3 on the eighth, a hole I'd finally found a way to master. It was a very sharp dogleg to the right. The first two rounds I had placed my tee shot down to the end of the dogleg and was forced to play a wood shot at right angles to the green. Each time I had caught the trap short of the green

216

and it had cost me two 5's. The hole was guarded on the right of the tee by a lot of wooded boundaries. On the next two rounds I surveyed before taking my tee shot, and elected to play far to the right, a route which cut the distance considerably and left me a short shot out of the heather. This short cut netted me two 3's on my last two rounds.

Some years later I had ideas of playing that hole in my same successful method only to find that the officials had added a lot more trees where I was accustomed to placing my tee shots. The British, however, still refer to that eighth at Muirfield as the "Hagen Hole."

Despite the 6 on the ninth, I still had a 35 for the nine holes. I took 40 to get back home for a 292 and the British Open Championship for the fourth time. I led by six strokes over runner-up Johnny Farrell. Leo Diegel placed third with 299. Behind him were Abe Mitchell and Percy Alliss with 300, and then a string of our American boys headed by Bobby Cruickshank at 301 with Jim Barnes, Gene Sarazen, Al Watrous and Tommy Armour stringing along behind.

I felt wonderful about that six-stroke win, for my other three British Open Championships had been close—just one stroke between me and the runner-up. It was a great day for the Americans, a fine comeback after the trouncing the British had given us in the Ryder cup matches ten days earlier.

That one, two, three finish that Leo, Johnny and I scored really stunned the British. Abe Mitchell and Percy Alliss did a good job . . . yet Mitchell, one of the world's greatest players, had too many three-putt greens. Leo had been afflicted that way, too, for after leading the field for two rounds, he ruined his chances by three-putting on eight greens. Eight three-putts by a golfer of Leo's skill is an unheard-of thing in championship golf, but it was perfectly understandable on the windswept links of Muirfield.

The British Open trophy cup was presented to me by Mr.

A. W. Robertson-Durham. Following the speeches and the enthusiastic, heartfelt greeting the British people gave me, I felt particularly honored when the golfing greats of all time—Harry Vardon, Jimmy Braid, J. H. Taylor and Sandy Herd—came up, shook my hand and said, "Well played, Walter."

Twenty-two American golfers paid their expenses to Great Britain in 1929 to try for the Open. And for the majority, as for me, it was not the first trip. Up through 1933 only seven American names were engraved on the British trophy. In 1922 the British Open netted the winner £75 or approximately $375. The real pay-off for us in those days was the glory of adding that Championship to our records and of getting our names on the mug. In fact I gave my $375 prize to my 1922 caddie, Skip Daniels. Six years later I gave Sarazen my caddie, and I replaced Skip with Walter Smith from Eddington. I won two British Championships with Walter, 1928 and 1929, beating Gene out by two strokes in 1928. So perhaps we could ask, what's in a caddie?

After Denny Shute's win of the Open in 1933, a period of thirteen years followed before another American name appeared on the British trophy . . . that of Slammin' Sammy Snead in 1946. Americans went to England to try for the win, but not in such numbers as in those earlier years. Those of us who won before 1934 had taken the cream of publicity and the glory of winning. American papers, which had followed our progress avidly and announced the winner in streamer headlines, began to give the British Open no more than a few inches of publicity.

Of course, there's another angle on the publicity accorded us in those earlier years. Individual golf writers on the various papers each had his favorite player. By concentrating on his favorite, following the play on the circuit and in the championships, the golf writer added to his laurels and reputation when the golfer won. Many of the old-time sports writers actually made their reputations on the top golfers they covered. Radio, television and international news tape coverage eventually cut down on the physical coverage by individual golf writers. Papers could cut expenses by subscribing to the ticker-tape service, and consequently golf competitions in more recent years are impartially presented by the newspapers. In our day, we relied heavily on the publicity we received—that publicity meant increased prestige with each championship we added to our records, and higher fees for our exhibition matches. With the impartial coverage today, the trend of competing golfers is to put greater value on the highest cash prizes, instead of the classic championship trophies.

The financial advantage of playing in the United States was obvious. Cash prizes had increased greatly, and where the number of clubs offering these prizes were strung along the circuit traveling expense decreased. As other countries became more aware of the drawing power of the game, new foreign titles were established to be won. New fields opened up outside the United States and England, where our boys of the twenties and early thirties had not competed. And more and more foreign players traveled over here to try for our higher and more numerous cash awards. Our championships and our tournaments increased in importance all over the world.

Our best golfers followed the circuit, enhanced the events, and thus made for themselves a new and more regular championship picture at home. In fact, some of our outstanding players today made their reputations by following the circuit . . . their efforts have been blessed with cash, yet they have not one major championship trophy on the mantel.

In spite of all the new fields to conquer offered our present-day golfers, I still hold that no golfer is a true champion until he has played and won the great British Open cup . . . until he conquers those windswept seaside links. Before Ben Hogan won the National Open at Oakmont Country Club in 1953 I got on the telephone to urge him to try for the British Open. He did

. . . and by winning added tremendously to his stature as a top golfer of all time.

In 1920, following my first attempt to win the British Open, I stood outside the club house of the Royal Cinque Ports Golf Club at Deal and speculated on just what had happened to my game. The dull, cold gray day seemed to echo my disappointment and disgust at finishing fifty-third in the field. I leaned dejectedly on a fence while members of the club celebrated inside . . . and I read the item in an English golf writer's column where he commented briefly that "Hagen's game was amusing, but he has contributed to the game by showing our players how a real golfer should dress. He was very well turned out."

I'd been disappointed at the treatment accorded professional golfers . . . all club hospitality was denied us. British Isle golf pros, so long accustomed to this treatment, did not question it. In the eight years following, I made a few dents in those traditions . . . but not enough.

Following the presentation of the trophy to me in 1929, I returned to London to celebrate my victory with the American boys at the Savoy. The next morning I sat in my very plush suite at the hotel waiting for the huge black limousine of the Prince of Wales to pick me up and carry me to the exclusive Swinley Forest Club near Ascot. I had been invited by the Prince to make up a "greensome" with him, Sir Philip Sassoon, Undersecretary of Air, and Aubrey Boomer, pro at the St. Cloud Club in Paris where we were to compete in the French Open later. From the fence outside the club at Deal, to golf with the Prince of Wales at the Swinley Forest Club was a giant step for me and for all golf professionals.

I had been told when I received the invitation from the Prince that he did not desire a gallery, he wanted to enjoy the game. I did my utmost to make an unobtrusive and hurried exit via the embankment entrance of the Savoy. Dodging my friends of the press and the other pros was quite a job. Upon my arrival the Prince congratulated me upon my win at Muirfield, and asked me to be his partner against Sir Philip and Boomer.

In a "greensome," or selected-drive four-ball foursome, all four players drive with each side selecting the ball it wishes to play to finish out the hole. They then continue playing alternate shots for the balance of the hole. We held consultations all through the round, coming to a decision as to which of us should play the second shot. The Prince, a keen student of the game, had taken instructions from leading professionals of Europe. Archie Compston had been the Prince's private instructor for a number of years, accompanying him on numerous trips to the Continent. At Coombe Hill a special locker room had been arranged for the Prince, which is named after him. I am being complimented with a similar arrangement at Grand Rapids, Michigan on Walter Hagen Day. However, my golf game, being what it is today, seems to need one of our up-and-coming young pros to play the course for me while I hoist a few hoots in the special locker room. My wrist action has held up longer than my legs.

At the first hole at Swinley Forest my drive was well down the middle. The Prince elected to play my ball and hit a beautiful five-iron to the green, thirty feet to the left of the flag. My approach putt was not good. I left the ball eight feet short and the Prince holed this putt for par 4 and our side went 1 up.

On the second hole, I hooked my drive into the heather and His Royal Highness, believe it or not, hit right down the middle for a good 225 yards. It was so good I didn't hesitate to play the next shot with his ball. I hit a mashie shot beyond the green and into a ditch . . . so the ball and I were really in bad. The Prince played a fine niblick shot to within six feet of the hole and I should have rewarded his efforts by holing the putt, but I failed. It wasn't too difficult a putt, but it looked much harder to me than a number of more tricky ones I'd holed at Muirfield. The Prince had made a beautiful recovery shot and set it up for me, but I guess the circumstances under which I was playing affected my touch on the green. However we halved the hole in 5.

We used my drive at the third; the Prince played a fair second pitch-and-run short of the edge of the green. I failed to lay it close enough for a 4 and again we took a 5 and halved the hole. Sir Philip nearly holed a 2 at the short fourth when Boomer gave him a splendid tee shot.

Both the Prince and I were short of the green and he played a good chip shot to the hole about five feet short. I missed the putt and we lost the hole to a 3. The Prince hit a screamer at the next hole—right down the middle—and I took my spoon and gave him a trip into the heather, for I got the ball on the toe and it sailed off into the rough. We had quite a time finding the ball. When we did it was in a thick patch but the Prince again played a good shot, knocking the ball on the green within twelve feet of the cup. I missed.

By this time I thought he must be getting rather suspicious about my victory in the British Open. Each time I missed a putt I looked at him and said, "Sorry, partner" and he smiled. We halved the fifth in 5's.

At one time he and I went 2 ahead, but on the fifteenth Boomer holed a long putt for a 4 and reduced our lead to 1. We held that, however, and the Prince and I won the match.

I was delighted that we'd won for I had played far from my best game. The Prince was a pretty fair golfer. He was then playing consistently in the 80's and was keen to improve his game. Following our lunch in the club house I watched him drive about fifty balls and gave him a few pointers . . . suggesting he get his arms out further and higher on his backstroke. I got him hitting a lot of good iron shots with a little hook, which he controlled very well. I had him hit from inside out. I used an old trick of putting down three balls and hitting the middle one. When he became a bit careless I asked him to put down his pipe instead of one ball . . . to insure against recklessness.

During our match all the club members withdrew and gave the Prince the privilege of the club for the day. Guards were stationed around the course to keep out the curious. At the fourth hole, however, one of the protection men spotted a man in the bushes . . . a cameraman who had sneaked in somehow. I had a queer feeling being so closely guarded and protected *from* publicity when all my life I'd been working to scrape somebody up to write about me.

A buffet lunch beautifully arranged on a long table in the club grill tempted me to act as waiter for our group. The Prince spoke up quickly, "I shall do the serving." He really got a kick out of serving the plates and waiting upon us. And I helped him along by asking for second helpings. I was impressed with his sportsmanship, his friendliness and his desire to see that we were all royally entertained.

He told me of playing golf on the courses in Vancouver and Victoria in western Canada. "I also enjoyed some rounds on a Long Island course near where the international polo matches were held," he said.

I learned he had been playing golf since he was fourteen but had only begun to take the game seriously in 1927. I imagine he is close to the most widely traveled golfer in the world, for he represented his country in every foreign land and enjoyed golf wherever he went. He had made a hole in one at three different courses: the sixth hole (220 yards) at Royal Wimbledon; the eighteenth at the Bahamas Country Club, Nassau; and a third on São Vincente Golf Course, Santos, Brazil. So it's no wonder if he was a bit quizzical about the shots I missed on the first nine holes we played.

The Prince of Wales's popularity in the British Isles was unquestioned . . . I appreciated the honor of his friendship. Our meeting the previous year after the British Open had undoubtedly been fortunate for me, for our friendship deepened with the years. We had a lot of good times together both in England and in the Bahamas, when he and his charming American wife resided there.

Nineteen twenty-nine was a pretty good year for me. I had the pleasure of bringing the British Open trophy home with me for the fourth time. I won the Metropolitan Open also for the fourth time and I wound up semifinalist in the PGA Championship. Leo Diegel trimmed me and went on for his second straight win.

For twelve consecutive years, beginning in 1917 with the North and South Open, I had managed to win a national Championship, so that Bob Harlow would have a tag with which to sell my name. Of them all, the British Open was my favorite. Bob would book me as the *only* British champion in the world. There couldn't possibly be two of us, but no one ever stopped to consider that. I'd endorse everything I could possibly use on the golf course, and then we'd hit the exhibition circuit. We had a regular caravan—three or four Cadillacs or Lincolns, my chauffeur heading the group in one, Harlow in the second, my caddie with my clothes and golf equipment in the third. I must have played, at one time or another, every golf course in this country. Guarantees didn't mean much to me. I'd play for the gate and pray that I'd acquired the type of personality and game to draw the crowds. After the matches we'd stuff the money in a suitcase and gun the motors to the next date.

The cash I collected through those years went almost before I had a chance to check its color. For instance, in 1933 I'd taken my son, Walter, Jr., across with me. Since we traveled on one passport he had flown across the channel to Paris with Douglas Fairbanks, Sr. while I finished some partying in London. The pilot brought back my passport on his return trip. I then joined Doug and Junior for some visits to the gay resorts in and around Paris.

We finally sailed for home on the USS *Manhattan*. Coming into New York the captain informed us we'd stop at the Statue of Liberty through the night, because of the heavy fog. This sounded ideal for me, and I immediately hired the orchestra for an all-night stand. I separated the teen-agers—Junior, the Quentin Roosevelt boys and their friends—from the adults. On the teen-age side cokes and hot dogs were served with astonishing rapidity, while on our adult side champagne cases were emptied with equal ease. The purser had agreed to give me credit for all filled cases of the bubbly we had left. I had few to return for credit . . . so few that I had to take care of my crew upon docking with $25 Junior had won on deck races.

After all the service tips to redcaps had been shelled out, my cab had to wait outside the hotel until I could pick up fast cash for the fare. Our party settled down in the hotel, and I called the desk to send up a couple of hundred dollars to be charged to my bill. Meantime Bob Harlow arranged the usual exhibition circuit, so our cavalcade could get on the road again . . . and start filling our suitcase with cash from the gate receipts.

CHAPTER XXIV: Caddies . . .

In my thirty years of golf, I have found no one who
was at all interested in copying the peculiar combination of jerks, twists, loops which I fondly call my
swing . . . it is based on excellent models. It reminds one of Walter Hagen's in that it works better
after a few Old-Fashioneds.

—W. K. MONTAGUE, *The Golf of Our Fathers*
[1952]

WHEN I returned from the British Isles after my fourth win, a
number of newspapers and magazines commented on the fact
that fifteen years had passed since my first big Championship
at Midlothian. And they pulled no punches in stating their
doubts about my ability to keep up the pace, since I would be
thirty-seven years old in December of 1929. Well, I'd performed a pretty fancy Charleston for the gallery after I'd shot
that record-breaking 67 in the second round of play in the Open.

Equally true, I'd decided to leave the record-breaking pace
from then on to the other fellows in the field, if they cared to
try it. I stuck to my philosophy of saving every stroke I could,
conserving energy to combat the weather, and concentrating
on each shot for any advantage I might find.

Except for that bout with the flu just prior to the challenge
match with Bobby Jones, I've been blessed with unusual health,
energy and physical co-ordination when I wanted to use it. My
theory has been to use it when I profited by doing so. Often
I've competed in various sports with no previous experience

226

whatever, and through sheer luck I've come out pretty well. I concentrated on rhythm and keeping an untroubled mind.

During World War II, many golfers acted as range or skeet shooting instructors for the services and the Army brass. This was not a surprising assignment, for their steady nerves, good eyesight, and meticulous care to detail fitted them well for this.

In the early 1940s, a Detroit contingent of outstanding golfers was invited by Colonel Coleman of Selfridge Field to participate in golf exhibitions in competition with various officers on the base. I made the necessary arrangements for the trip, and accompanying me to Mt. Clemens, Michigan, were Jim Demaret of Plum Hollow, Joe Devany of Oakland Hills, Frank Walsh of Red Run, Bill Graham of Bloomfield Hills, Emerick Kocsis of Lake Point, the late Charles Hilgendorf of Lockmoor and the late Charles Campbell. Since I did not enter the golf competition, the fellows insisted I engage in a skeet shooting match with the professional service instructor. I was given a gun, and to my surprise and that of the officers and fellow pros I hit fifty targets, which is twice around the trap, for a perfect score—or, several more birdies than all my brother pros combined had gathered around the golf course during the afternoon.

Guns were not entirely new to me. I'd done some shooting in many places around the world. At Eagle River, Wisconsin, I was invited to see the first live bird championship shoot, since I happened to be in the vicinity at the time. As at Selfridge Field, some joker handed me a gun and I went out there and won the shoot.

During my residence in Detroit, I. R. A. MacDonald, captain of his curling team of the Detroit Curling Club, invited me to join the club. I knew nothing of this sport, yet I went over with him a few times. After several hoots one evening they inveigled me into putting on an exhibition match with my good friend Ira and I actually knocked him off. This great curler from Nova

Scotia took a lot of kidding the remainder of the evening. Members kept asking him why he'd brought a "putter" like Hagen out there to score a bull's eye. Incidentally I was forced to join their curling club.

In the early twenties Jim Barnes and I were in England for the British Open, when Harry Vardon and Ted Ray challenged us to an impromptu lawn bowling match. Ted Ray was a terrific player. His control and accuracy were superb. I could easily understand why he was such a great putter. Jim and I lost gracefully. It was just as well we weren't playing tournament golf, because this was definitely one of Jim's off days. I had to depend on him, of course, but I was having an off day, too.

I never had much chance to swim. We had the usual small-town swimming hole back home, but I spent so much time on the golf course caddying that I missed swimming. I played center on the basketball team when I took my night classes at East High School in Rochester. I did get into a few hockey games . . . as a goal tender. Members of the Country Club of Rochester included alumni and former hockey players from eastern colleges. They arranged for traveling college teams to play on the rink at the club. We were never a match for the hard-skating, well-organized college teams, for age took its toll on the speed and agility of the alumni group and slowed our players down quite noticeably. We did manage to make decent showings in the games, but we contributed no outstanding victories as a team.

I liked skating. I went into the rink at Rochester and trained for weeks to enter the city speed skating championship. When I showed up the night of the competition I was told I was ineligible because my home was not in Rochester proper, but in the suburb of Brighton.

I became quite proficient on skates and finally worked up to jumping over seven barrels on ice. I had seen the great American speed skater in several exhibitions at Rochester . . . the

228

wonderful Edmund Lamy who held the Men's Outdoor championship in 1908-1910, the Men's Indoor in 1908-1910 and the U. S. Amateur for the one and one half mile (4.25.0) set January 27, 1910. Lamy became my idol and I worked diligently to become as speedy and as great a jumper as he. However, in one attempt I fell after covering the seventh barrel. I made no attempt to find an eighth barrel to increase my distance.

Once during my pro days at Rochester, a member made an appointment with me for a lesson. She arrived carrying both a tennis racket and her golf clubs and I learned to my amazement that she expected me to give her a lesson in each.

"I'm no tennis player," I told her. "I'll give you the golf lesson. I feel sure I can help you there."

"If you can play golf as well as this club believes," she informed me flatly, "you should be able to play tennis. I'll take a lesson in each."

Never one to resist a little buttering up, I took on the job. I found that I was ambidextrous in tennis as I was in baseball. I don't know how much she gained from my instructions in the game, but I learned that the game had no interest for me. All I actually remember about it was that we started with *love*, reached *40-all*, or *deuce*. I became *advantage in*, she won a point and we were back to *deuce* and finally back again to *love*. Somebody wins a set and what does it get him? Just a racket in his hand and another chance to run around hitting that bouncing ball. To me it was no game!

I also came in contact with some trout fishing experts. George Bonbright, Irving S. Robeson and Gordon Brewster, all members of the Country Club of Rochester, invited me trout fishing with them at a private club at Caledonia near Scottsville, New York.

They put a rod together for me and explained that my putting touch and feel for timing should make me equally skilled in fly casting. They spaced themselves, each taking a certain section of the stream, while I set my rod against a tree and followed Bonbright, rated number one in New York State.

"Where's your rod, Walter?" he asked.

I explained I'd learn more by watching him and imitating an expert than I would in trying to catch a fish my first time out. He was beautifully skilled in this sport and I watched him carefully. I noted his timing, the manipulation of his left hand on the line. And frankly this sport began to fascinate me. I could easily understand how timing and precision handling of the rod and line were relative to the timing and hesitation at the top of the golf swing. I fell for the idea of becoming an expert flycaster. I could scarcely wait to get back to Rochester to buy a smart-looking outfit at LaBourie's.

I bought the works: rod, reel, creel, flies by the dozen, tapered lines, hip boots and even a fishing jacket whose numerous pockets held every item a fisherman might dream of needing. I got a copy of *Field and Stream* and boned up on tying tackle. One Monday morning I set out through the dewy grass dressed in my finery. Through my mind flashed the picture of the golfer who turns up at the first tee with everything from cap to knickers and clubs all brand new. How well does he play? I found a section of a stream where I could be all alone. The magazine said to match the kind of fly on the stream at that time of day with the artificial fly. Resting my rod against a tree, I knelt on the bank and studied the flies on the surface of the water. I leaned through the tall grass for a closer look, slipped and went headfirst into the stream. I'd answered my own question . . . about the well-dressed golf novice.

Skull practice is the beginning of any game or sport. In golf, the novice can wait to hit a ball. First he must see the local pro and learn the rudiments of the game . . . know what kind of skill is required and how to gain it. Failing to recognize my own lack of knowledge in fly casting cost me an expensive dunking. I should have spent long hours standing in a field, casting for the center of a bicycle tire.

Performers, whether in sports or in some form of show business, have always interested me tremendously. For that matter I've run across a few amateurs who gave me many a good laugh. When Walter, Jr. was fifteen and we were returning from a trip to Europe, we became acquainted with Abe Lyman and his orchestra on board ship. In fact it was Abe's orchestra I had hired for that all-night party on the USS *Manhattan.* Some years later Abe came to Detroit and played at the Oriole Terrace on East Grand Boulevard following his performance in the Cass Theater in *Good News.* I invited a group of my friends up to my suite at the Book-Cadillac for cocktails, and to dinner and dancing later at the Terrace to Abe's music.

Crossing the downstairs lobby of the hotel about five that evening I saw a little colored boy dressed in the smart livery of a theater usher . . . bright red suit with brass buttons and a pert pillbox cap set jauntily on the side of his head. I stopped to talk to him and learned he worked at a nearby theater and that he could sing and dance. At my invitation he went up to my suite. I had him tell me about his song and sing a few lines softly. . . . I liked it and I'd never heard it anyplace before.

I had his prop, a huge chicken drumstick, sent up from the kitchen. I explained who he was to my guests and introduced his number. And believe me, he was great! His song concerned four fellows sitting at a table with a juicy roast chicken in the center. And I remember it went something like this:

The man from the East, he had the East Wing;
The man from the West, he had the West Wing;
The man from the North, he had the head and all the breast;
And I . . . lost . . . my . . . appetite!

231

As he sang, he gobbled down that big drumstick. He was a real hit. We picked him up again after his chore at the theater, bought a fresh supply of props at Sam Sufferin's place on Cass Avenue, and took the boy out to the Oriole Terrace with us.

I told Abe Lyman about the little fellow's act and he gave the youngster a big build-up to the night-club audience. The boy went on stage singing and taking bites of a drumstick, as he played the parts of each of the men at the table. He actually brought down the house. We fed him banana splits, gave him five dollars and sent him home in a cab. But first, I told him to find out from his mother what they needed at home, come to the hotel the next day and ask for me. I wanted to do something more substantial for him.

The following noon as I left the hotel, the doorman told me a young colored boy had been around at the back door insisting I wanted to see him.

"I do," I said emphatically. "Where is he now?"

"We told him seven o'clock was too early . . . to come back later in the day."

"When he returns, have him wait for me. I don't know his name or in which theater he works. He performed for me last night in a wonderful way and I want to thank him."

His cheerful little smile and engaging manners stayed in my mind, and I've regretted that he never came back. He was about thirteen years of age then, and he probably thought I was trying to brush him off. I wasn't. I'd still like to know his name and where he is.

Through the game of golf I've met a great number of fine young fellows all over the world . . . boys who began their business careers as caddies. I've heard two explanations of the origin of the word "caddie" as a tag for the boys who carry the bags of clubs. One version designates "caddie" as derived from the Scotch "cawdie," an errand boy of sorts in the streets of

232

Edinburgh. However, I prefer the second version, which gives the name "caddie" as a variation on the French word "cadet" meaning younger son or younger brother. It seems more appropriate for those thousands of boys all over the world who do such a fine job for golfers in every country. Most boys in the United States begin caddying at fourteen and usually go on to higher paying jobs at seventeen or eighteen. But in the British Isles caddies often continue in the work even when they become adults.

I've had caddies of all ages in the Isles. One of the younger ones, E. Hargreaves of Sussex, England, wrote me only this year reminding me that he'd caddied for me at Muirfield when I won the British Open for the fourth time. When Archie Compston beat me so badly at Moor Park in 1928 a big six-footer, J. W. Williams, who carried my bag, was easily past thirty-five. Whenever I played any of the windswept links in Kent, a wonderful old fellow of sixty years, Skip Daniels, was my caddie and constant companion. His well-worn black suit with its belted jacket, his weathered plaid cap and his cane, were as familiar to me as my favorite mashie-niblick. He would caddie only in Kent—at Sandwich, Deal and Prince's—and even there he picked his golfers. They had to be pretty special. He was of inestimable help to me when I won the Open at Sandwich in 1922. His encouragement, his steadiness and his completely accurate knowledge of the links, were qualities every good caddie should cultivate. He was tireless in his efforts during practice rounds.

Skip expected to caddie for me at Sandwich in 1928, but Gene Sarazen was trying for his first win and I agreed to lend him Skip. By that time Skip was getting quite old and he could not walk too fast, so he may have slowed Gene's game down a bit, for my caddie Walter Smith and I beat him by two strokes.

233

Bowlegged Johnny Anderson, the Scotsman who had been my caddie for the Open at Troon and whom I took over to the continent to help me around the courses in France and Belgium was another fine fellow.

Nagoya, a young Japanese boy . . . smiling, eager and energetic . . . was possibly thirteen when he carried my bag at the Komazawa course at the Tokyo Golf Club. In Tanganyika, Nairobi, an ebony-skinned native with huge rings hanging from his ears . . . some twenty more decorative rings of graduated sizes around his neck and arms . . . was equally efficient and interested in my game.

In Calcutta, India, some twenty or thirty urchins in their ragged yet colorful costumes, perched like gaily chattering birds in the trees surrounding the golf course, were frankly envious of their lucky pals toting our bags.

In Salisbury, Rhodesia, friendly young boys in shorts and T-shirts, their dark skin shining in the sun, strode barefoot around the hot sandy courses with our golf bags strapped over their shoulders. All over the world I met these boys and men of widely different races and colors who possessed the universal qualities necessary in a good caddie.

I caddied for ten cents an hour in those early days, but I ran across caddies in Africa where the head man received only seven cents. I may have been overpaid. Fees have increased through the years and caddies for the big tournaments and Championships now receive an average of thirty dollars for their services. If the golfer happens to win and hit the big prizes, the caddie should be, and usually is, rewarded with a sizable hunk of the cash. I made it a practice to pay my caddies well; and remembering back to my own experiences in the job, I knew how the quality of service improves with adequate payment.

The training a youngster acquires on the golf course, the association with a sport which later can be either his recreation or his vocation, is invaluable in building for better world un-

234

derstanding. International matches between our leading professionals and amateurs promote unity and peace and should be promoted wholeheartedly. Many of our finest golfers come up through the caddie ranks. Gene Sarazen, Byron Nelson were caddies. The winner of the 1954 National Open, Ed Furgol, once caddied at the Utica Golf Club at Utica, New York. Arnold Palmer, winner of the National Amateur at the Country Club in Detroit and of the Amateur Championship in the fabulous Tam O'Shanter tournament in Chicago at only twenty-four years of age, has spent some years in the caddie pen. Caddying offers youngsters ambitious to hit the championship ranks a wonderful opportunity to learn the rudiments of the game. They learn from the experts who visit the courses in all countries the skill and the fine points of competition. American caddies, too, through the generosity of Chick Evans and his Evans Scholarships can qualify for four-year college degrees.

When I began playing golf, caddies worked when only ten or eleven years of age and this, I believe, led to the skilled *young* players in the game between 1912 and 1930. As the age minimum was increased to fourteen, these boys who were capable of championship golf matured later in their game. As a result, many of the fellows did not begin to get into championship form until they were in their thirties. Right now, because of the widespread caddie tournaments, high-school and collegiate interest in the game, we're going back to find young fellows hit their championship stride at an earlier age. There are many promising young players like Gene Littler, Dick Mayer, Arnold Palmer and others still in their twenties who are playing good consistent golf. They seem, with the others of their age, to be the fellows destined to break the thirty-five-year age average of the boys of the past twenty years.

Golf has a way of leveling off the financial and social status of people, and ranking high the fellows with the "down the pretty" tee shot and the accurate putt.

235

I believe the most unusual caddie that appeared on my horizon was in the Belgian Congo in Africa. A tall, full-chested native stripped to the waist, wearing only the loin cloth peculiar to the tribe, toted Joe Kirkwood's heavy bag of trick clubs around a course studded with diamond dust greens. Strings of ivory ornaments hung around a short neck, rings four inches in diameter pierced contorted ears, a tight narrow band with cascading ivory ornaments and animal teeth encircled a head of short crimply-curled hair, and several rings banded fingers on both hands. The costume and decorative ornamentation was regulation in that country, but the eye-opening jolt to me stemmed from the fact that Joe's caddie was a lady!

I'm still wondering how Joe could keep his eye on the ball and choose the correct club for his trick shots.

CHAPTER XXV: . . . and Kings

It was some ten years ago that no sooner was a report about Mr. Walter Hagen's coming to Japan than I was really moved as if I was going to be able to meet a shooting star from the land of dream.

Till then, I had seen him in pictures and had heard of him in conversation, but when I actually saw him at Hodogaya playing a real golf game, I was totally fascinated. By the visit of Mr. Hagen, an immortal footprint on the history of golf in Japan was left. Even now I am still recalling about the way golf should be played when I think of the beautiful form of his and the white curved line of the ball in flight revealing his personality. His photo of that time is, even at present, adorning my workshop like the bright star of the dreamland.

ROKUZO ASAMI, *professional golfer,*
Hodogaya Country Club,
Yokohama, Japan

[1940]

GOLFING with the Prince of Wales and association with him on many occasions opened a lot of doors for me. One such door was flung wide in late August of 1929 when I received a most official-looking letter from the Honorable Treasurer of the Moortown Golf Club, Ltd., at Leeds, England.

The Honorable Treasurer, Mr. Norman Hurtley, informed me that an honorary membership in the famous and exclusive old golf club was being conferred upon me. He then requested that I sent them an autographed photograph which they promised to display prominently in the club house. I learned that the same invitation or honor had been conferred upon my good friend, the British professional, George Duncan. Since he and I with Abe Mitchell had been the threesome who crashed the gates at La Boulie in Paris in 1920, it seemed to me only fitting that we should take this same new step together. The idea had finally seeped through to the exclusive and ancient British clubs that having their outstanding professionals as fellow-members could be a distinct advantage.

My first encounter with the rigid social distinctions in Great Britain was the sight of the scoreboard at Deal in 1920, listing the pairing schedule. Before each amateur golfer's name was the title "Mister." The professionals were listed simply by name—I was W. C. Hagen. That method of listing continues in the British Isles to this day, but my resentment against it has been appeased by the wonderfully hospitable attitude and the genuine friendship I've known from the people there.

Needless to say I complied with the request for the photograph and thanked them for the honor accorded me. From that date on, whenever I was in England I was welcomed to those exclusive clubs. And I took my pro friends, both British and American, right in with me.

In the years that followed I was a regular visitor at the golfing house parties which Sir Philip Sassoon gave at his beautiful estate at Trent. Often, too, I took the Ryder Cup Team and their wives to Sir Philip's for some practice rounds on his private course. I met numerous members of the royal family, among them King George V and his sons, who later became King Edward VIII and King George VI. Both his sons were ardent golfers.

I had received that impressive letter from the Honorary Treasurer of Moortown while I was on tour with Horton Smith. We played eighty-two matches that summer of 1929 and took in $17,000 each. Our tour ended on the second of November just following Horton's win of the Oregon Open at Portland. As is customary we split our winnings during the length of the tour and for the second year running I got cut in on the top prize money in this event. I finished fourth or seventh when Horton won, but with Johnny Farrell I was more help, for I finished second.

During the season I won the Metropolitan Open for the fourth time, collecting top money of $750. I won the Great Lakes Open that year also, but even with my appearance money the take was not too big. I headed for California with my mind and my wallet envisioning the rich Los Angeles Open with prizes approaching $10,000 and the even bigger Agua Caliente with the largest purse offered at that time, $25,000. I definitely anticipated the feel of that healthy green stuff.

Back in Hollywood I took a beautiful suite at the famous Roosevelt Hotel, owned by a couple of motion picture producers, and known as the "Home of the Stars." I persuaded Mack Sennett to make a short golf comedy co-starring Leo Diegel and me. He agreed to pay us $3,600 each for our talents.

I gathered in very little cash from golf in California, perhaps because I could only star in one event at a time. Also, I may have been cast with too many stars. Gene Sarazen won the huge Caliente prize when he shot a 68 in his final round to beat out Horton Smith and Al Espinosa who tied for second. Gene pocketed $10,000 for this and he was sitting pretty.

I earned a total of $80 in prize money in five starts. Leo Diegel had trimmed me 3 and 2 in the semifinals of the PGA at the Hillcrest Country Club in Los Angeles in early December and had gone on to win the championship for the second straight year. As for me, well, at the end of three months in the California tournaments and the making of the golf comedy for Mack Sennett, I had my check for $3,600 and I could do some relaxing for a spell. I was never at any time hard pressed

239

financially for my golf factory was doing fine and the many endorsements kept some cash rolling.

During the winter I seriously considered a return to the British Isles for the Open of 1930. However, another idea on which I had been working for a couple of years unexpectedly came to a deal. I knew that exhibition tours in the United States would be at a low ebb that summer due to the Wall Street market crash the previous October. The fast-spreading depression put golfing interests in the background. People were too busy vainly trying to recoup huge losses or jumping out windows. For once I was very thankful that I had spent my money as it arrived rather than investing in the market to make a million.

So I felt particularly lucky when my negotiations for exhibition matches in New Zealand for $5,000 and in Australia for $10,000 were set up. Another offer from responsible people in Japan guaranteed me $6,000 for twelve matches in that country. Also I was to receive a bonus for each match in which I either tied or broke a course record in Japan. Breaking Japanese records became somewhat a habit, but I must admit the course records in that country were not too difficult to break. With these contracts to build on I figured it would be easy to fill engagements in Honolulu, Manila, Hong Kong and Shanghai . . . places I planned to play en route.

I knew that this would be an exceptionally advantageous year for my tour to the British possessions of New Zealand and Australia, since I would be the first four-time winner of their great British trophy ever to play golf in those two countries. I'd won it often enough to make an impression on the golf fans down under . . . and I decided to make that tour rather than play in the British Open Championship again. I persuaded Joe Kirkwood, who had made a lucrative trip back to his native Australia several years earlier, to pack his trick-shot clubs and go with me.

240

A gay farewell party on the evening of January 31 in Los Angeles lasted long enough for our friends to see us off at noon at San Pedro harbor. We were bound for Honolulu, our first stop. We planned to be away approximately three months, which would get me back in time to play in the National Open at the Interlachen Country Club in Minneapolis. I had not won the National Open since 1919. In 1928 I lost my PGA championship and for two years now I had been without a major American title.

The National Open was usually scheduled on dates so closely following the British Open that it became almost impossible to arrive in time to play a few rounds before the Championship started. Yet Bobby Jones, in 1926, won the British Open at Lytham and St. Anne's and immediately hopped a boat for the United States. Upon arrival in New York he headed for Columbus, Ohio, where he won our National Open. Ben Hogan repeated Bobby's feat in 1953 when he pulled off his double win at Oakmont Country Club and at Carnoustie for the British Open. Of course, Bobby's Grand Slam of 1930 tops both his own and Hogan's record.

Frankly, at thirty-eight I admitted to myself I could not do it. For the remainder of my serious golf I'd need to make a choice between trying for the British Open or our own National Open. And the time had come when I needed to win a major Championship in my own country much more than I needed another British win. I decided I'd go up to Interlachen immediately upon our return from the Australian tour, rent a cottage on beautiful Minnitonka Lake and get right into training.

While my winter in California had been far from successful financially, I had, however, enjoyed the scenery. My favorite spot for displaying the beauty of the particularly lovely girl I happened to be escorting was the gorgeous Blossom Room of the Roosevelt Hotel on Hollywood Boulevard. Many well-known orchestras filled engagements there and dancing has always been a favorite recreation for me. I loved the environment of the movie capital . . . the ease with which its people lived and the many varieties of entertainment offered. For the two winters prior to 1929 I had leased a house on King's Road above Sunset Boulevard. It became a favorite hangout . . . a popular Hollywood salon. As many as ten or twelve film beauties, either stars or on their way up, might drop in for tea. Thelma Todd, the curvaceous blonde whose untimely death saddened all movie fans, was often a guest. I knew June Collier, the Talmadge sisters—Norma and Constance, Bebe Daniels, Bette Davis. Miss Mary Broome was my introduction to the stars and starlets in those early days.

The house I leased was adequate for big-scale entertaining and I made good use of it. Built high on the hills overlooking Los Angeles . . . on clear days San Pedro and the Pacific Ocean were visible in the distance. At night the dancing and cocktail parties occupied my time, while my view into the valley showing a huge electric sign displaying "57 VARIETIES" made me feel right at home. An enormous drawing room with spacious verandas was built over a two-car garage, a wide staircase led to four bedrooms . . . that was my villa. I kept two Philippine houseboys, one of whom frequently donned chauffeur's livery and drove for me. I knew most of the male name stars of the day and frequently played golf with many of them . . . Douglas Fairbanks, Sr., Leo Carillo, Richard Arlen, Owen Moore, Harold Lloyd, Hoot Gibson, Wally Beery, Andy Clyde (with whom I did one film), Johnny Weissmuller, Humphrey Bogart, Pat O'Brien, George Murphy, Randolph Scott, Adolphe Menjou, Fred Astaire. And of course those two great golfers, Bing Crosby and Bob Hope, clowned around many a course with me. William Frawley, now teamed with Lucille Ball and Desi Arnaz in "I Love Lucy," once teamed with me in a pro-amateur two-ball foursome at Lakeside in Hollywood. We won a trophy which I hope he held on to tighter than I did any of mine. Yes, indeed, I found Hollywood a truly wonderful place to live!

Joe and I had departed from that exciting spot in January of 1930 . . . and were headed for Honolulu. We had a week layover there while awaiting our ship, the *Arangai,* to come in from Seattle and carry us on to New Zealand. We played three exhibition matches in Honolulu before embarking for our second stop, Pago Pago. While there we played an exhibition match on a three-hole course. We continued on to the Fiji Islands and there we were met and greeted by the Mayor himself.

On a sightseeing tour en route to his home we saw twelve or fifteen victims of a current intestinal virus epidemic being transported on stretchers by the natives to the outskirts of the city for burial. The heat was intense for we were just over the equator. At his home the Mayor asked our choice in drinks. My Scotch and soda was easy to provide but Joe's first serving of milk picked up a fly and had to be replaced. The Mayor's windows were not screened so I suggested that Joe's milk might be screened for his protection. We could readily understand the rapid spread of disease in the islands.

A passenger in second class contracted smallpox just prior to our arrival at Auckland and the entire ship's personnel and passengers were quarantined. Officials told us we'd be vaccinated and then remain in quarantine for several days to determine if the inoculation was successful. Since the voyage from Auckland to Sydney required about a week, we decided to remain on board ship and go on to Sydney. This meant, however, that we must pass up the New Zealand exhibitions and take a loss of several thousand dollars guaranteed us by the clubs there.

I'd heard that dousing a fresh vaccination with a generous supply of Listerine would counteract the effect of the vaccine. I applied Listerine to both my arm and Joe's in the secrecy of our cabin immediately after the physician departed. I had an old scar . . . a huge, murderous-looking thing . . . a good many years old, too, which I insisted to the officials was of more recent origin. Joe had actually been vaccinated only four years earlier but his small scar was unimpressive. The Listerine had ruined the chances of the one given him at Auckland so poor Joe had to be stabbed all over again. He was established on a quarantine island near Sydney for the additional eleven days while I relaxed at the hotel waiting for him. I had agreed not to play until our first scheduled exhibition, although I sent him a lot of balls so he could keep in shape and entertain the officials of the island with his trick shots.

After Joe's quarantine ended we took up our scheduled play. One of the most amusing incidents occurred at a large department store in Sydney where we gave an hour-long demonstration of form and playing technique of various clubs. We talked briefly about famous golfers we knew in America and Europe. I shot a few ping pong balls into the faces of the audience, then Joe performed a number of his unusual trick shots. Joe was born at Manley Beach near Sydney and many people in the audience knew him as a caddie and during his early pro days down under. When we'd completed our bit on the stage I announced we'd be around for a while, in case anyone had questions. I'll never forget the next few minutes.

I followed Joe off the platform down into the audience when a tall, straight, imposing lady, approximately eighty years old, steamed into the aisle and headed for my pal Joe. Her hat was the type George Washington wore crossing the Delaware and around her thin neck a narrow band of black velvet ribbon, like the one Mrs. Warren Harding affected, was knotted in a small bow.

"Oh, Mr. Kirkwood!" she called in a shrill falsetto. "Do you remember me?"

"Yes," Joe admitted bashfully.

244

"Remember when you used to caddie for me, Mr. Kirkwood? I'm so proud of your golf career. I've followed every Championship you've played." She nodded and smiled. "Mr. Kirkwood, what an ambassador you've been. In fact," she continued archly, "Mr. Kirkwood, my drawers are just filled with your achievements."

I walked quietly away and left Joe to blast his way out of that trap.

We played one match at Manley Beach. As we were driving to our hotel in the downtown district a huge policeman directing traffic at a busy intersection . . . a bobby with a big badge . . . turned to greet us and he was Joe's brother. Right then we all three went fishing.

We had an interesting trip through that vast country . . . shaped not unlike our own United States but much more sparsely settled. Three fourths of the population of Australia in those days was located in Brisbane, Sydney, Melbourne, Adelaide and Perth.

Officials of Canberra, located halfway between Sydney and Melbourne, home of Australia's Prime Minister, invited us to play an exhibition in their city. The Prime Minister, the Honorable Mr. Hughes, came down to welcome us and escort us to his residence, a beautiful building, the White House of Australia. During the afternoon we played a new and very beautiful course in fine condition and boasting a spacious club house.

Due to the smallpox quarantine our timing was running a bit behind schedule. We were now coming into Australia's fall season, which is our spring. Their fall and winter seasons to me provide the best golfing weather inasmuch as they have no great seasonal changes . . . just summer the year around. However, when fall arrives the golfers clean out the lockers, take clothes home for repairs and then head for the wonderful Australian beaches and resorts—proving that everybody must at least pretend to have a season for every kind of sport. But to my mind

245

they missed playing golf in their best weather . . . the winter months.

We left Australia by way of Townsville on the eastern tip and went by boat through the many islands to Manila. We stopped en route at Thursday Island, a fascinating spot. It was controlled by an Englishman whose main business was the building of boats for sponge and oyster fishermen. One native chap, working on the keel of a boat, impressed me tremendously.

In cutting the keel he followed a very old method of chalking a line, then fastening it to each end of the keel. He snapped the line sharply leaving an impression of a straight chalked line showing the thickness of the wood he was to take off . . . about one fourth of an inch. Using a grub ax as sharp as a razor, he then stood on the keel holding it steady with his bare foot and cut toward his toes along the chalked line. I quickly counted his toes to assure myself of his skill and accuracy. Not seeing any scars and noting the beautiful precision of his work, I thought, "Here I stand in the middle of no man's land admiring and envying the uncanny skill and accuracy of this native. I don't have a shot which comes even close to approaching his precision." The only part of his skill I could actually imitate was his stance . . . and I could use it only in putting.

Farther down along the beach crews of native women met the incoming boats carrying fishermen with their hauls of oysters and sponges. The girls opened the oysters searching for pearls which, by the way, were not as numerous as those produced in the cultivated oyster beds. The Englishman invited the ship's passengers for a tour of his castle and there he had on display the most gorgeous pearls I've ever seen. I did finagle him into letting me have one. I had it made into a stud which I still wear.

From Thursday Island we sailed on to Manila and up the coast to Kobe, arriving there on May 8—the very morning of the day our exhibitions were scheduled to start.

Our Japanese tour began that afternoon when we played our first exhibition at the Kobe Golf Club. Yataka Kanuma, secretary of the Japanese Golf Association, met us when we landed at Kobe and he accompanied us throughout our tour of the many fine courses in the Japanese islands. We played over several courses in the western district, including Naruo, Ibaraki and Takarazuka. Then we went up to Tokyo where we were widely advertised and headlined:

HAGEN AND KIRKWOOD ARE COMING TO JAPAN!
THE WORLD'S GREATEST GOLF CHAMPIONS!

We played to huge crowds of cheering spectators in the Tokyo area and many of the very fine professional golfers of the islands followed us. We played matches against the representative pros, such as Tomokichi Miyamoto, pro at the Ibaraki Country Club at Osaka; Kokichi Yasuda, pro at the Tokyo Golf Club; Chick Chin who later made several trips to the United States with the touring Japanese pros; Rokuzo Asami, pro at the Hodogayo Country Club at Yokohama. All these boys and their fellow-golfers made us welcome and entertained us generously.

While in Tokyo I had the pleasure of meeting the Emperor of Japan, Prince Asaka . . . and this later became most important. He had invited me to play a match with him on his private course and to give him a few instructions, but a damaging earthquake hit a day after our arrival. This earthquake, plus the fact that Japan was at war with China, prompted the Emperor to send his secretary, Mr. A. Orita, to our hotel to call off the match. His Imperial Highness sent me as a gift a beautifully engraved gold cigarette case, the thickness of two silver dollars. Shaped like a small book, it held only five cigarettes. He'd probably heard of my smoking habit and also of my thrifty custom of placing my cigarette carefully on the edge of

247

the green before I putted, then retrieving it after I'd taken my shots.

We left the comfort of the Imperial Hotel in Tokyo and moved to the Clay Hotel in Shanghai where the Japanese forces were keeping the city under a fairly constant barrage of artillery fire. A great friend of mine, Commander Baine, whose cruiser *Augustus* was docked in the harbor, invited me on board for luncheon. Only seconds after his car and chauffeur had picked me up, the Japs scored a direct hit on the steps at the front of the hotel where I had been standing. Later while we were enjoying lunch on board another badly aimed Japanese shell took the life of a sailor on deck.

We were invited to play a match outside Shanghai . . . a British course which bordered the estate owned by a brother of my good friend Sir Philip Sassoon of England. In order to reach the course we had to cross the line, a narrow-gauge railroad track on the outskirts of the city which was guarded on one side by the Japanese and on the other by British and Scotch soldiers. I don't suppose we were in any real danger but it was darned annoying to dodge back and forth with officials on the Japanese side stopping us and asking innumerable questions.

I wired the Emperor, Prince Asaka, to send down a man with an extra large badge I could wear as we crossed the border . . . a badge so large that the Japanese soldiers could see it for a longer shot than any I had in my bag. Since, in case of a mistake, it would be one shot from which I could not recover.

A Scotch soldier spotted me from his trench which paralleled the narrow-gauge railroad. He remembered me from an earlier trip I'd made to England, and he wanted an American cigarette. I just happened to have several extra packages and I readily handed them over to him and his buddies. We had a fine match and a grand turnout.

On the eleventh hole I played one of the best left-hand shots

248

I've ever made . . . it carried just short of the green on the Sassoon course. Joe was a trifle unnerved on the eighteenth when he strayed from the fairway on his tee shot and his ball landed on a mound used for burial purposes. The curious custom of interring the bodies on the surface of the ground and then covering them with soil created plenty of natural traps and bunkers. As Joe went for a five-iron second shot to the green, I kidded him by saying, "Don't take too much divot, Joe. A hand might be extended to you from the mound." I must confess we both got a shock when he took a hard shot and an elbow stuck up from the soil—which was right in keeping with Joe's play of the hole, an elbow in a roundabout way. After the match we gave the Jap officers a golf lesson in a clinic they had arranged.

Golf was in its infancy in Japan at the time of our first visit there. Our tour undoubtedly inspired many of the young professionals and amateurs to work harder at their game. We received scores of enthusiastic letters following our appearance, thanking us for including Japanese golf clubs in our trip and assuring us we had increased the national interest. Yes, they were our pals at heart.

I cabled Bob Harlow that we would arrive in Seattle by way of Victoria Island on June 16. We reached there on the day of Bobby Jones's great victory in the British Open at Hoylake, which led to his memorable Grand Slam. In November, months after our tour of Japan, I received from the Japanese Embassy in Washington a note informing me that a "wooden box containing a gift of silverware sent by His Imperial Highness Prince Asaka" was being forwarded to me.

In 1929, following my win of the British Open, I had toured in Europe playing matches in Germany, Hungary, Austria, Switzerland and France. Berlin was a gay and entertaining city in 1929 . . . so much so that I stayed up all night soaking up atmosphere and yet I was lucky enough to finish second in the

249

German Open the following day. From Berlin I flew to Vienna, the last few miles of the trip along the Danube River during the most gorgeous sunset I'll ever see. At the Dolder Grande Hotel in Zurich, Switzerland, I was hosted by a leading citizen of the town and had literally to tear myself away to keep an engagement with a beautiful little number I'd met in Berlin. Since I had been a free man the past several years, all these extracurricular activities were legal passes. I returned to Paris to pursue my education at the Folies Bergère. In each of the European cities I had played exhibition matches against leading professionals and had picked up about $12,000 in less than a month. Yet I had barely enough cash left when we steamed into the port of New York to tip the various stewards generously before I again began the regular round of exhibitions in my own country.

My financial circumstances following the tour Joe and I made to Australia and Japan in 1930 duplicated the European tour. Somehow I always managed to distribute the proceeds rather evenly throughout the various cities which had rewarded me so generously. However, I was fully persuaded that many foreign countries would gladly welcome us and pay the price to see our top golfers.

Professional golf in the United States was hard hit when Bobby Jones captured both the American National Open at Interlachen and the British Open at Hoylake. Tommy Armour won the Professional Golf Association Championship at Fresh Meadow Country Club at Flushing, Long Island. However, Bobby had taken the two big Opens and his amateur standing prevented the usual "world championship" challenge match which we pros liked to set up to sop up the gravy.

Frankly that "world championship" gravy reached the peak in the pay-off in 1928 when Johnny Farrell, National Open champion, and I as British Open champion were scheduled to play the best three out of five 36-hole matches in New York

City, Philadelphia, Detroit, Chicago and St. Louis. We realized around $10,000 each on the series, in which I managed to win three.

In 1929 when I again held the British title and Jones the National Open crown there was some talk of a "world championship" match between us. However, because of his amateur standing the USGA discouraged such an idea. I believe, had we been able to set up such a series, all attendance records would have been broken. I wouldn't venture a guess as to who would have come up a winner, so perhaps it was just as well that the USGA had no intention of sanctioning the matches.

PART THREE: The Green

INTRODUCTION

IT WAS a matter of just twenty-five years ago, back in 1914, that a kid golfer set out from Rochester to Chicago to make another stab at the United States Open Championship.

He was undecided at the time whether to be a professional ball player or a pro golfer. His stand at Midlothian was to give the answer. And Hagen won—the first of a dozen major titles he was to gather down the years. Chick Evans was on Hagen's heels at the Midlothian test, but could never quite catch up.

In August, Chicago and Midlothian and Hagen's vast army of friends and admirers are giving the veteran a big show over his first championship course. This will be a round robin best ball affair and it promises to be one of the golfing classics, given to one of the great names of golf for all time. It will be a tribute to Hagen, who has written more than his share of golf history since he dropped his last putt at Midlothian twenty-five years ago. . . .

I always thought that Hagen's greatest crash in golf told a truer story of his nature than any of his successes. He left England in 1920 to play in his first British Open at Deal. He went over as U.S. Open champion, a title he had won at Brae Burn the year before.

He drew major headlines of the tournament. But in his first test he finished in fifty-third place. He couldn't break 80. He started with a big gallery and finished with his caddie and a lone scorer. But he finished without alibi or a complaint. Not only that, he walked up and posted his terrible 72-hole count in front of a big British crowd. As he gave in the figures he turned to this crowd with one remark, "I'll be back."

He came back to win four British titles. . . .

Hagen had everything it takes. He was a magnificent swinger with wood and iron—one of the great recovery masters and a brilliant putter. Hagen made well over a million in golf—and spent it all. Money has never meant anything to him, except something to get rid of quickly. How he ever took the beating that he gave himself is beyond any one's imagination. Only a few years back I saw him arrive at Pasadena, California for the Pasadena Open. He reached the club house in a dinner suit. He had been up all night—no sleep and no food. They drove him to the third tee to catch his two playing partners. He had to play the first two holes alone. Yet he finished that round with a 71. Later in the afternoon he finished the second round in a sixsome, just at the edge of night.

"I can't lift my feet," he told me. "I can't pivot a lick." But he had a 72 that second round.

I've seen him report from an all-night gathering with friends just in time to start and still break 70. Not once—but many times. Only recently in the PGA at Pomonok where he used up little sleep, he was still good enough to go out in 31, five under par.

Hagen was always the first to congratulate some young golfer winning his first big tournament. There is no envy in him, no hate and no greed. He has always been generous to the last turn—too generous for his own good. His feat of winning the PGA four times in succession—twenty-two consecutive matches against the great of the game—will never be equaled in our time. He is still a great golfer—and just as great a fellow. The party they are giving him at Midlothian should be one of the all-time tops—for Hagen deserves it.

—GRANTLAND RICE
[1939]

Beyond a doubt Walter is the master of the man-to-man struggle form of competition in the realm of golf. Apparently he revels in meeting those situations where either a slip on his own part, or else a deserving effort on the part of his opponent, has forced the issue squarely up to him. Certainly there is no more heroic figure at rescuing desolate and forlorn hopes, and there are but a scant few who are capable of watching the brilliant coups and still retain the composure necessary to play golf free from strain that means broken concentration, hurried swings, and in consequence, errant shots.

—INNIS BROWN, *The American Golfer*
[1926]

A SUMMER fishing trip on board Larry Fisher's yacht the *Margaret F* was an important break for me each year. A 72-foot cruiser carrying a crew of four, its guest list usually comprised Jack Truss, Eddie Esch, Al Wallace, Tom Doyle, Harry Cunningham, E. E. (Red) Thompson and Harley Earle. Our yearly cruise from Detroit through Lake Michigan into Canadian waters eventually found us anchored in Georgian Bay off the villages of Tobermory or Little Current. All members of the party were expert fishermen, or bragged that they were, and various wagers were made. The largest fish, the first fish, the heaviest fish and so on would get the winner $25 on each count. We all had side bets with each other, too, a sort of round robin deal.

On a particular day one summer we were anchored in unknown waters during our trip north and separated, two to a boat, to try our luck. Jack Truss, my temporary partner, and I fished for some hours before I finally hauled in a bass, not too big and not so small, just par. We became a bit tired and returned to the yacht to enjoy a nice cool hoot while the others continued fishing. Since we were the first ones in, I decided to play safe for at least one of my bets. My bass had originally weighed three and one-half pounds but when I finished stuffing him with lead sinkers his weight and my chances had increased considerably.

The other fellows returned to the yacht a few hours later and not one had had even a bite. Therefore I won all wagers. Yet after several rounds of relaxing refreshment I was still having trouble collecting my bets. I called to John, the chef, to verify my fish.

He was no help. "Mr. Hagen," he said, "do you mean the one you put the lead in?"

Believe me, the ribbing really started and after that little "stuffed fish" episode they watched me closely each day. I even had them cleaning my fish and counting the lead sinkers in my tackle box to make sure I tried no more funny stuff.

Each year as we visited the small villages on the northernmost post of our cruise we were presented with big brass keys to the Town Hall and in return we threw an open party. All the townspeople turned out, including many Indian squaws with papooses strapped to their backs. We arranged chairs upside down for makeshift bunks for the babies . . . and everybody danced while the sheriff acted as bartender—the night was really gay. We were always sure of our welcome the following summer and of additional brass keys.

Those Canadian waters were popular with other visitors from various parts of the country and we had pleasant times renewing old acquaintances each year. The Webber brothers, Tom and Jerry of the great J. L. Hudson store in Detroit, had a cottage up there and were congenial hosts. The 140-foot yacht owned by Burt Massey, head of the Palmolive Soap Company, was a familiar sight each year. George Eastman, for whom I had caddied for many years in Rochester, anchored his yacht there and we had many wonderful chats about old times. And that brings me to a business deal he helped me with which resulted in something far better for the city of Rochester than for me.

Since my schooldays baseball had been in my blood. During my years in golf I followed my favorite teams avidly. While playing Joe Turnesa in the finals of the PGA in Dallas in 1927 I heard that the Rochester Red Wings baseball team was for sale. I sent my manager Bob Harlow up there with $10,000 for an option on the team. When the Championship ended and I'd won I grabbed my clubs and took the fast route to Rochester.

I found I'd purchased fifty-three players, one of whom had made good from my early baseball days when we were city champions. He'd been scouted in those early days and sent to Baltimore where he was a club mate of Babe Ruth. Well, here we both were back in the game in our home town. I was beginning to think of myself as a baseball magnate. I intended to forget the advice Larry Fisher gave me when I mentioned the deal to him.

He told me, "Walter, stick to your golf. Don't divide your interests. I approve of your golf club manufacturing venture, but not this baseball deal."

Despite Larry's advice I went ahead with the deal. However, my bank balance was far from enough to see me through. I needed a new ball park so I decided to call on my old friend George Eastman.

I telephoned him and he invited me for breakfast the next morning to hear my plan. He was a fine gentleman, then about seventy years old. He greeted me warmly, recalling my caddie days at the Country Club of Rochester and complimenting me on the success I'd made as a pro. I explained why I was in Rochester. He listened carefully, but I could feel his lack of sympathy, for I sensed he thought I wanted him to buy in with me. This I would have loved, of course. However, I went on to tell him then that he had done so many fine things for his city—building libraries, schools, conservatories and a theater— that I was suggesting that he build a fine stadium for all the athletic events, including track meets, football and baseball. I reminded him of the need in Rochester for such a stadium, at the same time pointing out that a new stadium would be an asset for me after I took final possession of the Rochester Red Wings.

Mr. Eastman told me he was leaving in a few days for a hunting trip in India, his last he believed, because of his age. He said he would consider my suggestion and look into it upon his return. If he found it feasible he would gladly see what could be done to provide the stadium.

I followed through with the Rochester deal as long as I could. That fall I attended a meeting of the members of the American, National, International and other associate leagues at the Commodore Hotel in New York City. Judge Landis presided and to my extreme pleasure I was unanimously approved as president of the Rochester club in the International League. Well, the cycle was complete and I was back in baseball again . . . but my stay was short. My money was fast giving out. I finally got out of the deal, after I'd lost $37,500; but after my demise as a club owner Mr. Eastman returned from his India trip and he did build for Rochester a very fine stadium. I felt I'd accomplished something, for my loss must have helped pour a bit of concrete around the stadium or at least scatter a few cinders on the track.

In December of that year and following my return to my own line of work I read an article in the *American Golfer* discussing the size and shape of players in relation to their game. The writer remarked on "Leo Diegel, a sturdy young man about Hagen's height but a bit slimmer . . . of German-American ancestry"; on "Mike Brady, with the shoulders and neck of a wrestler"; "Willie Macfarlane, a tall slender scholarly looking man from Aberdeen, Scotland"; "Johnny Farrell, the slim black-haired, smiling youngster"; "Hagen, the cold nerveless strategist . . . Irish-American . . . black-haired, Buddha-faced."

I'll have to admit the size, shape and hair color of the men in the game never bothered me in the least. But the ladies who play and follow the game, well, that's a different picture. They were helpful to my game . . . with their attractive pitch-and-run contours. In fact, I think I'd make a pretty good judge for the Miss America contests. Inasmuch as we're told to keep an eye on the ball, I always had that other eye peeled for my feminine gallery and did I dress for them! That's where my imported Austrian sweaters, Japanese silk shirts with the French cuffs and British cashmere coats were valuable . . . to attract the glances of the feminine ticket purchasers.

I met beautiful and charming women all over the world . . . a roving eye was my Geiger counter; my claim was staked with a devoted appreciation of their potentials and ability to make my travels and my leisure moments more enjoyable. In India I met the dark-skinned high-caste girls of Calcutta in their luxurious brocade robes and sheer silk shawls . . . their necks and arms bedecked with the heavy jewelry they wear so well. Geisha girls in elaborately embroidered kimonos costing hundreds of dollars, with scented posies tucked in their modish coiffures, moved with studied grace and daintiness as they served our "cocktail" tea.

Strongly contrasting in physique and coloring but equally attractive were the British and Australian women who attended the golf matches. Their attractive fresh complexions, vibrant health and *joie de vivre* make them rate high in the world of beautiful women.

On the island of Bali slender, full-bosomed dusky-toned beauties clad only in floor-length sarong-type skirts cooked our meals and kept our cottages . . . their silhouettes affording relaxed viewing for our putt-ing tired eyes.

From Banff to Zanzibar I've traveled and every place I've found the beauty of the country made much more inviting by the loveliness of the native women. The letter A of the alphabet was omitted for I happened to miss that wonder spot, Alaska, although I've met a few Eskimos. A sophisticated, charming and beautiful Argentine woman whom I met in Paris one summer invited me to consider a life of ease in her native land against a future of knocking the little white balls around the pasture. I remembered Larry Fisher's advice, fortunately, that I should "stick to my golf and not divide my interests." And who is he to talk?

Despite all the places I've seen and the wonderful experiences I've enjoyed in each I'll still settle for the United States and our gorgeous American women. Two of my favorite cities are New Orleans and Minneapolis. I was host many times to the languorous beauties of New Orleans, either at the Roosevelt Hotel or at one of the numerous famed French restaurants. Seymour Weiss managed the Roosevelt at that time and Huey "The Kingfish" Long lorded it over his home state. Although we never had any trouble rounding up plenty of the New Orleans belles to provide the necessary pulchritude, my policy of open house parties at my hotel suite had to be abandoned for the Senator's bodyguard insisted on screening the credentials of every guest when he was present.

Parties in Minneapolis usually followed a duck hunting trip and I always served my own game, succulently roasted, garnished with wild rice and prepared by the chef of the Radisson Hotel. In the twenties and thirties, and I'm ready to state this for the record, those second- and third-generation Norwegian, Swedish and Danish girls were among the most beautiful and the healthiest I've ever met. Nicollet Avenue and the Flame Room of the Radisson glowed with their fresh blond beauty . . . Nothing gave me more pleasure than catering to those healthy appetites. I must confess Minnesota beauty still appeals to me, for at the PGA at Minneapolis in 1954 I posed for a picture with the very lovely Miss Minnesota. The fact that the picture made the cover page of *Golf World* was due, I'm sure, to her talents and not to mine.

Parties have always been my favorite way of life and I punched the cash register keys with a golf club during the day to be able to afford the luxury of entertaining when I'd finished the round. My parties usually were impromptu affairs . . . the open house policy. My friends all over the world came to know and to enjoy my kind of hospitality and to keep me right in there banging away at a golf ball. A party began with a few pals and their ladies trailing along with me to the hotel after an exhibition match or a tournament. Having worked up a lot of social warmth after a couple of hours, members of the original group got busy on the telephone and invited others to come and partake. It wasn't pure coincidence that many very attractive ladies found their way to my parties for I definitely encouraged this interest in golf. I entertained every night that I could entice a few pals around my sideboard, not too difficult a feat, I can vouch. And I'll admit right here that I could make one highball last longer in my own glass than any Scotchman ever born.

There was one party, however, which I planned with extreme care. It took place at the Royal Alexandra Hotel in Winnipeg, Manitoba, Canada. The Blue Hills Golf Club in Kansas City, Missouri had advertised an open invitation tournament and then canceled it at the last minute. I accepted the responsibility for the matches and put up the cash. I invited Chick Evans down from Chicago and he won. I was second so naturally, beating all the pros, I took $800 of my own money and broke even. Chick being an amateur could not accept the prize cash. Following the Blue Hill tournament I started a tour of western Canada by way of Winnipeg.

I played my first three exhibitions at Winnipeg and got away to a fine beginning financially by picking up about $1000. Frank Pierce, genial host who managed hotels for the Canadian Pacific had supplied me with a luxurious suite in the Royal Alexandra. A chance remark of a girl employee at the hotel to the effect that "Hagen will take a bundle of dollars out of Canada" led to my throwing the big party later.

We moved west playing to enthusiastic Canadian golf fans. I played exhibitions in Moose Jaw, Saskatoon, Edmonton, Medicine Hat, Victoria Island, Vancouver and Calgary. My reception everywhere was friendly and I was enjoying the wonderful country and its people. However, the remark of the girl at the Royal Alexandra still rankled ten days later when we rounded out the tour. I wired Frank Pierce reserving the royal suite and asked him to round up my golf pals and their ladies for a big party. I also got in touch with my favorite Winnipeg hostess and asked her to make sure the employees from the Royal Alexandra were in attendance at the affair.

The party was a success all right. About thirty guests, Canada's leading golf personalities and Winnipeg's most beautiful girls, had been invited, but more than one hundred attended. The hotel chef served a marvelous dinner . . . and the beer and ale in the ice-filled bathtub, champagne in ice buckets, a well-stocked liquor cabinet kept the music going round and round. At the height of the festivities I found one beautiful girl still waiting for me and we stepped out to finish off the evening at a popular night club, where I picked up my second check for the evening. Although I had taken in over $3000 during my ten-day tour, I went back across the border with less money in my slacks than when I started. But I felt I'd helped cement the good neighbor policy with our Canadian friends.

Getting acquainted with people has always been rather easy for me, as it is for any athlete in the public eye. Yet I once inadvertently made the meeting of a charming young lady a rather painful incident. I was playing on a course at Lake Placid Club in New York when I hooked a tee shot sharply and it struck the thigh of an unusually pretty girl just off the fairway. I walked over immediately and apologized, but as I told her, it's rather difficult to gauge the seriousness of an accident like that unless one checks personally. We had cocktails later that day in the club house. Romantic affairs had a pleasant habit of developing quickly in those days and I usually managed to overcome any obstacles barring the way to my "pursuit of happiness."

CHAPTER XXVII: Competitors

The sun don't shine on the same dog's tail all the time.

—SAM SNEAD, *Life Magazine*
[1954]

AROUND 1900 when I was caddying at the Country Club of Rochester, golf was considered an "old man's game." Only the more prosperous citizens could afford the club membership fees, the colorful costume and the leisure the game demanded. There was just one public course at Rochester, the Genessee Valley Course. The majority of the iron heads for clubs were handmade in the British Isles and imported here.

In general use at that time, too, was the gutta-percha ball which had replaced the "feather" ball around 1848. The old "feather" ball had contributed to the fact that golf was considered a fair-weather game. That ball, made by stuffing feathers tightly into ovals of leather, sewn baseball fashion, became soggy and weighty when wet. Rain often spoiled the golf club grips because no caddie bags were in use then to protect them.

Late in 1899 Dr. Coburn Haskell, an American, introduced the controversial rubber-core ball but golfers were slow at first to take advantage of the greater distance and accuracy offered over the hard gutta-percha ball. However, when Alex Herd played the Haskell ball at Hoylake in 1902 and won the Brit-

265

ish Open Championship, the ball immediately jumped into universal popularity and use. Following the introduction of the Haskell ball we had in use many balls of varying specifications until May 1921 when a ball of 1.62 inches and 1.62 ounces was universally accepted. Several years later, 1924, those specifications were changed in this country due to a series of tests, both mechanical and through use, to a ball of 1.68 inches and not more than 1.55 ounces. There was as much difference between this ball of 1924 and the original Haskell rubber-core ball as there had been between the Haskell and the old gutta-percha.

I was doubly fortunate in being born when and where I was. I was familiar with the game from childhood and, more important, I happened along in my early playing days just when the implements and the facilities were being greatly improved. That was a transition period in golf, just as a similar transition occurred around 1924 and again some fifteen years later with the introduction of the precision-balanced steel-shafted clubs and the hopped-up rabbit ball we now use.

Golf courses in the United States in my early days were mainly *au naturel*, far removed from the scientifically designed courses of today. The rough was just what the name denotes—rough. Those roughs of grass and weeds alternating with uninhibited bushes and trees contrast strangely with the trim, barbered rough of our best courses today. On those early fairways the grass was cut or scythed, the greens were mowed. Today's greens are carefully rolled and contoured and today's traps instead of bunkers are artfully spotted so as to increase the challenge and reward the accuracy, judgment of distance, and skill resulting from the latest improvements in the implements of the game. The transition of the early 1900s to the rubber-cored ball necessitated a changing of the courses. Holes were lengthened, bogies and pars lowered. So the hopped-up ball and the steel-shafted clubs manufactured today make the expertly planned courses a definite must in the game if the skill of low-scoring golfers is to be tested.

At Brookline in Boston in 1913 I played for the first time in competition in bad weather. As more tournaments were established in the United States in those early days, weather was just another hazard. Blustering winds, rain and, in the British Isles, even sleet and snow were taken in stride. If we were lucky we played before the storm struck. If not, we played through it. Today's golfer resembles today's baseball player in his tendency to run for shelter if a storm of heavy wind and rain breaks. Indeed, many clubs employ big horns or sirens to call players off the course until the weather improves. Matches are even canceled if the weather is not too promising. Weather played a great part in our scores, which often soared into the high 70's or 80's . . . since we had to play regardless of sun or storm.

Curiously enough, also, the type and the limited number of clubs we carried then contributed to the greater skill we acquired in the varied types of shots we were compelled to make with them. We had no wedge, the most popular club among golfers today. As late as 1921 we were playing wedge shots with a niblick . . . or the equivalent of an eight-iron . . . or with any club having sufficient loft to pitch cleanly out of a trap and over projecting heights.

Jim Barnes and Fred McLeod were highly proficient with this so-called "pitch and run" shot. I picked it up from McLeod, who was definitely a master, and it was one of my best and favorite shots.

That pitch-and-run shot helped me win the British Open at St. George's both in 1922 and 1928. In 1928, on the fifteenth —a tedious two-shot par 4 hole—a wind of gale velocity made it play long. My brassie shot caught a cross trap short of the green, but I was blessed with a good lie in the sand. If I had exploded the shot out of the trap I would have had little or no control, and it would have been hard to hold my ball near the

267

hole since the green sloped away from me. I used a seven-iron to pitch-and-run to the sloping left side of the green. My ball rolled around and down and almost holed. Using the pitch-and-run made the big difference in my score on this hole, giving me three pars on those final holes and the win of the Open by one stroke.

Chick Evans, Francis Ouimet and I appeared on the golf scene in 1913 when the game was ruled by such great old-timers as Harry Vardon, Alex Smith, Ted Ray, Johnny McDermott, Gil Nicholls, George Sargent, Alex Ross, Tom McNamara, Willie Anderson, Alex Herd, Jim Braid, J. H. Taylor and Walter Travis. We three—aged 23, 20 and 21 respectively—were competing against those fine golfers who were in their 40's and 50's. And here, despite our youth, this early association with their manner of play paid off. We profited from watching and practicing their skilled and proficient games and also from the tough competition afforded by the greatest golfers the game has ever known.

With the uncanny accuracy of Harry Vardon as our pattern, we young golfers strove to follow in his footsteps. He was a superb stylist and I have yet to see his equal in hitting full brassie shots around the pin. He could place a brassie shot within feet of either side of the flag with the same accuracy as with his irons.

I am inclined to agree with the sports writers who claim that my best shots were made with the seven- and eight-irons and the putter. I know that during my competitive years I was more familiar with the rough and the woods than with the fairway. This never bothered me too much for I got a lot of practice. I could pitch and run or putt to equalize the advantage the boys might have picked up over me with their middle-of-the-fairway or to use the English expression "down the pretty" shots. Too often when a championship tournament is being played on a very long course the experts assume that the prodigious hitters are going to have the advantage. I've seen these long hitters go for a slugging fest and knock themselves right out of the tournament, while the low scores were turned in by the moderate hitters, usually the boys who can approach and putt. Johnny Farrell was an excellent example of fine approach shots and accurate putting winning over the long-ball hitters. His approach and putting won the Shawnee Open for him in 1922 and also let him finish in the money in every tournament he played during 1923-24.

For instance I recall the PGA of 1938 at Shawnee Country Club on the Delaware when Paul Runyan beat Slammin' Sammy Snead in the finals 8 and 7. Here was a player, Runyan, being outdriven by forty yards or more on various holes and yet he gave Snead a terrific lacing. And this was no pitch-and-putt course they were playing.

There is one hazard which has not changed since the game of golf originated. That is the quality of the player's opponent. In competitive golf, particularly, the character and temperament of the opponent, the kind of game he habitually plays, are big factors in winning or losing one's match. The quality of the opponent is recognizably more important in match than in medal play, as I believe Bobby Jones learned in our challenge match when he "played Hagen instead of the card" or par. He was led to do so because of the fact that I was very wild. But he overlooked my short game.

Too many tournament players are inclined to disregard the value of studying and gauging the temperament of opponents in match play. Following the circuit year in and year out I learned early to use the characteristic type of play of each opponent to my own advantage, not forgetting of course the value of pars or better on every hole. Nevertheless, I couldn't always measure the accuracy my opponent might have on a given day. At times we all played way over our heads. I imagine that Mike Souchak realized the truth of that when he shot his record-breaking 27 on the back nine in the Texas Open at San Antonio in 1955, and went on to establish a new all-time scoring record of 257.

I never allowed my opponent's shot or ball to interrupt my shot or my concentration. Should his ball lie a few feet from the hole I always figured that my shot or the location of my ball might possibly make his putt a bit more difficult . . . and it often did.

In those early days when Harry Vardon was our pattern, we strove primarily for accuracy. We were content to get a hole in par, because par was usually good enough to win. Yet as the quality of opponents shifted, into the game of golf just as into baseball, came the era of sluggers . . . and the sensation boys. It's a sure bet that if enough of the sluggers are out there trying to make the longest drives and hitting every second shot directly for the flag, two or three or even four are bound to make it pay off and come up with amazingly low scores.

Shortly the entire field of golfers realized that winning a championship meant taking risks or letting the golfers who take the gamble walk off with the titles and the cash. And it's an odd fact that even though they gamble they don't always win but they force the type of play, until everybody is taking desperate chances in order to pull off a miracle. In my early competitive career a man took chances of that sort only when he was behind and the holes were disappearing fast. And believe me, even then we could string up a nice line of birdies if we were forced to do so.

Jack Doyle, known some thirty years ago as the Sage of Broadway, often asked me for an opinion as to who would win the big golf championships. And though I knew every golfer hitting the circuit and had played against most of them time and again, I could never with any accuracy guess how they'd line up when the Championship ended.

Making book on golf matches has always been a popular pastime in Great Britain. In 1924 the British bookies sent circulars over here quoting ridiculous odds on the top players of the game. I was listed as a 10-1 bet and Al Wallace, my Detroit pal, sent a check for $1000 for a bet on me. I won the British Open that year at Hoylake but the bookies neglected to pay off. Al finally recovered his "grand," due to the efficiency of Scotland Yard. However, British law required only that the bookies pay back the amount of the wager. Betting on golf matches has always been frowned on by the United States Golf Association in this country. Calcutta pools used to be a part of every major championship, but so much money became involved that officials tried to discourage the practice.

Golf fans, like boxing and baseball fans, enjoy comparing the top players of the twenties and thirties with the ranking golfers of today. And in golf we've plenty of statistics for the comparison. I have chosen for a basis the American National Open, since it is open to and participated in by both amateur and professional golfers from the United States and abroad.

In 1901, playing with the old gutta-percha ball, Willie Anderson won the National Open at Myopia Hunt Club with a score of 331. With the introduction of the rubber-core ball Lawrence Auchterlonie cut twenty-four strokes off Willie's score for his win of the Championship in 1902 at Garden City. Alex Smith shot a blistering 295 at Lake Forest in 1906, the first man to break 300. But it remained for the great George Sargent to set a record of 290 when he won the Championship in 1909 . . . that score was unbroken until Chick Evans' 286 at Minikahda in 1916. I had tied Sargent's 290 with my first win of the National Open at Midlothian in 1914, but I hadn't been able to crack the record. And Chick's 286 stood unbroken until 1936, when Tony Manero posted a 282 with his win of the Championship at Baltusrol. During the years from 1916 through the mid-thirties the scores remained pretty consistent. So it seems that the Haskell rubber-core ball gave more impetus to our game in that early transition period than the steel-shafted clubs, the speedy rabbit ball and the professionally designed and groomed courses gave to the game in the thirties. Skill, accuracy, form and competitive toughness must combine with these finer implements of play in order to lower the scores.

In 1937 Ralph Guldahl shot a 281 to win the Championship at Oakland Hills in Detroit and since that time only once has that score been broken . . . Ben Hogan's miracle 276 at the Riviera Country Club in California in 1948 . . . and it has been tied once, Julius Boros in Texas in 1952. Other than Hogan, no golfer of today has shot below 281 in the National Open and even the great Hogan won two of his four National Open Championships with 287's.

I would gladly challenge a team of Snead, Hogan and Cary Middlecoff to play a 72-hole Open against Bobby Jones, Gene Sarazen and myself . . . if the good Lord could cut a couple of tens off the years of my team. And I'd guarantee Bobby, Gene and I could post the winning scores. I believe the failure to cut more strokes off that 286 of Chick Evans' 1916 score is due to the type of golf the fellows today are playing. I believe their game lacks the accuracy, the consistency—or should I say, the finesse—of the game we played. Give my team this rabbit ball, my beautifully precision-balanced steel-shafted clubs and I think we could really cut down those scores posted in the past ten years of the National Open. At least we'd come close!

Gene Sarazen was twenty when he won his first Championship title; Chick Evans was twenty-four when he won both the USGA Amateur and the National Open; Bobby Jones and I were each twenty-one when we won our first Championships. Due to the war and his tragic accident Ben Hogan was thirty-six when he won his first National Open; Craig Wood was forty; and Ed Furgol, 1954 champion, is thirty-eight. The champions of today are taking their titles after they're thirty-five or forty. What I'm trying to stress is the fact that the golfers of my team were meeting top competition and winning championships and titles while we were youngsters. Today's golfers appear to need years of competition and seasoning before they come through with the trophies of the major Championships.

Perhaps it may seem that I stress too much the winning of major Championships . . . of getting one's name on the cups. I want to stress the importance of consistent competition. I'm speaking primarily of pro golf now, for I like to see our big-time pros follow the circuit, not just go for the events offering the most money. Of course, even here, there's a difference. In our early days of competition the prizes offered were so small as to be financially insignificant. In the twenties we spent many thousands of dollars crossing the pond to enter the British Open . . . to win the comparatively small prize money of less than $500. We made not one trip, my contemporaries and I, but five to ten trips. If we held a title, we deemed it important that the current contenders have a chance to knock us off.

I'd be the last fellow in the world to go sentimental where the long green stuff is concerned. I played golf to live . . . in the manner to which I easily became accustomed . . . that's for sure. But during the money-making circuit I entered every tournament where a championship title was the winner's reward, regardless of the amount of prize money offered. I got quite a kick out of collecting medals and getting my name on every trophy.

Some of my toughest competitors didn't get their names on many trophies or get listed as champions but they were great golfers. I'm thinking of fellows like Tommy McNamara, Tommy Kerrigan, Harry Cooper and Bobby Cruickshank . . . plus Mac-Donald Smith and many more. These fellows loved the game and they contributed much to its popularity and its color. They were always considered possible winners.

Although in our one challenge match I was successful in defeating Bobby Jones, I believe his attitude toward the game

273

. . . his quiet, cool, analytical type of play was more discon-
certing to me than the explosive, erratic temperament of many
other golfers. However his game in our particular match wasn't
at its best.

I shall not attempt to rate the golfers in the field when I was
playing in top form. I'll just say that at one time or another
they all gave me trouble. But Gene Sarazen seemed to give me
the most, despite the nine more years of experience I had. He
was cocky and self-confident, but he had plenty of moxie and
determination and could concentrate solidly on his game.
These qualities made him a great competitor, as he still is after
thirty years in the big league of golf. He has proved, as a Senior,
that he can often beat the best of today's players.

In the early twenties Chick Evans, Francis Ouimet, Jim
Barnes, Jock Hutchison and Johnny Farrell were tough boys
to beat, too. Of these Jim Barnes bothered me more than the
others, perhaps because I had to play him more often.

Henry Cotton paired with me at Muirfield for the British
Open in 1929. He looked like a great hitter but he wasn't getting anywhere with his game. He needed to acquire polish for
the kind of golf I believed he could eventually play. I suggested
that he come to the United States that winter and barnstorm
with our leading pros . . . so that he might learn to blend his
game with our American standards of play. He came, but got
no immediate results. I saw him again later that winter and he
didn't seem too well pleased. However, he agreed with me that
one trip around the circuit wasn't enough and that he should
try again. It was this persistence and painstaking practice which
paid off for him. He has a great record as a fine golfer.

Tommy Armour, another great warrior of today, crossed the
Atlantic with me on his first visit to this country . . . following my first try for the British Open in 1920. On the boat I
watched Tommy take some practice swings and I could readily
understand his being listed on the bulletin boards in the British

Isles as *Mr.* T. D. Armour. However, he was fresh from winning the French Amateur and since he was a bit short of cash I invited him to be my guest at the Westchester-Biltmore Club in Rye. I introduced him to Mack E. Bowman, president of the organization, who gave Tommy a position as secretary there.

While he worked at the club we played many rounds of golf, with my good friend, the late Jay O'Brien, betting on Tommy against me. I had to give Tommy as much as two and three up Nassau on each nine holes yet I still had enough money left from our betting to buy drinks for the round-table locker room boys at the finish of each round. Looking back on Armour's tremendous record—winner of the National Open, 1927; PGA Championship, 1930; British Open, 1931; Canadian Open, 1927, 1930, 1934; Western Open, 1929 and a good many other Opens across this country—I am sure his rapid rise to golf championship play was due to his serious study of the game. He could not have been copying my swing.

In considering past and present outstanding golfers and trying to name the clubs and shots they used best, I know I'm really in trouble. Not too many appear to me to excel in any particular shots, as the really great old-timers did; they seem rather to be able to put together a combination game which has enabled them to hit the top championships. As for me, I'm barred . . . I needed a hunting license to find my birdies.

I keep remembering the backspin Jock Hutchison could put on a ball; Jim Barnes's deadly accuracy; Alex Smith with his five-iron and "pitch and run" shots; Tommy McNamara's deadly putting skill; Tommy Kerrigan's long drives and sure-win putts; and the way Bobby Cruickshank, with his jovial personality, could literally laugh a ball into the cup. And of course, I can't forget Old Man Par always directing me with a jaunty wave of the Flag!

I find that in making out the list which follows I tend to recall certain shots made by these competitors which occasionally made plenty of trouble for me. Well, for what it's worth, here are best clubs and shots by a few of the great.

One-iron——Denny Shute, Billy Burke, Jimmy Demaret
Two-iron——Henry Picard, Craig Wood, Bobby Jones
Three-iron——Tommy Armour, Alex Herd, Ben Hogan
Four-iron——Billy Burke, Francis Ouimet, Jimmy Demaret
Five-iron——Willie Macfarlane, Harry Vardon, Bobby Locke
Six-iron——Jock Hutchison, Ralph Guldahl, Lloyd Mangrum
Seven-iron——Johnny Farrell, Gene Sarazen, Lew Worsham
Eight-iron——Chick Evans, Leo Diegel, Julius Boros, Sam Snead
Nine-iron and wedge——Gene Sarazen, Johnny Revolta, Ben Hogan
Chip——Jim Barnes, Fred McLeod, Mike Brady, Byron Nelson
Putter——Ted Ray, Cyril Walker, Bobby Locke, Horton Smith
Driver——Al Watrous, Bobby Jones, Ben Hogan
Brassie—Harry Vardon, Bobby Jones, Byron Nelson
Spoon or four-wood——Paul Runyan, Harry Cooper, Johnny Farrell

I have not attempted to list the fellows in first, second and third order—from my nineteenth-hole position that would be an impossibility. Every one of them had his day on the course when he could take all contenders. So, duffers and free-swingers, I'll let it go at that.

CHAPTER XXVIII: Gasparilla
Open, 1935

Sir Walter's favorite stratagem was the reverse approach. . . . When faced with an easy shot, he pretended to be racked by doubts. He'd study his lie;
he'd walk ahead to survey the green; he'd finger his
clubs uncertainly; he'd shake his head; he'd address
his ball and back away to change clubs. Then he'd
drop one dead to the pin. The gallery would go wild
and his opponent would be shaken.

But on an impossible shot The Haig would whip
out an iron without hesitation and blithely swing
away—also dropping dead to the pin. The gallery,
appreciating the immensity of the feat, again would
go wild. The opponent, who could appreciate it
even more, would begin to wonder whether he was
playing man or fiend—a fiend who could get super-
natural help.

—ARTHUR DALEY, *The New York Times*
[1954]

IN CHECKING on my golfing record after I returned from the
Australian trip in 1930 I found I had yet to win the Canadian
Open. I had competed only once, in 1912, when I finished
eleventh, just ahead of the great Alex Smith. Some of our boys
had been making the trip up there rather often. Among my
contemporaries, Leo Diegel had won the Canadian Open four
times; Tommy Armour, twice; Al Watrous, MacDonald Smith
and Clarence Hackney had a win each.

Throughout my competitive days many of my followers appeared to believe I should win or come close to winning every tournament I played. Believe me, I've lost plenty I should perhaps have won. However, I did manage to win many of the big ones. When I let it be known I had entered the Canadian Open a few of these trusting fans thought the trophy should be shipped down to me. But they don't come that easy.

Before our tour "down under" I had fixed my sights on the National Open Championship at Interlachen in July only to have Bobby Jones pick it off to add to his collection. The largest field to qualify in the history of the Open competed in 1930, a total of 1177. When I won it first at Midlothian in 1914 a field of only 129 qualified and at the time of my second win in 1919 field qualifiers had increased to 142. Of course, in those early years the qualifying rounds were played at the Championships proper whereas today players qualify sectionally throughout the United States, due to the tremendous number of entries. So with this increase in entries in 1931 I knew I'd have my work cut out for me if I were to add the Canadian Open Championship to my list.

My game in Toronto was sharp enough to give me a 292. I was standing in the locker room celebrating and idly watching the crowd at the last hole, when a chap came running up from the eighteenth green to bring me a bit of jarring news. He reported that Percy Alliss was faced with a thirty-foot putt, similar to the one I'd holed on the eighteenth. If Alliss holed it he would tie me. Well, he made it. He had finished with five consecutive 3's.

Canadian officials insisted on two rounds for a play-off. Just before play began the following morning Larry Fisher telephoned me from Detroit to say that he, E. E. (Red) Thompson, Harley Earle, Jack Truss and Carl Snyder, then manager of the Book-Cadillac Hotel, were flying up in his plane to watch me finish. He instructed me to win the trophy so he could bring it back. However, they were delayed in taking off and missed the morning round, which was just as well for we ended up tied with 73's!

In the afternoon round Alliss was leading by two strokes at the fourth. When I reached the fifth I was surprised to see the gang from Detroit lined up back of the green. Alliss and I got our par 4's and I walked over to the boys knowing I would get kidded plenty.

"How do you stand now?" they asked.

"Alliss is leading me by two strokes," I told them.

"How can we take the cup home with the kind of golf you're playing?" Larry Fisher inquired.

"You're just in time to see some good golf," I said. "I'll get the trophy for you."

Nothing happened on the sixth and seventh; then I shot two consecutive birdies on the eighth and ninth to pull up even. I looked over at my pals and for the first time I saw grins on their faces. We stayed even going to the seventeenth when I holed a putt for a 3 and I was one stroke up. So I was leading him for the first time . . . and a very pleasant feeling came over me for now Percy was running out of holes.

We both placed our second shots to the home hole and I was inside of him. He was about twenty feet from the hole. He missed and we tied the hole in 4's. The boys took my Canadian trophy back to Detroit and I took off for some fishing on Muskokia Lake with Leon Sage, a long-time pal from Rochester, New York. We spent the next few weeks as guests aboard the yacht of the chain store magnate, J. C. Penney.

In the PGA in September of that same year Peter O'Hara scored a first-round knockout over me at the Wannamoisett Country Club at Providence, Rhode Island. Over the Keller Golf Course at St. Paul in the PGA of August, 1932, John Golden beat me on the forty-thirder the seventh extra hole. And incidentally that was one of the longest extra hole matches in our PGA history. I did not play in the PGA the next year because Denny Shute and I toured Europe playing exhibitions following the Ryder cup matches and the British Open.

By the way, I darn near won the British Open for the fifth time. That is, I'd have been close if my game of the last two days had been as sharp as it was the first two. I was leading the field at the end of the second day with 140. However, with 79 on the third round I was tied with Denny Shute at 219. In my last round I blew up with the wind and Denny finished with his fourth consecutive 73 to tie Craig Wood at 292. He beat Craig in the play-off to become the new British Open champion and I finished sixth.

I remember old Andrew ("Andra") Kirkaldy at the British Open at St. Andrews that year. Andra was seventy-two years of age and no longer active in golf, but he followed his favorites as avidly as ever. He had been a beautiful golfer to watch in his competitive years—his powerful physique being especially noticeable on his iron shots. In 1894, when J. H. Taylor became the first English professional to win their Open, he "challenged the world" for a fifty-pound a-side prize. Andra Kirkaldy accepted the challenge and won by a hole.

In 1933 Andra sat in a big armchair near the steps leading down from the club house to the eighteenth green . . . with a huge black umbrella protecting his weathered face from the sun. He remained there until one of his favorites came to the green, then he hurried down to hover over the play and to hold the pin for those of us he was particularly interested in. Abe Mitchell, playing the eighteenth, placed his second shot just over sixty feet from the hole. As was his custom Andra went down and held the flag. When Mitchell played his third shot old Andra removed the flag. Some spectators were rather upset about Andra's holding the flag, for had he left it in place it would have stopped the ball and given Mitchell a shorter putt.

Had his ball been inside the sixty feet he would have been

subject to a two-shot penalty if his ball hit the flag, but Abe had been well outside the limit . . . at which time the removal of the flag is optional to the player. Because of the gallery controversy over Andra's action the golf committee ruled that the competitor should send his caddie if he wanted the flag taken. Andra stayed in his chair unhappily watching from the sidelines but when his favorite golfers came into view he continued to edge slyly up to the green. He was a wonderful old fellow . . . picturesque and rugged.

Several weeks later, in July, Henry Cotton challenged me to a match over his home course at Ashridge, Berskshire. Cotton, one of the outstanding and promising young British golfers, made it tough for me. At the twenty-seventh I found myself 1 down, but I finished strong and finally won the match 3 and 2. Later that summer he became professional at the Waterloo Golf Club in Brussels, Belgium and asked for a return match, to be played at Waterloo. I needed rest far more than golf at that time but I agreed to play. I had been shooting my best golf in the past few weeks and I believed my luck would continue.

The Waterloo course was accessible to all of Belgium and Henry managed to work up a lot of enthusiasm among golf fans in the area. A large gallery gathered early to watch us play, but Henry had his worries. An hour before starting time I had not arrived. Now it was a question of getting Hagen to make an appearance.

He began trying to reach me by calling the hotels in Brussels and the Savoy in London. Meantime my plane had taken off from London but we had run into a terrific storm and by-passed Brussels for Antwerp. While waiting for the storm to blow over I gave Henry a call to tell him where I was and that we'd be taking off again as soon as the storm subsided. He was relieved to know I was that close—approximately fifty kilometers—and promised to hold the gallery another hour or so since I felt so sure I'd make it. Fortunately for us, the big gallery stuck around and I arrived just before Henry decided to return the gate receipts to the customers. I always managed to arrive at a golf course before the cash had to go back to its original owners.

Through an interpreter I apologized to the gallery and described my trip in the rickety old plane in the storm and the slow lumbering taxi from the airport. They readily forgave me and we started the match. I played the first eighteen holes in 67, good enough to win any match. But Cotton was playing better, equaling the course record of 66. I fought hard but he played the last eighteen in 67 and took me into camp 6 and 5.

So Cotton and the British won their second Battle of Waterloo. When Napoleon went down to defeat a century earlier the news did not reach England for several days. Some historians say that Rothschild's own carrier pigeons brought him the news. He capitalized on it and built the foundation of the vast Rothschild fortune. But Cotton got all the birdies in my defeat and the news was flashed to London by wire in a few short minutes.

Despite the fact that many sports writers insist I never shot a stroke of golf unless a greenback showed, I did play a lot of golf for charity, both in this country and abroad. Frankly, I never asked, when I was playing exhibitions for profit, what the guarantee would be. I played for whatever the sponsors could dig up for me, whether by guarantee or gate receipts. There were years when my game itself did not pull down too many big purses but I had enough subsidiary interests to keep my income in the champagne and caviar bracket.

Well, there's big money up now with nearly one million dollars available for our five thousand pros who follow the tournament schedule. The circuit is well-planned, making it easy for the fellows to proceed from California across the south to Florida and from Michigan and points east and west to Texas in short financial leaps. Top money in tournaments along the circuit today will make some pros from $20,000 to $100,-000 richer. However, the competition has more than tripled, too. More hands are in there grabbing.

Records show that the five top money spots today average from $20,000 to $35,000 a year. And despite the increased number of tournaments and the several hundred thousand more dollars offered, landing in those five top spots is just as tough as it ever was. There are pros traveling around, just as Tommy Kerrigan and I did in 1913 in Florida, trying to pick up enough tail-end money to pay for hamburgers and caddie fees.

Following the golf circuit is a far different life from that of athletes who play their games in season. I loved the travel and the fellowship . . . the palms of Florida . . . the seaside of California . . . the fierce wind blowing off the firths of Scotland . . . the beautiful green pines and holly of North Carolina . . . the wonderful bracing air of Minnesota . . . the Latin glamour of New Orleans. I liked meeting the film stars of Hollywood . . . visiting the White House in Washington . . . hoisting a few with members of the Royal and Ancient at St. Andrews . . . making up a foursome with the rich and the famous in Miami, Palm Beach and Belleair. Most of all I enjoyed all the thousands of golf fans all over the world who became my friends and my pals . . . who helped me spend the long green I played so hard to make. I wouldn't have changed the life I lived for any other in the world . . . regardless of money.

Well, time runs out on all of us and all the sunshine and fresh air the golfer soaks up won't ward off the day when his legs tire painfully after thirty-six holes and his back twinges sharply when he takes a full swing. In fact, I bent an elbow in the grill before a round to keep my fingers from shaking a bit after last night's fun. Yet I managed to win another big Open in

283

1935, despite the fact that I'd announced my retirement from active competition late in 1933. I was on the early side of forty when I won the Gasparilla Open with a record-making first round of 64 for that championship course.

I had pulled into the Belleair-Biltmore Hotel in late evening the day before the start of the Open and at sun-up I found myself still in my tuxedo after an all-night party. I decided I'd change clothes quickly and hit a few golf balls before motoring over to the event at Tampa. My starting time was nine o'clock and this was one of the mornings when that hour came too early. I had my chauffeur get some practice balls ready for me at the side entrance of the hotel and also start the motor of my car so I could make a quick getaway. I sent him out to retrieve my shots.

I usually hit a few iron shots to warm up, but since he was way out there some 200 yards I decided to take my four-wood. I topped my shot and it ran along the ground about 100 yards. I changed to a two-iron, again topped the ball slapping it about the same distance. I went back to my four-iron, which I usually wound up with. I topped my shot, hitting it another slight 100 yards. I waved to the boy to come in.

"That's enough practice," I told him. "Pick up the balls and put them in the car. I've had enough for today. Let's go."

Entering the Gandy Bridge crossing Tampa Bay we had another topping shot . . . the left rear tire went flat. However, my driver changed it quickly and we were on our way.

At Tampa I found an old friend, Mr. Gibson, waiting to escort me into the locker room and introduce me to some special corn liquor he had for an eye opener . . . and which I needed right then about as much as I needed another golf club for my practice strokes earlier in the morning. However, to be sociable, we had one for the first tee. As I came out of the dark locker room into the bright sunlight I recognized three of my good old baseball pals—members of Connie Mack's Philadelphia Athletics—Mickey Cochrane, Cy Perkins and Jimmy Foxx, waiting to see me tee off. I greeted them and went on.

I had one thought in mind and that was to play well to the right on the parallel Number Two fairway, since there was a boundary on the left side of the first hole. And I certainly had little or no confidence that early, in my game. Should I hook I was afraid of taking a two-stroke penalty on my very first shot. However I got my tee shot off all right and I was on my way.

Coming back to the club house on the ninth I put my second shot on the green about twenty feet from the flag and as I was walking up to the green I looked over to my left and spied Mickey Cochrane, Cy Perkins and Jimmy Foxx in the gallery. Having no recollection whatever of my earlier meeting with them I immediately went over and shook hands and greeted them. They laughed uproariously, sure that my score must be as funny as my memory.

"Hey," Mickey said, "what's all this? We saw you at the club house just before you teed off."

I tried to recall the meeting but I guess the morning sun was too bright for me.

"Well, how are you doing, Haig?" Jimmy Foxx asked.

"If I hole this putt," I told him, "I'll be out in 29."

"Wait a minute, Walter," Mickey said. "You mean 39!"

I missed the putt but I was out in 30. I came back in 34 to finish in 64, a new course record, which paved the way for my winning the event with a score of 280. Strangely enough I can hardly recall any of the shots I played on that first nine.

Some joker had run a column in the Tampa paper that morning showing mutuel odds, horse racing fashion, on the players entered in the Gasparilla Open.

I was listed: "Walter Hagen, 25-1, golf's Man O'War; old fellow working well."

I believe my odds should have been closer to 50-1.

CHAPTER XXIX: Pitch and Run

The Haig was great for reasons other than his ability to boil three shots into two. He had that certain something only the magnificently great possess. It was something that Ruth had and Dempsey. . . . It was that distinctive quality known simply as personality. . . . It was little conceits of camaraderie which endeared The Haig to all with whom he came in contact on and off the bunkered battleground. It is old stuff now that Hagen escorted the British professionals out of the servant class and that he made the United States pros so clothes-conscious they became models of sartorial arrayment. . . . Every year about this time when "greatness" is bandied about with careless disregard of its true meaning and this writer is sometimes asked to name the greatest golfer ever to come within his focus, he always makes the same reply—Hagen.

—LESTER RICE
[1951]

IN AUGUST OF 1939 the Midlothian Country Club in Chicago honored me on the silver anniversary of my first win of the National Open back in 1914. Club members initiated an invitational round robin event composed of eight teams of the leading golfers. The boys were paired as follows:

Denny Shute and E. J. (Dutch) Harrison
Paul Runyan and Horton Smith
Henry Picard and Johnny Revolta

Tommy Armour and Jimmy Thomson
Byron Nelson and Dick Metz
Ralph Guldahl and Harold McSpaden
Ed Dudley and Billy Burke
Gene Sarazen and Walter Hagen

We played for a purse of about $10,000 with Ed Dudley and Billy Burke taking top prize money. All Gene and I could harvest out of it was $275 apiece. I got quite a thrill out of the event. The course had been somewhat revamped since I played it in 1914. On the back of each green the committee had placed a sign giving the yardage of each hole and the score I had made when I won my first Championship. While going around with Sarazen I became very disconcerted at my own scores at times and quite embarrassed at how many times I was taking a beating from myself that day.

Two other clubs accorded me anniversary honors, the Oak Hill Country Club in my home town of Rochester, New York in August of 1934 and the Red Run Golf Club in Detroit in 1947. Hagen Day in Rochester celebrated the twentieth anniversary of my victory at Midlothian. My dad saw me play in an event for the second time in his life—the first time he had followed me in the National Open in Toledo, Ohio in 1931. A reporter asked Dad who would win the Hagen Day tournament.

"My son, Walter, will probably win it," he said. "He usually does."

His prediction proved wrong. Leo Diegel won with a 276 and I finished in a tie for tenth place with George Christ, my boyhood pal and former assistant at the Country Club of Rochester where he was pro in 1934. However, my brother pros made up a purse which they presented to my dad so he won.

I was glad to have him see me play again and of course I'd have been happier had I won for him. My mother never saw me play in an event although she occasionally saw me knocking a ball around the Country Club of Rochester course when I was a boy. After I began making money in golf I arranged for my family to live in Orlando, Florida. After a few years they became so homesick for their own home town that all the fragrance of orange blossoms could not keep them away from Rochester.

In September of 1947 members of the Red Run Golf Club presented me with an honorary membership and two very fine gifts—a gold diamond-studded money clip and a target pistol with which to commit "hara-kiri" if I ever caught myself on the golf course again. The result is I'm still alive. However, I made good use of the pistol just a short time ago when I lent it to my good friends Loraine and Fred Wiswedel, who were traveling west to hunt uranium.

During the early 1940s I played a great number of Red Cross Fund benefit matches. I recall one match in March of 1941 when Bobby Jones, Tommy Armour, Gene Sarazen and I were invited to play an exhibition for the Bahamas Red Cross under the distinguished patronage of my good friend, the Duke of Windsor and his Duchess. Gene and I teamed against Tommy and Bobby and took a beating. This was one of the last times Jones played golf but his game was as sharp as ever. Gene, Tommy and Bobby departed by plane for the United States shortly after our matches but I stayed over for a week as guest of the Duke and Duchess. The Windsors were gracious hosts and I enjoyed my visit immensely. Back in this country I found a story going the rounds . . . another one of those stories which had a basis of truth plus a bit of minor distortion.

The Duke had acted as referee during our Bahama matches. On the sixteenth hole I walked over to study my chip shot. I called out laughingly, as I looked at the Duke standing on the green close by, "Caddie, take the flag." He walked over and took the flag. Some newspapers ran the story that I called

288

out "Eddie" not "caddie," a slip which would have been so easy for me to make.

Several years ago a blind shot I once made was recalled to my mind by a Denver sports writer, Starr Yelland, in a radio-by-telephone interview.

"Walter," he said, "do you remember playing in the St. Paul Open over the Keller Course when your second shot at the eighteenth missed the green, ran underneath and back of the viewing stand?"

"I certainly do," I answered. "But that was a long time ago. How can you remember that?"

"I was there," he told me.

A viewing stand had been erected for the spectators around the eighteenth green and I was coming to the eighteenth, a long par 4 hole, at the finish of the Championship. Just as Starr Yelland recalled, my second shot had by-passed the green to the right and lay directly back of the stands. Officials began calling people down from their seats so that I might play safely over the stands.

"Let them keep their seats," I said. "Just have them bow their heads as low as possible. I'll play it right over them."

I executed my shot perfectly and actually the ball stopped a foot from the hole. I'm inclined to believe my blind shots have been responsible for quite a few of the low scores I made.

A couple of "firsts" stand out in my mind, too. Mr. R. Otto Probst, one-time president of the Erskine Park Club at South Bend, Indiana requested and received from me a pair of golf shoes which I had worn while winning a national championship. He had them silver-plated and mounted on a mahogany base in my exact putting stance . . . to serve as a trophy for the annual approach and putting competition of the Erskine Club.

I also received the perhaps dubious honor of having a poem written about me when I failed to qualify for the PGA Championship at Pinehurst Country Club in November of 1936. It made me believe I rated along with the famous "Casey at the Bat."

The Once Over or Mr. Hagen Recalls
BY
H. I. Phillips

I remember, I remember
   The drives so straight and far
The balls that sailed right down the line
   And meant a certain par;
The ones that went three hundred yards—
   The gallery's sharp "Oh!"—
The plaudits of the multitude
   Back in the long ago.

I remember, I remember
   The way I used to swing;
A mighty and unerring sock
   That kept the ball awing;
My spirit flew in feathers then
   But it's so heavy now
I need no summer pool to cool
   The fever on my brow.

I remember, I remember
   When golfing was but play;
When it was childish exercise
   To take the PGA.
When headlines screaming "HAGEN WINS"
   Were always kept in type
And grabbing major Championships
   Was nothing but a pipe.

I remember, I remember
When I adored the grind,
And I was never better than
When coming from behind;
When play-offs were my fondest dreams
And I was coolest in
The pinches of a match that took
An extra hole to win.

I remember, I remember
The days my spirit flamed
And one thing was a certainty—
I couldn't be outgamed!
I doted on the warfare then
But now I'm through, I fear . . .
Like —ell I do! Remember, boy,
There'll be another year!

Sports writer and television emcee Ed Sullivan reminded me not too long ago of a series of experiments which Babe Ruth and I were put through at Columbia University for information on reflex action. The University scientists were seeking facts on the differences in the reflex action of a man whose eyes were accustomed to playing with a moving ball and one accustomed to a stationary ball. The results showed that the Babe was faster in pegging all the moving objects while I outranked him in judgment of distance and accuracy of division lines of space. I suppose the tests proved seeking golf birdies was my best game, for I could never have made a hit as often as the Babe.

Gene Sarazen and I teamed up for a number of four-ball tournaments from 1934 through 1941 but we never managed to win, although I did win the Inverness Four Ball Tourney in 1936 with Ky Laffoon as my partner. I picked Gene as my play-

ing partner in the Ryder Cup Team matches in 1933 at Southport where we broke even with Britishers Percy Alliss and
Charles Whitcombe; and again in 1935 at George Jacobus'
home club, the Ridgewood Country Club in New Jersey, when
we won 7 and 6 over Perry and J. J. Busson. We were tough on
each other as competitors but good friends when we took on
the other boys. That friendship stemmed from the fact, I believe, that he enjoyed a good practical joke as much as I and he
wasn't above pulling one on me when he could.

On New Year's Day back in 1938 I was hoisting a long cooling drink in my Galaface Hotel room in Colombo, Ceylon
when I received a surprising telephone call. A man's voice,
speaking badly bent English embellished with a heavy foreign
accent never before used on words, somehow got across to me
that he had been following my matches and would like to meet
the "great Hagen." I invited him up . . . and who should
open the door but Gene Sarazen. He had fooled me with his
lingo, just as he fooled a few million viewers in 1954 when he
played a similar character on a television show, "Masquerade
Party." Gene and I were just crossing paths, for he was on his
way to play exhibition matches in Bombay, India while Joe
Kirkwood and I were headed for Calcutta.

Joe told me a good one on Gene. The two of them teamed
up for a tour of South America in 1934. On one particular
night in Rio Gene came dashing up to their hotel room searching for Joe. He told Joe he'd met a croupier of the hotel's
gambling game in the lobby and Gene asked Joe to go with
him to try his luck. Joe dropped in with him, gave the place
the once over and returned to his room. Some time later Gene
came up again, excited as could be, his hands filled with paper
money and another huge roll of bills in his pocket.

"Here," he told Joe, "you keep this for me. I'm going back
and get some more easy money."

His luck continued and he returned to the hotel room a second time with his hands and pockets full.

"I won't have to work again as long as I live," he said. "I don't think I'll continue this tour. I'm taking the next boat back home and buy me a big farm."

"Let's count it and see how much you've got here," Joe suggested. "It looks like a mint, I'll admit, but you've got all colors and sizes of bills here."

So the two of them got busy with their pencils and to Gene's dismay he found that some of the paper he'd thought equivalent to our dollars was worth very little after exchange. The entire roll was about enough to buy a ticket home. He was so disgusted he wanted to give it back to the gamblers.

"No wonder they're so free with their money," he complained bitterly. "It isn't worth anything."

Another pal of mine, Jim Barnes, involved me in a slightly embarrassing incident back in 1915 when I was trying to win the Panama Exposition Open in San Francisco. Jim and I were barnstorming on the West Coast and the fact that we had entirely different ideas as to how the nights were to be spent created some conflict between us. Jim, serious about his game and eager to win the Open purse with its $1000 first prize, insisted on retiring at nine o'clock each evening. His early retiring did not bother me for I had met a pretty young thing who worked in a florist shop in the hotel lobby. I was content to let Jim rest his more mature bones in bed, but being only twenty-two at the time, I preferred to fill my evenings with the theater, dancing and romancing until the wee hours of the morning.

Jim particularly disliked my night-owl hours because he insisted on leaving the hotel room door unlocked for me. Being a spectacularly careful man, he hid his watch and money under his pillow to keep them safe. He persisted in explaining to me that traipsing around all night was no way to train for the coming Championship. He said that during our tour he'd had to play most of the golf. The side bets we had won from our opponents . . . well, he thought we had collected because he had done most of the work. I attempted to persuade him that I would be in shape when the bell rang for the Championship, but what did he care about that? We were on our own in the Championship. He was not thinking kindly of me when we arrived at the club for the Panama Exposition Open.

My partner and I had a woman scorer. She stayed about one hundred yards back of me on the first hole. After I'd played my second shot and holed for a par 4 I looked back and saw her standing on a cross trap still the same distance away.

After she caught up with us I told her, "You needn't stay so far behind."

"I'm afraid I might disturb your play," she said.

I decided she had acted as scorer in some previous matches where profanity had been used rather freely. I explained that she would not bother us and that she could come up closer.

At the ninth, a short par 3, I played a five-iron to within ten feet of the hole and had that putt for a 29 for the nine holes. I saw Jim Barnes going up the eleventh fairway . . . striding along with the usual four-leaf clover in the corner of his mouth. Remembering Big Jim's exasperation with me the past few days, I told my scorer that Mr. Barnes might like to know I had this putt for a 29 out. I suggested, a bit facetiously, that she go across and inform him of my possible score, letting her believe my pal would be elated. So she wobbled hurriedly across the railroad bridge, while I leaned against the railing to hear and to see his reaction. She kept calling his name excitedly to get Jim's attention and when she finally came even with him, she imparted the information. He looked first at her and then at me . . . in the distance.

"What the HELL do I care about what Mr. Hagen does?" he shouted in disgust.

After that incident, my lady scorer was even more cautious and she certainly was not interested in carrying any further messages for me. The fact that I went on to win the $1000 first prize money did not make Jim's disposition sweeter, either.

Women in golf—not just as scorers but as very fine competitors in the game—go way back in history. Mary, Queen of Scots and her ladies-in-waiting first engaged in tournament play around 1542. Queen Mary was a frequent visitor to Seton Butts and Seton Links and awarded fabulous jeweled gifts to the winners of the tournaments.

Although the ill-fated Queen may have made the first awards to the ladies of the game, our women golfers have taken innumerable prizes in the golf world since that time. Mrs. Glenna Collet Vare, six times winner of the USGA Women's Amateur and holder of many other championships has been my playing partner in many exhibition matches. She is truly a great champion, a credit to the game—with a form which is admittedly an asset to any feminine golfer.

Marion Hollins, Edith Cummings, Bernice Wall, Mrs. William A. Gavin, Mrs. Dorothy Campbell Hurd, Maureen Orcutt, Virginia Van Wie with present-day Patty Berg, Dorothy Kirby, Babe Didrikson Zaharias, Betty Jameson, Louise Suggs, Edith Quier (now Mrs. Harrison Flippen)—they've all been fine champion golfers and to paraphrase a bit, like the great Alexa Stirling they were all sterling players.

Recently we have added a new field—Jane Nelson, Barbara Romack, Mrs. Scotty Probasco, Polly Riley and our new Open champion Patricia Ann Lesser. Another name to be reckoned with is our own Wiffi Smith of St. Clair Shores, Michigan and I predict that the golfing world will hear great things of her . . . in the very near future.

I learned the method of putting largely from Walter
Hagen in 1937. The term he used for taking the club
back and still keeping it square was that you
"hooded" the face. He proved to me that this backswing applies true topspin to the ball and is in fact
the only type of backswing with the putter that will
apply true topspin. Hagen in his heyday was probably the world's greatest putter and I was happy to
learn from him.

—BOBBY LOCKE, *Bobby Locke on Golf*
[1954]

SINCE MY EARLY caddying days, when I'd heard Mr. George
Eastman and other well-traveled members of the Country Club
of Rochester talk of hunting big game in India and Africa, I
had wanted to experience that thrill. Reading Teddy Roosevelt's book detailing his adventures on safari in Africa had
heightened my desire. I figured big game hunting was the type
of sport where, if I missed a shot, I'd be one down and no
more to go.

Early in 1937 I lassoed Joe Kirkwood for another world tour
. . . this one to be far wider in range than our trip to Australia
in 1930, for now we planned to encircle the entire globe. Playing each continent in season meant that our tour would extend
for at least a year and a half.

Joe told me, "We'll pick up some real dough, Walter, if
you'll get your mind on golf and do a little work."

I explained that my idea was to play just enough golf to take
us where we wanted to go. I know I had been concentrating

more on plans for our tour than on my golf game for at the PGA at Pinehurst in November of 1936 my game went sour and I half-topped most of my shots for the first time in my life. I hadn't prepared for golf that year very well. All summer I had spent the time building some fancy duck blinds at my place in northern Michigan. I practically installed hot and cold running water in those blinds to convince the ducks that passing them up was just plain silly. In mid-November I headed back for Detroit and planned some social activities. At a party in my suite at the Book-Cadillac I waited for the shank of the evening to announce plans for the world tour I would begin in January of 1937. Early the following morning I took off by plane to meet Joe in Los Angeles to map out our itinerary.

I felt sure the combination of our games would be as spectator-pleasing as it had been in the past . . . that his trick shot routine and my seeking for the birdies would again be a drawing card. Many times we came close to missing engagements, mostly due to difficulties in traveling connections, but we always managed to cajole the waiting fans into a fine humor with Joe's trick shot routine despite the delay. I had seen his routine so often that I could duplicate a few of his tricks. In fact, my familiarity with them came in quite handy for both of us some months later at Calcutta, India.

We sailed from Los Angeles late in January and the first leg of our voyage covered some of the same places as had our earlier tour in 1930. En route to New Zealand we stopped over for matches in Honolulu, Pago Pago and the Fiji Islands. The smallpox quarantine had forced us to cancel our matches in New Zealand in 1930 but apparently the generous fans had forgiven our defection for they turned out in great numbers at Auckland. We had equally good galleries at the famous hot springs resort of Rotorus, Wellington, Christchurch and back at Wellington the second time.

From there we embarked for Sydney, Australia, some 1500 miles distant, where we played exhibitions at Sydney, Brisbane, Townsville, the capital city of Canberra, Melbourne and Adelaide before taking a new Douglas Trimotor the 2,200 miles to Kalgoorlie, situated on the edged of the Great Victorian Desert in western Australia. Kalgoorlie courses really tested our ability, for the fairways were gravel, the roughs were coarse stone and the putting greens were smooth-rolled fine gravel.

At Perth, located on the extreme western side of the great island continent, I was really on my game. After three-putting on the first hole for a five, I managed to collect several birdies along the rest of the way. One sports writer commented in the Perth *Sunday Times:* "Hagen's game was so accurate the ball might have been controlled on a piece of string." Joe, however, was a trifle bitter over the slim galleries and doubly irritated because a number of the enthusiastic fans crashed the gate and cut down considerably on the receipts. I had shot 65's on two consecutive days over these strange and unusual "down under" courses and I didn't take Joe's beef too seriously . . . particularly since we had hit these parts in their off season for golf.

Our boat had sailed from Sydney by way of the island of Tasmania and we were happy indeed to rejoin our belongings on board at Perth. Since I was captain of the American Ryder Cup Team scheduled to compete against the British at Southport on June 29, 30 we had planned this leg of our tour so that I might reach England several days before the American boys arrived for the matches. En route we made brief stops at Bombay and Aden before sailing into the Suez Canal Zone.

There, through the courtesy of E. E. (Red) Thompson of the Chrysler Export Division of Detroit, we were met by a representative of the company with whom we motored the ninety miles over the desert to the beautiful city of Cairo. Joe and I mounted camels, shortly after our arrival, for a sightseeing trip around the great Pyramids. Believe me, those camels with their slow rolling gait over the sandy wastes made my stride around a golf course resemble that of the speedy Roger Bannister or John Landy.

Cairo boasted two very fine courses with beautifully designed and equipped club houses. We had cocktails on the terrace at one club house . . . enjoying the sight of lovely girls swimming in the chartreuse-tiled pool. We dined at the second club, situated some yards away and entirely surrounded by polo fields. Our British friends and the wealthy Egyptians appeared definitely more polo- than golf-minded, although we did have a delightful visit with many of our English golfing friends during our short stay. We motored back to the Suez Canal early the following morning to rejoin our ship.

The tiny island of Malta is one spot I'll never forget. As we approached the Grand Harbor entrance the steep cliffs seemed to rise vertically hundreds of feet high. I was told that the island was part of a geological "great fault," a series of mountainous rock formations rising from the sea. Upon leaving the ship we climbed the steep road to the scenic village hundreds of feet above sea level. At the top, we had a wonderful view of the entire island . . . the narrow, cultivated terraces along the contours of the hills . . . the blue waters of the Mediterranean in the background. We did not play golf there, although a course was available. However, I could imagine driving a ball from the top of one of those rocky cliffs and seeing it hole out into the sea.

From Malta we sailed to Marseilles, where many of my friends have been initiated by the Riviera croupiers. We went by rail to Paris where Joe and I played an exhibition match at St. Cloud before flying to London to take up headquarters at my old stomping ground, the Savoy Hotel. Our American Ryder Cup Team took the British at Southport for the first time on British soil, and following our team matches I played

299

in the British Open at Carnoustie in early July. Henry Cotton polished off everybody with a 290. Oddly enough, I had won my first National Open twenty-three years earlier with that identical score (Midlothian in Chicago, 1914) when I tied the lowest score ever posted up to then for seventy-two holes of golf—George Sargent's 290 of 1909.

After the British Open I returned to London and the Savoy where it was my good fortune to breakfast with Mr. Charles Sorensen, then an executive of the Ford Motor Company. He very graciously offered to provide me with a Lincoln car and a chauffeur for the length of my stay in the British Isles. When he learned that Joe and I planned to barnstorm throughout the Isles for several months he extended the same courtesy to Joe.

Mr. Sorensen's generosity caused the Ford Motor Company's British Sales Division a bit of a slowdown for our travels tied up six cars. Because of border laws we were forced to use two sets of cars in Ireland, while our first set had been left at Glasgow, Scotland when we crossed by boat to Belfast. From Belfast, following our exhibition matches, we motored to Dunkalk where we left our second pair of cars and picked up the third pair in which we drove south to Dublin and across to Sligo, playing exhibitions at numerous towns along the way. At Sligo when we crossed the border we were met by the drivers and the two cars we had left at Dunkalk, in which we returned to Belfast. Mr. Sorensen laughingly told me some weeks later that we had tied up practically the entire supply of cars the Ford Motor Company had in Scotland and Ireland.

I had purposely planned our barnstorming of Scotland for the last two weeks of August and early September because of the grouse season. Such a temptation no man could resist, particularly if he had entree to some of the great moors surrounding the ancient castles of Scotland. I had just that in my good friend, Mr. Robertson who owned a beautiful estate outside the town of Inverness, known as Leys Castle. He arranged a day's shooting for his several other guests and myself on the surrounding moors. His kennels boasted many fine retrievers and his handlers released the dogs one by one to retrieve our birds. They had brought along, also, a small donkey with two huge hampers strapped across its broad back and in no time at all those hampers were filled with braces of birds. The shooting was that good.

We returned to the castle in mid-afternoon for refreshing showers and gathered later for cocktails around the large swimming pool on the terraced lawn. The cocktails tasted particularly enjoyable because of the many lovely mermaids in gay colored bathing suits who were draped gracefully along the pool's edge. I could not help wondering about the name Leys Castle.

I took time out for a bit of salmon fishing on the Ness River and was rewarded with one weighing eleven pounds. And that reminds me of a small village where I stopped overnight on my way to Mr. Robertson's estate. I had registered at a small pub, the home of an elderly gentleman and his two maiden sisters. Upon seeing my name they immediately struck up a conversation and insisted upon taking me across an ancient bridge to the small church in the village. There, to my surprise, was my name, WALTER HAGEN, carved into the cornerstone of the quaint church. Since no explanation was forthcoming we can only assume the Vicar was a golf fan. My host promised, if I would stay over the next day and play an exhibition on the village course, he would see to it that I enjoyed some excellent trout fishing from their private stream. We fished early the following morning and in the afternoon I played over the local course, consisting of nine holes with the greens surrounded by wire netting to keep out the sheep. I was forced to chip onto the greens over the wire or sneak through it. The two maiden ladies had done an excellent job, in true female fashion, of

301

spreading the word of my exhibition, and the villagers turned out with well-filled baskets from which they spread a fine lunch at the club house following the match.

We fished at Lochlee for a couple of days, then played at Dundee, Edinburgh and Leith. On our way south to London we played matches at Northampton, Birmingham, Nottingham, Sheffield, Hull and Leeds. Returning to the Savoy Hotel as our headquarters, we motored along the west coast for exhibitions at Manchester, Liverpool, Bristol and the resort towns of Southampton, Brighton Beach, Dover, Hastings, Sandgate and Folkstone.

I took the Ryder Cup Team to Cardiff in Wales for exhibition matches and from there I flew over to the Isle of Wight, played one exhibition there and returned by plane to London. However, my most memorable jaunt into Wales was made by train to the northern section, near the town of Rhyl. We had played our match on Sunday afternoon and boarded the train expecting to relax with a nice cool drink when we were informed that the town through which we were passing prohibited such liquid refreshment. The town, with a jaw-breaker name, the mere sight of which makes one's mouth dry was: Llanfairpwilgwngyllgogerychwyrndrobwil-llandisillogogogoch.

I was delighted to learn through a news item this year that the club car is now allowed to open its bar once the train passes the city limits . . . which would be, in my estimation, about when the conductor finished pronouncing the little town's long name.

We played many more exhibition matches in the British Isles during our stay, but by the middle of September our time was running short. We were booked to sail from Marseilles on the Italian Line taking us through the Straits and down the West Coast of Africa to Capetown for matches in South Africa. On our way to board the boat we played in France, Belgium, Germany and Switzerland.

My good friend Harvey Firestone also came aboard at Marseilles to sail with us to the African Gold Coast where he was met by a small craft manned by some employees of his huge rubber plantation. We rounded the Cape of Good Hope about the first of October and I had my first view of wonderful old Table Mountain crested with its one lone tree.

We played exhibition matches in Capetown, Port Elizabeth and East London against the leading amateurs in the various cities, among them the well-known Clarence Olander and Otway Hayes. We encountered playing conditions in Africa very different from any I had ever met before. The first exhibition we played at Johannesburg was against Sid Brews and a nineteen-year-old youngster, Bobby Locke, and I was amazed when I reached a 600-yard hole with a drive and a two-iron. I overplayed greens of around 450 yards with a drive and a seven-iron. The light air made golf in that sector of the world a different game. I had to discard all ideas of distance I'd garnered through the years and learn a new brand of golf. Sid Brews and Bobby Locke took us that day.

Another oddity in Africa was the diamond dust of the greens around Kimberley, the diamond capital of the world. Here, with me, the hazard was mental, for every time I bent over to pick up my ball from the cup I felt like pocketing a handful of the green. At the luxurious hotel where we stayed in Johannesburg, I brewed coffee on the beautifully landscaped roof and looked with envy at the dozens of diamond mines in the distance.

Joe and I had occasion many times to play against Bobby Locke, then a young amateur and a darn good player. We met him at just the right time . . . during his amateur days, when he couldn't cut into any of our prize money. That's once when I took advantage of Bobby. I think, perhaps, seeing us take in all that dough was partly responsible for his turning professional a year or so later.

Sid Brews, pro at Houghton Golf Club, was by far the outstanding pro golfer we met. We took a couple of beatings from Sid and Bobby, for at first they were just too tough for us on their own home courses. However, I later teamed up with Brews, when we were challenged by three of the outstanding players of his home club . . . three businessmen among them a Chrysler dealer and a meat packer . . . and believe me, they were tasty red meat to me. I was the lion, Brews was an excellent partner—and between us we gave them a shellacking which resulted in one of the best gate returns we had taken.

Kirkwood and I traveled north along the East Coast of Africa playing exhibitions in the major cities of Bloemfontein, Pietermaritzburg, Ladysmith, Durban and inland to Johannesburg, Victoria, Bulawayo, Salisbury and Beira. At Beira we took a boat to the island of Zanzibar, then back to Dar-es-Salaam and up to Mombasa. After playing exhibition matches in each of these cities we motored into Kenya and at the Muthiaga Golf Club about three miles outside of Nairobi we were met by the Honorable Secretary, Mr. Clark.

While we were changing to golf apparel the Honorable Secretary and several members of the club took a peek into my golf bag.

"Have you a gun with you?" one of them asked.

"I don't need one in my golf game," I said. "Do I?"

"Yes, you may," I was told, "because yesterday several lions ran across the course. However, we decided if you should deviate too far and get into the heavy growth off the fairway, we'll penalize one shot, since it's far too dangerous to hunt a lost ball."

I had always believed there were enough shots in my clubs I'd carried thousands of miles around the world, but now it occurred to me I might need another kind of shot. As it happened the match was played without our seeing any lions but knowing they might be back in the bush taking in our game added an extra hazard to the course.

304

The following day we drove inland to Nakuru on the way to Lake Victoria. I learned from the Honorable Secretary of the Nakuru Golf Club that my good friend the Prince of Wales had visited their city on a recent good will tour. The local citizens had studied up on royal etiquette and had arranged a gala affair in the Prince's honor at the club. Decked in their most formal attire, the ladies and gentlemen awaited the arrival of the honor guest. To their surprise and dismay he appeared in golf knickers, ready for a game on their eighteen-hole course. Later in the evening, as the party progressed, the members missed their future king and my story teller, the Honorable Secretary, was selected to hunt for him. At a small night spot featuring the hot jazz of the era the Prince of Wales was found, seated on the platform with the band, happily and with unusual talent playing the drums.

The Honorable Secretary and I had quite a long wait for one of our opponents for the first match I played at the Nakuru Golf Club. From the course we could see his ranch on the second plateau of the nearby mountain. A herd of elephants had stampeded through his acres, knocking down his barn and other farm buildings, and were threatening his home. Before he was able to stop the stampede, he told me later, he had killed eleven of those huge beasts. Unfortunately ivory tusks of elephants in that part of Africa were brittle due to the lack of mineral vegetation, and had no commercial value. So he salvaged nothing to pay for the repairs to his buildings.

Although he showed up a couple of hours late for our match his ordeal with the elephants had not hurt his game. A huge giant of a man—so husky looking I decided he could have wrestled those elephants to a standstill—he didn't actually need a gun. And his tee shots were terrific . . . on one hole his drive carried 345 yards, right over the green into the brush. We never did find the ball.

Nakuru was a pretty city, situated on the edge of a salt lake which was the nesting place of thousands of flamingoes. The low marshy banks of the lake were covered with mud mounds built about a foot in height . . . and in these odd mud nests the flamingoes housed their young. I took many feet of colored movies of these beautiful birds . . . one in which literally hundreds of them were in flight . . . a sight I have yet to see equaled. I was told that the lake had no life in it . . . other than a kind of vegetation upon which the flamingoes thrived . . . no tide to raise the level of the water, hence their mud mound nests were never endangered. Yes, Nakuru was a beautiful city . . . the lake and the flamingoes at its edge and snow-capped Mt. Kenya towering 17,000 feet into the clouds to form an impressive backdrop.

CHAPTER XXXI: Safari

> Hagen is a man with two personalities. For this rea-
> son he is even more interesting than had he been
> the fantastic, carefree, irresponsible person . . . he
> played to his public. How else would he have made
> more than a million dollars during his heyday as a
> player and at sixty be so firmly entrenched in the
> golf manufacturing picture that his royalties support
> him the way he wishes to live. And he never goes
> anything but *first class, deluxe.*
>
> —BOB HARLOW, *Golf World*
> [1952]

ONE OF my main ambitions on this tour was to get in some big
game hunting in Nairobi. Up to now I had enjoyed some grouse
shooting in Scotland and some small game hunting in South
Africa. So, after playing our exhibitions at Nakuru, I returned
to Nairobi where I was the guest of a rancher named Harris
whose acres of cattle-grazing meadowland began about nine
miles outside the city proper. His ranch, boasting approximately
23,000 head of dairy cattle, was also a very modern pasteuriz-
ing plant. However, his milk produce was carted throughout
the day and night by slow-traveling buffalo teams to the railway
station at Nairobi to be shipped to various connecting cities. Mr.
Harris' great importance to me lay in the fact that he was an
expert hunter-guide. During World War I he had been employed by the government to shoot wild game for the army food
supply. Hartebeest, eland, impala, wildebeest, water buffalo and
various species of deer were plentiful on the veldt surrounding
his ranch. I was very lucky in being backed up by such an ex-

cellent marksman. The water holes on his land were for the use of his own cattle but those holes attracted numerous wild game and endangered the lives of his stock. Because of the inexpensive labor available—four cents a day for the regulars and eight cents for the head men—he was able to employ a great number of natives to protect his herds. We relaxed comfortably in the patio with cooling drinks while the natives were sent out to locate the wild game. Notified by runners of the location, we drove out for the shooting in an open type station wagon, shaded by a canvas canopy and having blown-up inner tubes for seats.

On December 21 while on safari we lunched at a spot about sixteen miles from the Harris ranch . . . a vicinity where the natives had seen a pride of lions earlier in the day. We, however, saw none, although I was surprised when Joe presented me with a delicious birthday cake which "Mommy" Harris had baked and which we enjoyed in the shade of the acacia trees. "Mommy" Harris presented us with an even greater surprise when we returned to the ranch that evening. From her kitchen window she had shot a huge nine-foot lion which she had seen peering through the panes, hungrily sniffing the aroma of our dinner steaming on the range. I could easily understand the lion's interest for she was an excellent cook and those tantalizing odors kept me hanging around the kitchen, too. She was frequently visited by giraffes who had a fondness for her carefully tended flowers. The natives built a twelve-foot fence to guard the flower beds but with their long necks the giraffes were still able to reach over and feast. So "Mommy" was kept busy with a broom when not preparing those wonderful meals for us. Each evening, as my contribution to conviviality, I uncorked a bottle and served their favorite drink—half and half. This mixture, half milk and half rum or whisky, I found very enjoyable.

I was quite lucky in my hunting while a guest at the Harris ranch, for I got one lion, several bull zebras and trophy heads of water buffalo, impala and kudu, none of which to my great disappointment ever arrived in the States. I shot other game, such as hartebeest and wildebeest but they were of little value as trophies.

Following the sojourn at Harris' I left Nairobi for Mombasa and Joe and I sailed a few days later for Colombo, Ceylon where we spent New Year's Day of 1938. Making the Galaface Hotel our headquarters we proceeded to play a number of exhibitions on the island. Since we had a series of matches scheduled for Madras and Calcutta, India I suggested to Joe that we take a German tramp steamer up the coast from Ceylon. He turned down my proposition, however, and took off by plane over the mainland while I boarded the tramp steamer alone. I did not remain alone for long . . . for I occupied the first mate's cabin and cockroaches three inches in length were in full possession. Due to the terrific heat I lived and slept only in shorts. At night I could feel the roaches playing tag over and under me. I kept my luggage as tightly closed as possible and even wished for chewing gum or paste to seal the crevices tighter, for the roaches seemed able to sneak into anything.

I did get a kick out of the trip, for the crew were all members of Hitler's navy and prior to each meal they stood at attention before a mammoth picture of the Fuehrer and "Heil-ed Hitler" with smart precision. I stood along with them although my salute resembled that of our own newest army recruit. The captain spoke enough broken English for me to understand him and we had many talks on the bridge. In the evenings the main entertainment was a game played with cards approximately four by six inches in size. I never did learn the game too well, despite the captain's earnest effort to instruct me. All I needed to remember after each session was the amount of money I owed and to try to change my American cash into the correct number of German marks.

On the second day out from Colombo we sheared a pin in one

propeller which took several hours to repair so we were bobbing around quite a bit. From the bridge I saw a torpedo boat surface and signal our boat, the *Ochenfeller*. The captain explained to me that the torpedo commander had inquired if we were in trouble and had informed him that they were sounding the depths of water from Singapore to the Island of Ceylon. He, the captain, apparently had no hesitation in telling me this since he considered me a real German—just one of the boys. Furthermore, I knew if I didn't play the part I'd be good feeding for some of the hungry sharks.

I connected with Joe again at Madras and we were off to the golf course. I was delighted to meet my good friend E. E. (Red) Thompson from Detroit who had been primarily responsible for our hospitable entertainment at Cairo. He was making a trip through India, having come up from Bombay. We had a short visit during which time he and I were invited on a snipe shooting trip following my exhibition match that day. Walking through the valleys and wading through the rice fields while the beaters drove thousands of birds over us gave me one of the rarest experiences in my years of hunting. We shot until the guns were actually hot.

Kirkwood and I had a contract for a week of exhibition matches in Calcutta and it was there that he, in doing his trick shots, took a full swing to catch a ball in mid-air with a niblick and loosened a chip off his shoulder. His shoulder was put in a cast and I took over his routine, with Joe directing me from a chair on the first tee. I performed pretty well although I did have difficulty with two of the shots. Not one of the many spectators was willing to part with his watch for me to use as a tee nor was anyone enthusiastic about my driving a ball from his toe. I finally put down my own watch and got the shot off all right.

During Joe's incapacitation I had to follow through and play his routines to fulfill our contract. Just to increase the interest

I agreed that if I didn't tie or break the course record I would give a party to all members of the two clubs. Since Calcutta had an odd arrangement in golf courses . . . the two clubs were situated directly across the highway from each other . . . one had a beautiful club house with two eighteen-hole courses and the second had a beautiful club house with one eighteen-hole course. Toward the middle of the week it looked as if Joe and I were stuck with an expensive party. I was playing an exhibition match on Friday afternoon with two leading amateurs and they had eight scratch men as amateurs in Calcutta. I had my work cut out for me to play better ball than the two of them each day. However, that Friday afternoon I got lucky and managed to hole out for a 65 and a course record. So the club members footed the party bill and Joe could keep his pocket buttoned.

The Rajah of Calcutta, a great golf enthusiast, had followed the matches all week. He wanted to entertain us with a safari into the mountains near New Delhi about two hundred and fifty miles north. Since Joe's shoulder was still in a cast I decided to go up and shoot with the Rajah.

The arrangements made for the comfort of the Rajah and his guest about knocked my eyes out. We had a retinue of servants, who, due to the various castes or class system, were designated by the color of the dot on each native's forehead. We had water carriers, fire builders, cooks, food servers, hide tanners for our game, white hunter-guides and two thousand native beaters. I had an entourage of fifty natives to care for my daily comforts, and a tent consisting of seven rooms was erected for my occupancy alone. The Rajah's tent had fourteen rooms. Our tents had been set up days prior to our arrival at the foot of the mountains and a mesh-type fence, made of cut timber stacked with the leaves and small branches left on, surrounded us like a corral.

Early each morning the two thousand beaters, armed with

pans and tin pails as noise makers, chased all the game within an area of two to ten miles out into the clearings before our machans. We had hoped for panther or tigers but all we saw were bears. We managed to get four or five bears a day. As we moved to a new camp a few thousand natives worked ahead of us making a road and clearing for a new camp, completely disregarding the rice fields and the cultivated areas.

My pals back home would scarcely have recognized me perched on a sort of man-made precipice, twelve to fourteen feet high, called a machan . . . in the midst of a hundred-yard clearing. A rail surrounded this machan and I sat on a basket-type stool with my gun bearer standing close by holding a huge umbrella to protect me from the intense heat. This clearing was one of many, a few hundred yards apart, made by cutting down all trees and vegetation within the space so the view would be unobstructed. I liked hunting but somehow, sitting up there so comfortably, I was more interested in the great variety of birds with the most colorful plumage I've ever seen.

At one location during our safari a native woman who had ventured a short distance from her corral home to gather wood was seized by a hungry tiger. A white hunter and some natives trailed the animal back into the mountains where they finally found parts of the woman's mutilated body. I tried to follow them, mounted in a wobbly basket-seat on an elephant. I was guiding the animal by tapping him gently with a large stick about the size of a baseball bat when he evidently became frightened at something along the trail. Believe me, those elephants are not as slow-moving as I had been led to think . . . for this one began swishing his huge trunk around and stomping up the path with furious energy. Right then I decided to go back to camp. I had quite a socking match with the elephant trying to convince him to return with me. First I hit him rather gently between the eyes with no results. Then I socked him harder and harder until he finally turned back toward camp with me still hanging precariously in the basket.

With my English hunter-guide I drove out in the Rajah's car in the afternoon to look over the water hole near where the woman's remains had been found. Freshly imprinted pug marks gave evidence the big tiger was still hanging around. That night I decided to go out after him on my own, since the Rajah refused to accompany me. I drove out to the water hole that night in his open car carrying a double barrel 471 rifle as big as a cannon. Two natives in a second car followed me and, after I had backed my car into the foliage with the headlights focused on the water hole, they drove to a spot about a mile up the trail to park and watch the proceedings. I attached a miner's light to my head so I could focus my gun when and if the beast would appear.

The darkness was intense. I could not light a cigarette lest the light frighten the animal away. I could not shift my position, for the least sound or motion might disclose my presence to the acute hearing of any wild game. That water hole had looked so different in the bright sunlight . . . with the afternoon shadows making inviting shade and the twittering of the many birds giving it a gay sort of atmosphere. Now, the deep silence of the dark moonless night with the stars obscured by the trees made it a strange and forbidding place. This was a lonesome spot for a crowd-loving fellow like me! Quite a difference from the usual type of spot in which I chose to while away an hour or so. Frankly, I was scared!

I sat there on the front seat of the car for perhaps two hours. Suddenly I heard the roaring of a tiger . . . a tremendous roar, echoing and re-echoing in the darkness. In the deep forest the roar was magnified to a volume which rang far and wide. I shook and I quivered after each reverberation. A short silence and then another tremendous roar which seemed to come from the forest directly back of me. I had the uneasy feeling that the tiger was much nearer than I liked to think. I waited again . . . another roar . . . and I shook with it. It was impossible for me to turn and look back. I had the overwhelming fear that he was actually in the back seat of the car with me. Apparently the natives in the car up the trail shared my apprehension for suddenly the lights of their car came on, the motor started with a welcoming burst as they headed back to camp leaving me behind in darkest India to cope with my visitor. However, the lights and the motor noise frightened the tiger for he plunged through the darkness away from me and I sank weakly into the seat to recover my composure. Then I lit a cigarette and took off up the trail to the safety of the camp and the protection of my English guide and my fifty natives. All I could remember was the pounding of my heart and the welcoming sound of the retreating car of the two natives as they sped back to camp. I was darn glad of an excuse to beat it out of the water hole area and that was my last try at spotting for wild animals at night.

However, my greatest fight was yet to come, and it was a direct result of the safari, for I picked up malaria germs. Ten days later I landed in a Calcutta hospital with three physicians in attendance—an Englishman, a German specialist and a native medicine man. During the next week I ran a temperature of 105.6 degrees. At intervals of semiconsciousness I was incessantly concerned with the notion that the nurses stood me on my head against the wall at night. I had lost practically all my hair. In fact, after taking a peek at myself in the mirror I darn near ordered a toupee. But thanks to the good Lord, that purchase wasn't necessary for he soon replenished my head covering.

Kirkwood and I sailed from Calcutta with brief stops for exhibition matches in Rangoon, Penang, Singapore, Kuala Lumpur. We hopped over to Java where we played the capital city of Batavia to enthusiastic galleries. Enticed by the beautiful dancing girls of Bali Bali we gave an exhibition there, also. Then by boat to Manila and on up to Hong Kong and Shanghai. Following those exhibitions we headed for our second trip to the Japanese Islands where we played at Kobe, Osaka, Kyoto, Tokyo, Nagoya and Yokohama. In May we sailed for San Francisco via the Hawaiian Islands and arrived back in the States around the first of June. We had covered well over twelve months of land and six months of water during our tour and this country looked mighty good to us.

I've been pretty lucky all my life and I believe it was never better brought to my mind than during that world tour. As a youngster I had been inspired by the stories of George Eastman and Teddy Roosevelt . . . stories of big game safaris in Africa and India. And here again luck had not let me down. Mr. Harris, at whose ranch I had lived in Nairobi, and who had been my expert guide had also acted as guide for Teddy Roosevelt on one of his African hunts. Early one dawn he escorted me out to the very spot where Teddy had shot two huge buffalo, of which the President had been so proud. However, none came my way that day.

On one of the safaris I made with the Rajah in India, my English hunter-guide and I had been exchanging various facts about our lives.

"Where were you born, Mr. Hagen?" he asked.

"Rochester, New York," I told him, feeling sure he had never heard of the place.

"Did you know Mr. George Eastman?"

"Quite well," I said. "But Mr. Eastman passed away some years ago."

"That's too bad," my guide said. "He was a fine gentleman. I was guide for him on his hunting trips in India in the early 1900s."

That's when the young caddie Walter Hagen was toting Mr. Eastman's golf clubs around the course at the Country Club of

Rochester while listening avidly to tales of those very same safaris. I'm sure all my pals will permit me to indulge in that very trite expression, "It's a very small world, after all."

In 1938 when Joe and I returned from our long tour I considered myself still an integral part of the golf picture. We played a few exhibitions at Pebble Beach and at Santa Barbara, then flew to Denver for the National Open at Cherry Hills, which Ralph Guldahl won. I did not play in the Open for I failed to qualify by one stroke. On the seventeenth hole of the last qualifying round my second shot, a seven-iron, landed in the cup between the flag and the rim, then popped out and pulled up some thirty feet away. Had my ball stayed in the cup or even popped out close enough to the pin for a birdie, perhaps I'd have been some added competition for Guldahl. As it was all I got out of the shot was a par 4.

That shot reminded me of another I'd played at the Savannah Country Club in Savannah, Georgia a good many years earlier. On the very first hole my second shot rolled out over the edge of the green into a shallow trap. There I found my ball in the bottom of a small peanut bag. The weight of the ball stood the bag in an upright position, so I could see the ball. Rather than take a penalty, I elected to play the ball in the bag. Instead of blasting, I played a sort of chip shot. Well, out of the trap came the bag and when it hit the green . . . I almost dropped myself, for my ball trickled out of the bag and rolled neatly into the cup for a birdie. I could have used a freak shot like that to qualify for the National Open at Cherry Hills in 1938.

In these later years when my career was coming to a finish I felt a desire to go back and check on myself . . . perhaps to count my medals and review what I'd done. In fact, I believe I had the urge to find out if I had used my talents to the best of my ability.

I have always believed that the championship golfer reaches

316

his peak at thirty-five years of age, although I will admit that many of our greatest have gone on playing a fine game long past that age. When the mid-1930s rolled around, the pressure of those younger fellows with the brisk strides and the power swings was making me realize I was a few years past forty. I no longer had the urge to spend time practicing . . . it was too much strain on my social life.

The most obvious fact about my game in the late 1930s was that, although I had acquired greater control and accuracy with my wood and iron shots, I was having greater difficulty dropping my ball in the hole . . . my putting touch was decidedly off. I tried out different stances . . . I tried standing with my feet close together . . . I tried standing with my feet wide apart. I tried bending over a bit more and I tried standing straight. Actually, my main trouble was just a whisky jerk.

I got a big kick out of the young golfers coming up in the game who stepped up and rapped every putt for the hole. They expected to hole a putt of from twelve to fifteen feet. They had the confidence I'd possessed in those earlier years . . . and to my mind confidence is the greatest asset in accurate putting. Well, I had come to the years when I frankly attempted to keep my game consistent rather than try the bold shots which had characterized my peak-time play. Eighteen holes a day more than satisfied me.

I recalled the days when I had played with John D. Rockefeller, then in his eighties, when he had paced himself for nine holes a day. I remembered the British Open in 1929 when Uncle John Ball had paired with me in the first round of his last appearance in competition . . . he was sixty-eight years of age. And my mind went back to the fine old gentlemen at the Country Club of Rochester, garbed in the colorful outfits of the early 1900s, who had played the game for recreation, exercise and a few side bets. People in that part of the century were convinced that golf was a game exclusively for the older men.

Well, I contributed my part to make golf a highly competitive and lucrative game for the youth of the world. And by 1941 my own ambition, my own tireless seeking for new courses to conquer, had made competitive golf entirely too strenuous and too demanding for me.

CHAPTER XXXII: The Nineteenth Hole

> You're only here for a short visit. Don't hurry. Don't worry. And be sure to smell the flowers along the way.
>
> —WALTER HAGEN
> [1956]

I SUPPOSE every joker who knows one golf club from another is familiar with my tendency to get around the course as quickly as possible and bend an elbow at the nineteenth hole, a favorite on any course. In my time I've had occasion to line up with the boys at some three thousand courses and I believe I'm fully qualified to mention the indispensable hospitality contributing to the fast friendships built up around the table or in the locker rooms.

As far back as Harry Vardon's book instructing novices how to hold a golf club, there have been volumes by both players and sports writers extolling the fine points of the game, the most difficult courses, the champion players and the kind of equipment best suited to player and course. Most of those books make pretty fair reading. I contend that the anecdotes of raconteurs at the nineteenth hole make far spicier reading. However, those stories are not the sort which win the approval of the general public. So I shall merely recall a few of the well-known nineteenth holes and a number of the fine fellows with whom I enjoyed some pleasant hours.

For instance, there is the nineteenth at Pine Valley in Clementon, New Jersey—a familiar spot presided over by the ageless master of mixology, the great Tucker himself. Here after a round over the difficult, troublesome course I sat at the long maple table, on which was centered the Crump cup, with Joe Kirkwood, Emmet French and Bob Harlow while we discussed the tough fourteenth.

At Boca Raton Tommy Armour, the Silver Scotchman, and I relaxed in comfortable beach chairs under a huge colorful umbrella while he directed his perspiring pupils. Tommy and I teamed up here, and in many another spot, to send bar profits sky high.

At the Augusta National, Colonel Robert Jones and his famous son, Bobby, and I teamed up with Stan and Bob Barbour on the cool veranda overlooking the eighteenth hole to sip a minted Tom Collins while reviewing the play on that tedious and difficult twelfth hole.

The "Out of Bounds," as the nineteenth at Pinehurst was called, saw me relaxing with Bob and Page Stranahan, Bob Harlow and Dick Tufts, our genial host, presiding. The talk covered everything from that great finishing eighteenth hole to the price of tea in China . . . but usually each topic was concluded with an argument as to whose bottle would fill the glasses for the next round of liquid refreshment.

At Olympia Fields Number Four course, where their famed nineteenth hole received us weary golfers after many a practice round prior to a championship, we'd sit around a table in the largest and one of the most beautifully carpeted locker rooms in the world. There we discussed our best shots and forgot the bad ones with Harry Radix, donor of the original Vardon trophy, Scotty Fessenden, Bill Mortell, Charley Bartlett, Bob Smith, Bob Adam and Herb Graffis, representing the Fourth Estate.

It's as difficult to escape from the nineteenth at Oakmont as it is to get out of the cross-raked traps on the course. The great

Bill Fownes came out to watch one day when Jimmy Thomson and I were teeing off for a practice round prior to the Open Championship.

"Jimmy," Bill said, "I've placed traps all along the left fairway on the first hole, even out as far as three hundred yards. The last one is just for you."

And then Jimmy hit one that carried completely over that last trap. I don't believe Bill ever did forget that incident.

At the Canterbury Country Club in Cleveland, Ohio the tiled patio would host such greats as Tris Speaker, the immortal center fielder; Tom Towel, my Cadillac agency friend; Billy Burke with his favorite cigar; while the press was represented by Francis Powers. After hoisting a few this restful hole often appeared to be built over the same rolling terrain as that last fine eighteenth. Our talk usually covered the three toughest consecutive holes in golf: the short but treacherous par 4 fifteenth over the barrancas; the 600-yard par 5 sixteenth; the very long par 3 seventeenth . . . all great finishing holes.

From the veranda of the Baltusrol Country Club the beautiful terrain rolls toward the lake which divides the tee and the green of the picturesque fourth hole. Then there's that wonderful finishing hole where I stood during the 1954 Open Championship with friends who had watched me defend my first National Open back in 1915.

A broad vista window overlooks the rolling Pacific from the nineteenth at Cypress Point, where Bing Crosby made a hole-in-one on that sixteenth. At the nineteenth here I've relaxed with some of the finest fellows in the world. Richard Arlen, Roger Lapham, Jack Neville and I enjoyed many rounds together.

Plum Hollow's nineteenth hole features the throne of a commode autographed by all my pals who played a Red Cross Benefit in the early 1940s. Bob Hope was my partner and competitors Ebbie Goodfellow, Detroit's Mayor Edward Jeffries, Jim Demaret, Sam Byrd and Harold Johns sat around the table after the matches to praise the great golf promoter Russ Gnau for his successful efforts in scheduling these and many other such exhibitions.

A large round table near Al Watrous' pro shop—trapped on the left and right by high lockers, the flag carrying the usual shape and color (a circular leather box with five dice inside)— that's the scene at the nineteenth at Oakland Hills, Detroit. Raising his hand to signal the waiter would be Chris Brinke as he sat kibitzing with Al and me. While on my right would be my great friends Bert Davis and Eddie Vail, the automotive industry's Yeager timekeeper. On my left there was always the smiling Ike Ross, his good-humored face the uplifting and cheering contrast to my own Buddha-like countenance.

In all my wandering around the globe I never really owned a home. This, my first, is situated on a knoll facing west on Long Lake near Traverse City, Michigan. My picture windows look out on the silvery blue water across to the island some half mile distant. To the north, one hundred yards through the trees and the knee-high broad-leaf ferns, my guest cottage gleams white and inviting at the head of the steps leading to the dock walk. One hundred and fifty yards out into the lake the dock beckons hospitably with its easy chairs and umbrella-shaded tables. From the dock my eyes can take in the *Dor-Mee* rocking easily at anchor nearby . . . the American flag flying proudly from the flagpole on the hill. The sun is shining and the cool breeze from the lake makes just being alive a luxury. My Hawaiian shirt—bright with flame, gold and woodsy green—harmonizes with my golf slacks. My hair is about half and half, as the saying goes, but it is still holding its own.

After all the noise and the clamor . . . after the clubs are cleaned and stacked . . . the silence which follows the last round played seems strange, bewildering, yet wonderfully peaceful. However, this silence, to me, often reverberates with the roars and the applause of the fans who followed me for so many years. I got my name in the record books and for every golf ball I hit I got to know someone . . . caddies, kings, golf fans and even a few phonies.

I still hold close to my heart the wonderful memory of the cheers and the applause . . . what sweet sounds they made! Now instead of counting strokes on each hole I count the tall slender white birches, the spruce, the hemlock, the maples and the cedars on my acres at Long Lake . . . the nineteenth hole on The Haig's course. And I am keeping places ready around the table for my many friends . . . an inviting hospitable, relaxing nineteenth hole for those who might stray my way to kibitz.

For me the record books are closed. The cheering galleries? Well, they have mostly gone on their way . . . to follow the new champions around the course. Reliving all my years of golf has been a pleasant chore and I hope my story will furnish some enjoyable reading for my many fans all over the world. Joe Kirkwood told me a tale recently about a trip he made to India about 1948, some ten years after our world tour. He was strolling down a street in Rangoon when he noticed a group of natives carrying articles for a sacrificial offering into a beautiful old temple. Food, old furniture, small coins . . . all of great value to these poverty-stricken people . . . the most they had to offer their god, Buddha. They placed the offerings before the altar, bowed low and backed away. Joe watched until all had left the temple, then curiosity forced him to examine more closely the articles piled there. In the midst of it all he found a photograph of Walter Hagen, which I had autographed in 1938, and it had been cherished for ten long years before being placed on that altar.

There may be something symbolic in that tale. Perhaps the long years I followed the sun, the part I played in helping make golf history, my records in the book, the Championships I won will be the incentive for some young fellow to come along and

323

beat my records. And my story, a long time in the writing and set down here for the first time, is my offering to the sport I love . . . to the many fans, the great competitors, the fine champions of the game, *golf*.

An Afterword

by MARGARET SEATON HECK

The uncertainties of match play leave scant margin for error and that's why an observer is left open-mouthed with wonder at the realization that Walter Hagen won the PGA five times in all, including four times in succession. The Haig was supreme in these man-against-man competitions because he knew every psychological trick in the book. One of his favorites was to keep an opponent waiting on the first tee. But once Wild Bill Mehlhorn was prepared for him. With studied carelessness he greeted the debonair Hagen; "Hello, Walter, I didn't expect you for another hour."

The Haig grinned, whipped off his coat and stepped to the first tee without even a practice swing. He shot an eagle 3 on the first, a birdie on the second and was two under par at the turn. He won the match, 6 and 5.

—ARTHUR DALEY, *Sports of the Times*
[1951]

ON MY DESK he had placed a press release from the Professional Golfers Association, listing the events for the year 1955 and announcing prize money for the winners of approximately $950,-000. At the bottom of the page he had written: "If I were only 21! How about it, Maggie? WALTER, THE HAIG"

During the two and one-half years of work on this book I have read thousands of newspaper articles and magazine features extolling the feats of the "Fabulous Hagen." Record books, some yellow with age, dating back to his early years in the game down to his last appearance in competition have been my constant companions. Then, too, there are the hundreds of tales which his friends and acquaintances have written or told me. I have listened for many, many hours while The Haig Himself recounted his own version of the amazing exploits which comprised his long championship-winning career. To me, it has been a priceless experience.

A great number of these personal stories are included in *The Walter Hagen Story* . . . hundreds of others which certainly deserve telling, must of necessity remain in my files due to publishing wordage limitations and Boston censorship. Walter had his reputation with the ladies; his colorful ways of finding relaxation from the rigors of the rough. Some of these might perhaps shock the more strait-laced but the majority are charming tales of the humorous, fun-loving Hagen personality.

One of my favorites concerns Walter's celebration following his win of the PGA Championship in 1925 at Olympia Fields Country Club in Chicago. By three in the morning when the conviviality ended, all cats were black in his eyes and every guest cottage looked like every other. He chose the one he believed to be his, unlocked the door and switched on the light . . . to find a terrified little old lady of seventy-odd years clutching a robe tightly about her frail body.

He hurriedly apologized and with that innate charm peculiar to him explained that he had been celebrating his victory of that afternoon.

"You poor boy," the little old lady murmured soothingly. "You've had a hard day. I followed you during the entire Championship." She darted around the room arranging glasses, ice cubes and so on on a tray. Placing it on a table by the sofa, she said, "Now what you need is a good stiff nightcap. Then we'll sit here and talk over some of those fine shots you played today." And that they did, with Walter making his exit with the rising sun.

To The Haig there are no intruders on his time . . . just welcome interruptions. He believes firmly in never doing today what can be put off until three weeks from today. He is undoubtedly the world's greatest procrastinator. During the years we have worked on his book he has never failed to leave his desk at the first sound of a turning door knob. There have been many days when we worked for twenty minutes and entertained his friends and admirers for four hours.

Every visitor invariably begins his conversation with, "Walter, tell about the time . . ." and he will relate each incident with zest and enjoyment no matter how many times he has told it. He has the memory of the proverbial elephant and the grace of a large gazelle as he acts out the story. Yet with all his delight in good talk and friendly argument, he is a wonderful audience for an interesting guest.

Anyone who has ever met him knows him for life. When these friends hit Detroit or Traverse City the first telephone they ring is Walter's. At noon he may get a call from a retired heavyweight champion and an hour later from a Chicago policeman he met years earlier who wants to go hunting or fishing with him.

His tact, his generosity, his infallible courtesy and kindliness allow no awkward situations to arise in his presence. Take for instance, the young man dining with his best girl in a Midwestern city night club who called out as The Haig neared his table, "Hello, Walter, how are you?"

Walter paused by the table, shook hands warmly, and asked, "And have you corrected that slice yet?"

He told friends later he had not known the young fellow but, "I've been in a similar spot when I wanted to impress my girl. And you never let a nice young fellow down."

He has a horror of being "sold" something. He turns a skep-

327

tical eye and a doubting ear on any long-winded sales talk. But he makes an immediate purchase when he happens upon a product which strikes his fancy. He bought an expensive raincoat last fall like one which was left in his Cadillac by mistake. Someone sent him a particularly delicious baked ham and he ordered a half-dozen as gifts for friends kibitzing with him several weeks later.

Walter Hagen is possessed of tolerance, an often exasperating patience and a sound German stubbornness. His keen sense of humor makes him a great tease and joker. His attention to detail remains as constantly fastidious as when he selected his first cashmere sweaters and his famed fleecy coats. Beautifully monogrammed shirt, paisley ascots, hand-crafted shoes, custom-tailored suits in the same browns, gray or blue . . . the Walter Hagen of yesterday and today.

A wonderful and hospitable host, The Haig, who likes to dine shortly before midnight on a thick steak and Chef salad. And one sunny afternoon in the summer he cut a pretty fancy Charleston on the boardwalk near his boat dock. He even boasts a smart slalom, but to date he has not demonstrated this skill. Football and baseball on television broke up many an afternoon of our collaboration. He is greatly interested in the promising young golfers coming up and always ready to give of his experience and skill to help them along.

Letters come to him from all over the world requesting his autograph and reminding him of shots he played in various tournaments or matches. The name of Walter Hagen, the brilliance of his golf history, are as awe-inspiring to people meeting him for the first time today as they were to the devoted galleries trailing him around the courses in his championship days. Others stride the fairways—the eager and the skilled—seeking the elusive crown of Golfdom, but only The Haig had the personality to wear it combined with the forceful persistence to win it.

328

1914   United States Open Champion
1915   Massachusetts Open Champion
       Panama Exposition Champion
1916   Western Open Champion
       Metropolitan Open Champion
1917   Western Open Runner-up
1918   North and South Open Champion
1919   United States Open Champion
       Metropolitan Open Champion
1920   French Open Champion
       Metropolitan Open Champion
       North and South Open Runner-up
1921   American PGA Champion
       Western Open Champion
       Michigan Open Champion
       United States Open Runner-up
       World's Low Record Round of 62 at Belleair, Florida
          in West Coast Open
1922   British Open Champion
       New York State Open Champion
1923   North and South Open Champion
       Long Beach Champion
       Texas Open Champion
       British Open Runner-up
       American PGA Runner-up
1924   British Open Champion
       Belgian Open Champion
       American PGA Champion

North and South Open Champion
Unofficial Championship of the World.
    Defeated Cyril Walker, 72 holes match play, 17 and 16

1925 American PGA Champion

1926 American PGA Champion
Western Open Champion
Eastern Open Champion
British Open Third-Place finisher
Unofficial Championship of the World.
    Defeated Bobby Jones, 72 holes match play, 12 and 11

1927 American PGA Champion
Western Open Champion
Unofficial Championship of the World.
    Defeated Gene Sarazen, 9 and 8
North and South Open Runner-up

1928 British Open Champion
Unofficial Championship of the World.
    Defeated Johnny Farrell, 3 out of 5 matches

1929 British Open Champion
Texas Open Champion
Metropolitan Open Champion

1930 Michigan PGA Champion

1931 Canadian Open Champion
Michigan Open Champion
Western Open Runner-up

1932 Western Open Champion

1935 Gasparilla Open Champion
Sacramento Open Runner-up
American Open Third-Place finisher

OTHER Florida West Coast Champion (three times)
TITLES Silver Lakes Open Champion
Miami International Four Ball Champion, with Leo
    Diegel as partner

Toledo International Four Ball Champion, with Ky
    Laffoon as partner
Missouri Open Champion
Captain, Ryder Cup Team: 1927
                              1929
                              1931
                              1933
                              1935
                              1937
                              1939

GOLF GLOSSARY

BIRDIE. One under par for a single hole.

BITE. Backspin imparted to a ball.

BRASSIE. Number two wooden club, used off the fairway where distance is required.

BUNKER. A natural hazard on a golf course; in this country, a large sand trap.

CADDIE. Person who carries player's golf bag, derived from French *cadet,* younger brother or son; as a verb, act of carrying golf bag.

CLEEK. Number four wooden club, used in circumstances similar to those requiring a spoon.

CLUB. A utensil of golf; place where golf is played.

DORMY. As many up as there are holes to go.

DRIVER. Number one wooden club, usually used off the tee only—and where distance is required.

EAGLE. Two under par for a single hole.

FAIRWAY. Cultivated grass between the tee and the green.

GREEN. Ultra-cultivated grass in which the cup is situated.

IRON. Refers to any of the iron-headed clubs, excepting the putter.

LIE. The lay of the land or grass upon which the ball is situated; the manner in which a golf club sets upon the ground.

LINKS. A form of a golf course, laid out upon wasteland by the sea, usually windswept and having natural hazards. All British Opens, the oldest Championships in the world, are played on links. Rare in this country.

MASHIE. Name of an iron, approximately a five-iron. This is the only holdover, excepting the niblick, from the days when all clubs had individual names. Seldom used today except in facetious reference to time—a player speaking of his "mashie" infers he has played golf a long time.

MATCH. A system of play in which (a) two players play against each other, (b) two players play against two others, (c) a team of players plays against another team.

MATCH PLAY. A system of play in which the result is determined by who wins the most holes.

MEDAL PLAY. A system of play

332

in which each player adds his score, the lowest score determining the winner.

NIBLICK. Number nine, iron-headed club, used where accuracy is the sole requirement.

OPEN. *National Open.* Annual Championship* of the USGA.

The Open. The National Open when speaking of golf in the United States.

The Open. The British Open when speaking of golf in Great Britain.

OPEN. A tournament open to both amateurs and professionals.

PAR. The score an expert should make for (a) a single hole, (b) an entire course, (c) an entire tournament.

PGA. Professional Golfers Association, association of the pros in the United States. Their annual championship is referred to as the PGA.

PUTTER. Club used for holing the ball on the green.

* CHAMPIONSHIP. A tournament of regional significance, i.e., the National Open.

R. & A. The Royal and Ancient Golf Club, ruling body of golf everywhere in the world outside the United States. The R. & A. club house is in St. Andrews, Scotland.

SAND TRAP. A hazard consisting of an undulation in the ground filled with sand, sometimes re-referred to as a "trap."

ROUGH. All uncultivated grass—lining either side of fairway.

SPOON. Number three wooden club, used where great distance plus loft and accuracy are required.

STICKS. Slang for clubs.

STYMIE. The situation when an opponent's ball lies in the direct line of player's ball.

TEE. The mound of earth off which each player starts a hole; also, the wooden peg upon which the ball is placed when driving off.

USGA. United States Golf Association, ruling body of golf in this country.

WEDGE. A form of niblick, used from heavy lies and out of sand trap.

ACKNOWLEDGMENTS

Many people have contributed to the contents of this book:

Sports writers all over the world who wrote so generously of my golf career;

The late Bob Harlow, my manager for thirteen years, who kept my scrapbooks in his own inimitable fashion;

H. B. ("Dickie") Martin, whose determination to see my life story fill the pages of a book, gave me the initial push;

The thousands of golf fans whose letters have encouraged me and reminded me of incidents they wanted to have me tell;

My writer, Margaret Seaton Heck, whose tenacity in extracting the facts and the stories from me and whose diligence in research, correlation and collaboration put the completed story in the hands of the publisher.

And I wish also to thank the many golf writers and fellow professionals whose words about me are quoted throughout the book.

W. H.

Index

Adam, Bob, 320
Ade, George, 122, 123-24
Africa, tour of, 302-9
Agua Caliente Tournament, 239
Alexander, Grover Cleveland, 33
Alliss, Percy, 209, 214, 216, 217, 278-279, 292
American Golfer, The, 157, 259
Anderson, Carl, 45
Anderson, Jimmy, 136
Anderson, Johnny, 234
Anderson, Tom, Jr., 20, 25
Anderson, Willie, 20, 268, 271
Arlen, Richard, 242, 321
Armour, Tommy, 43, 105, 117, 147, 151, 152, 158, 159, 163-64, 178, 184-85, 188, 207, 210, 212, 217, 250, 274-77, 287, 288, 320
Arnaz, Desi, 243
Asaka, Prince, 247, 248, 249
Asami, Rokuzo, 237, 247
Ashridge, Berkshire, 281
Astaire, Fred, 242
Auchterlonie, Lawrence, 271
Augusta National Golf Club, Georgia, 320
Australia, tour of, 2, 113, 240-41, 243-246, 298
Australian Open Championship, 110
Ayton, Laurie, 123

Baer, Max, 86
Baine, Commander, 248
Balff, Ray, 111
Ball, Frank, 132
Ball, John, 131, 317
Ball, Lucille, 243
Baltusrol Golf Club, N. J., 46-7, 156, 271, 321
Barbour, Bob, 320
Barbour, Stan, 320
Barnes, Jim, 21, 28, 32, 44, 45, 47, 54, 66, 67, 68-9, 79-80, 81, 98, 100, 106, 125, 130, 137, 147, 158, 159, 207, 210, 212, 216, 217, 228, 267, 274, 275, 276, 293-95
Bartlett, Charley, 320
Beach, Rex, 79, 122
Beebe, Marge, 88
Beery, Wallace, 242
Belgian Open Championship, 136
Belleair, Florida, 49, 61, 121, 123
Bender, Chief, 33
Berg, Patty, 295
Blackwell in the Midlands, 164-65

Blue Hills Golf Club, Kansas City, 262-63
Blue Mound, Milwaukee, 48
Bobby Jones Story, The, 155-56
Boca Raton Club, Florida, 320
Bogart, Humphrey, 242
Bonbright, George, 229-30
Boomer, Aubrey, 208, 211, 220-22
Boros, Julius, 272, 276
Boston, Mass., 199-200
Bowman, Mack E., 275
Brackenbridge Park, Texas, 99
Brady, Mike, 19, 44, 46, 54, 57-9, 159, 178-79, 207, 260, 276
Brae Burn Country Club, Mass., 19, 52, 56-9, 254
Braid, James, 67, 82, 212, 218, 268
Brews, Sid, 303-4
Brewster, Gordon, 229
Brinke, Chris, 322
British Amateur Championship, 67
British Golf Association, 127
British Isles, tour of, 2, 300-2
British Open Championship, 27, 83, 90, 92, 93, 138, 149, 165, 186, 196, 212, 213, 217, 218-20, 241, 251, 254, 265-66, 273, 275
    1920 Deal, 8, 18, 60, 61, 63, 64-71, 79-80, 163, 220, 254, 274
    1921 St. Andrews, 80, 81-2, 98, 188
    1922 Sandwich, 26, 98-102, 233, 267
    1923 Troon, 126-28, 135, 188, 234
    1924 Hoylake, 126, 130-35, 145, 146, 271
    1925 Prestwick, 79
    1926 Royal Lytham, St. Anne's, 4-5, 7, 156, 194, 241
    1928 Sandwich, 80, 193, 195-99, 214, 233, 267-68
    1929 Muirfield, 157, 163, 212-18, 221, 222, 224, 233, 249, 274, 317
    1930 Hoylake, 240, 249, 250
    1933 St. Andrews, 210, 280
    1937 Carnoustie, 300
    1950 Troon, 213
Broadmoor Golf Club, Seattle, 98
Brook, Indiana, 123-4
Broome, Mary, 242
Brosch, Al, 98-9
Brown, Innis, 256
Burke, Billy, 121, 158, 209, 276, 287, 321
Burke, Jack, 80

Index

Bussom, J. J., 211, 292
Byrd, Sam, 321

Cadillac, Michigan, 6, 175
Cairo, Egypt, 298-99, 310
Calcutta, India, 234, 260, 292, 297, 309, 310-15
Calcutta, Rajah of, 311-15
Campbell, Alf, 20
Campbell, Charles, 227
Canadian Open Championship, 20-1, 28, 275, 277-79
Canterbury Country Club, Cleveland, 321
Carillo, Leo, 242
Carnoustie Links, Scotland, 82, 241, 300
Catalina Island Open Championship, 201, 202, 203-4
Cedar Crest Country Club, Dallas, 163, 164, 183-86, 258
Central League of New York, 22
Cherry Hills Country Club, Denver, 316
Chicago, see Midlothian, North Shore, Olympia Fields Club
Chin, Chick, 168, 247
Christ, George, 14, 19, 22, 287
Christy, Andrew, 14-5, 18, 19, 20, 21, 22
Chrysler, Walter, 55
Clemson, Dick, 33
Clemson, George, 33
Cleveland, Ohio, 99
Clyde, Andy, 242
Cobb, Ty, 55
Cochrane, Mickey, 121, 285
Cocoanut Grove Cocktail Lounge, Palm Beach, 26
Coleman, Colonel, 227
Collett, Glenna, 111
Collier, June, 242
Columbia Country Club, Chevy Chase, 47, 98, 166
Compston, Archie, 7, 9, 187-94, 195-201, 207, 208, 221, 233
Coombe Hill Golf Club, Surrey, 66, 67, 221
Cooper, Harry, 148, 159, 178, 181, 210, 273, 276
Corbett's Glen, New York, 9
Corcoran, Fred, 186, 205
Cotton, Henry, 139, 213, 215-16, 274, 281-82, 300
Country Club, The, Brookline, Mass., 25, 27-32, 35, 37, 39, 67, 68, 163, 267
Cravath, Gavvy, 33
Croome, A. C. M., 72
Crosby, Bing, 242, 321

Cruickshank, Bobby, 128, 147, 184, 210, 213, 214, 216, 217, 273, 275
Cullen, Mrs., 13
Cummings, Edith, 295
Cummings, George, 21
Cunningham, Bill, 97
Cunningham, Harry, 256
Curtis, Harry, 141
Cypress Point Club, California, 82, 321

Daily Mail, London, 62, 64-6, 199
Daley, Arthur, 277, 325
Dallas, Texas, 148, 272; see also Cedar Crest Country Club
Daly, F., 213
Daniels, Bebe, 242
Daniels, Skip, 218, 233
Davis, Bette, 242
Davis, Burt, 322
Deal Links, see Royal Cinque Ports Golf Club
Deer, Ray, 106
Demaret, Jimmy, 52, 98, 227, 276, 321
Dempsey, Jack, 9, 86, 97, 182, 202, 286
Denver Country Club, 202
Deschamps, Pierre, 73-6
Detroit Athletic Club, 4, 54
Detroit Golf Club, 167, 235
Devany, Joe, 227
Diegel, Leo, 80, 137, 147, 156, 159, 178-81, 182, 201, 208, 209, 212, 214, 215, 216, 217, 224, 239, 260, 276, 277, 287
Doyle, Jack, 270
Doyle, Tom, 256
Dudley, Ed, 202, 209, 212, 287
Duncan, George, 66, 67, 71, 73-4, 100-1, 188, 197-98, 208, 213, 238
Dutra, Olin, 158, 209

Earle, Harley, 256, 278-79
East, Victor, 110-11
East High School, Rochester, 228
Eastern Open Championship, 156
Eastman, George, 17, 258-59, 296, 315
Edward VIII, 239
Eisenhower, Dwight D., 138, 166
Elliott, Gene, 108, 117, 118, 119, 125
Equinox Club, Manchester, 22
Erskine Park Club, South Bend, 289
Esch, Eddie, 256
Espinosa, Al, 159, 185, 212, 239
Europe, tour of, 2, 249-50, 302
Evans, Chick, 2, 38, 45, 46, 47, 123,

158, 159, 235, 254, 262-63, 268, 271, 272, 274, 276
Evening Express, London, 189

Fairbanks, Douglas, 196, 224, 242
Fairbanks, Douglas, Jr., 196
Farrell, Jack, 184
Farrell, Johnny, 132, 147, 158, 159, 184, 185, 200, 201, 208, 212, 214, 216, 217, 239, 251, 260, 269, 274, 276
Ferrier, Jim, 98
Fessenden, Scotty, 176, 320
Fiji Islands, 243, 297
Firestone, Harvey, 303
Fisher, Larry, 52-3, 55, 256, 258, 261, 278-79
FitzSimons, Reverend Simon, 48
Flagler, Henry, 26
Ford, Edsel, 55, 167-68
Ford Motor Company, 300
Formby, England, 130
Foster-Armstrong Piano Company, 13-4
Fownes, Bill, 321
Foxx, Jimmy, 121, 285
Frawley, William, 243
French Amateur Championship, 275
French, Emmet, 80, 207, 320
French Lick Country Club, Ind., 106, 137
French Open Championship, 18, 72-6, 80, 81, 136, 220
Fresh Meadow Country Club, Flushing, 250
Furgol, Ed, 235, 272

Gamber, Clarence, 202
Gandy Bridge, Florida, 118, 284
Ganzil, John, 141
Garden City, L. I., 48, 271
Gasparilla Open Championship, Tampa, 277, 283-85
Gassait, Jean, 207
Gavin, Mrs. William A., 295
Genessee Valley Course, Rochester, 265
George, Dow, 147
George V, 238
George VI, 239
German Open Championship, 250
Gibson, Hoot, 242
Gnau, Russ, 322
Golden, John, 185, 208, 212, 214, 279
Golf House, New York, 19
Goodfellow, Ebbie, 321
Goodman, Johnny, 158
Graffis, Herb, 320
Graham, Bill, 227

Grand Rapids, Michigan, 143, 195, 221
Great Lakes Open Championship, 239
Green Grass Widow, 88
Greenwich Country Club, 81
Greenwood, George, 66
Guldahl, Ralph, 272, 276, 287, 316
Gullane, 212
Gunn, Watts, 159

Hackney, Clarence, 277
Hagen, Cora, 10
Hagen, Edna Strauss, 90, 108, 117, 118, 119, 120, 130, 135, 136
Hagen, Freda, 10, 142
Hagen, Lottie, 10
Hagen, Louise, 10, 287-88
Hagen, Mabel, 10
Hagen, Margaret Johnson, 48-9, 51, 56
Hagen, Walter, Jr., 49, 98, 224-25, 231
Hagen, Walter, Golf Productions Corp., 141-44, 186
Hagen, William, 10, 42, 287-88
Hammond, Spec, 105
Harding, Warren G., 7, 47, 166-67
Hargreaves, E., 233
Harlow, Bob, 3, 81, 110-11, 126-27, 146, 148-49, 151, 169, 188-90, 194, 199-200, 224, 225, 249, 258, 307, 320, 334
Harmon, Tommy, 184, 185
Harris ranch, Nairobi, 307-9, 315
Harrison, E. J. (Dutch), 286
Harry's Garage, Rochester, 13
Haskell, Dr. Coburn, 265
Havers, Arthur, 126-28, 132, 188, 208
Hawkins, Norval, 54-5
Hayes, Otway, 303
Hefflin, Karl, 186-87
Herd, Alex, 79, 82, 218, 265, 268, 276
Hialeah, Miami, 147
Hilgendorf, Charles, 227
Hillcrest Country Club, Los Angeles, 239
Hodogaya Country Club, Yokohama, 237, 247
Hogan, Ben, 16, 86, 98, 109, 183, 219-20, 241, 272, 276
Hollins, Marion, 295
Hollywood, California, 87-8, 144, 187, 201, 239-43
Homans, Eugene, 159
Honolulu, 240, 241, 243, 297
Hope, Bob, 243, 321
Hornsby, Rogers, 182
Hot Springs, Arkansas, 202
Houghton Golf Club, 303-4
Howard, R. E. (Bob), 62-3, 64-6, 126
Hoylake Links, *see* Royal Liverpool

Hoyt, Fred, 58-9
Huggins, Miller, 182
Huggins, Percy, 109
Hunter, George, 124.
Hurd, Dorothy Campbell, 295
Hurtley, Norman, 238, 239
Hutchison, Jock, 54, 66-7, 80, 81, 99,
    100, 123, 188, 210, 274, 275, 276
Hylan, John, 102

Ibaraki Country Club, Osaka, 247
Ingleside Club, San Francisco, 44
Interlachen Country Club, Minn., 241,
    250, 278
Inverness Country Club, Toledo, 80,
    81
Inverness Four Ball Tourney, 291
Inwood Country Club, Long Island,
    88, 98, 139-40
Izod, A. J., 90

Jacobus, George, 292
Jameson, Betty, 295
Japan, tour of, 2, 113, 168, 238, 240,
    247-49
Jeffries, Edward, 321
Johannesburg, South Africa, 303
Johns, Harold, 321
Johnson, George, 48
Johnston, Harrison, 159
Jolly, H., 208
Jolson, Al, 56-7
Jones, Bobby, 4-5, 9, 19, 62, 77, 78,
    86, 99, 109, 128, 144-59, 182,
    194, 213, 226, 241, 249, 250, 251,
    269, 272, 273-74, 276, 278, 288,
    320
Jones, Colonel Robert, 320
Jurado, José, 197

Kalgoorlie, Australia, 298
Kanuma, Yataka, 247
Keeler, O. B., 62, 157-59
Keffer, Karl, 21
Keiser, Herman, 98
Keller Links Country Club, St. Paul,
    279, 289
Kent, Duke of, 211
Kerrigan, Tommy, 44, 54, 80, 147,
    273, 275, 283
Kimberley, South Africa, 303
Kirby, Dorothy, 295
Kirkaldy, Andrew ("Andra"), 100,
    280-81
Kirkwood, Joe, 77, 80, 102, 109-14,
    123, 125, 126-27, 147, 168, 207,
    236, 241, 243-49, 292-93, 296-
    316, 320, 323
Klein, Willie, 178
Knocke-sur-Mer, Belgium, 136

Kobe Golf Club, Japan, 247
Kocsis, Emerick, 227

La Boulie, Versailles, 72-5, 136, 238
LaBourie's Sporting Goods, Rochester,
    11, 230
Lacoste, René, 182
Laffoon, Ky, 291
LaFitte, Eugene, 74-5, 136
LaFitte, Pierre, 207
Lake Forest, 271
Lake Placid Club, New York, 264
Lakeside Golf Club, Hollywood, 243
Lambert, Bill, 10
Lamy, Edmund, 229
Landis, Judge Kenesaw M., 259
Lang, Al, 125
Lapham, Roger, 321
Lardner, Ring, 7, 122-23
Leonard, Dutch, 34-7, 38
Lesser, Patricia Ann, 295
Little, Beekman, 17, 22
Little, Lawson, 98
Littler, Gene, 235
Livermore, Jesse, 90-1, 92, 93, 130
Lloyd, Harold, 201, 242
Locke, Bobby, 109, 276, 296, 303-4
Long, Huey, 261
Long Beach Open Championship, 201
Longwood, Florida, 141
Loos, Eddie, 147
Los Angeles Open Championship, 202,
    239
Louis, Joe, 86, 147
Lowell, Dr. William, 109
Lyman, Abe, 231-32

MacDonald, Bob, 38, 123
MacDonald, I. R. A., 227-28
Macfarlane, Willie, 78, 144, 158, 177,
    210, 260, 276
Mack, Connie, 284
Mack, Joseph, 54-5
Mackie, Jack, 139
Mallory, Molla Bjurstedt, 182
Malta, 299
Man Who Cheated, The, 87
Manero, Tony, 158-59, 164, 184, 271
Mangrum, Lloyd, 276
Manley Beach, Australia, 244, 245
Marquard, Rube, 121
Martin, H. B. (Dickie), 28, 48, 61,
    65, 66, 71, 81, 121, 334
Massey, Burt, 258
Massy, Arnaud, 100, 132, 207
Mayer, Dick, 235
McCarthy, Joe, 121
McCutcheon, John T., 123
McDermott, Johnny, 27, 44, 47, 61,
    207, 268

McLean, Edward, 166
McLean, George, 128, 159
McLeod, Fred, 47, 147, 166, 207, 267, 276
McNamara, Tom, 44, 47, 207, 268, 273, 275
McSpaden, Harold, 287
Mehlhorn, Bill, 144, 147, 159, 178, 181-82, 188, 197, 201, 202, 207, 208, 325
Meighan, Tommy, 123
Menjou, Adolphe, 242
Menominee, Michigan, 169-70
Menomonie, Minnesota, 170
Metropolitan Open Championship, 48, 60, 81, 224, 239
Metz, Dick, 287
Miami Biltmore Club, Coral Gables, 104
Michigan Open Championship, 98
Middlecoff, Cary, 272
Midlothian Country Club, Chicago, 36-8, 39, 40, 44, 46, 52, 56, 115, 163, 226, 254, 255, 271, 278, 286-87, 300
Minneapolis, Minn., 261-62
Minnikahda Club, Minneapolis, 47, 271
Mitchell, Abe, 9, 66, 67, 71, 73-4, 79, 114-15, 132, 171-72, 188, 197, 214, 217, 238, 280-81
Miyamoto, Tomokichi, 247
Molter, Harry, 86
Montague, W. K., 226
Moody, Helen Wills, 182
Moor Park Golf Club, Hertfordshire, 9, 188-94, 233
Moore, Owen, 242
Moortown Golf Club, Ltd., Leeds, 208, 238, 239
Moran, Pat, 33, 39
Morning Post, London, 193-94
Morse, George, 124, 152
Mortell, Bill, 320
Muirfield, Scotland, 212-218, 221, 233, 274
Murphy, Bob, 4
Murphy, George, 176
Murphy, George (actor), 242
Murray, Midge, 19
Muthiaga Golf Club, Nairobi, 304
Myopia Hunt Club, 271

Nagoya, 234
Nairobi, Africa, 304, 307-9, 315
Nakuru Golf Club, Africa, 305-6, 307
Namm, Benjamin, 151
Naruo Golf Course, Japan, 247
Nary, Bill, 99
National Club, L. I., 82

Nelson, Alfred, Co., 211
Nelson, Byron, 86, 98, 163-64, 235, 276, 287
Nelson, Jane, 295
Neville, Jack, 321
New Orleans, La., 261
New York Yankees, 121, 124, 182
New Zealand, tour of, 2, 240, 243-44, 297
New Zealand Championship, 110
Nicholls, Gil, 44, 46, 131, 151, 152, 268
Nippon Club, New York, 168
North and South Open Championship, 54, 83, 110, 126, 130, 136, 140, 156, 164, 224
North Shore Country Club, Chicago, 105, 184
Northcliffe, Lord, 64-6

Oak Hill Country Club, Rochester, 18, 20, 287
Oakland Hills Golf Club, Detroit, 19, 54-6, 61, 69, 136, 174, 272, 322
Oakmont Country Club, Pa., 45, 84, 102, 219, 241, 320-21
O'Brian, Jack, 52
O'Brien, Jay, 275
O'Brien, Pat, 242
O'Hara, Peter, 279
Olander, Clarence, 303
Olympia Fields Club, Chicago, 144, 177-82, 320, 326
O'Malley, Ward, 161
Orcutt, Maureen, 295
Oregon Open Championship, Portland, 239
Oriole Terrace, Detroit, 231-32
Orita, A., 247
Orlando, Florida, 147, 288
Ormond Beach, Florida, 161
Ouimet, Francis, 27, 28, 31, 37-8, 46, 47, 158, 159, 268, 274, 276
Owasco Country Club, Auburn, 22

Packard, A. T., 173
Pago Pago, 243, 297
Palma Ceia Golf Club, Tampa, 49
Palmer, Arnold, 235
Palmer, John, 12
Panama Exposition Open Championship, 18, 44-5, 293-95
Parks, Sam, Jr., 85, 158
Pasadena Estates, Florida, 119, 121, 142, 146
Pasadena Golf and Country Club, St. Petersburg, 96, 107-8, 118-23, 124-25, 144, 146, 147, 148, 151, 154-55

Pasadena Open Championship, California, 255
Pearce, R. S., 125
Pebble Beach Golf Club, California, 82, 316
Pelham Golf Club, New York, 128-30, 186
Penney, J. C., 279
Perkins, Cy, 121, 285
Perkins, Erickson, 10-11, 48
Perkins, Thomas Philip, 159
Perry, Alfred, 211, 213, 292
Perth, Australia, 245, 298
Philadelphia Athletics, 285
Philadelphia Nationals, 33, 34-5, 39
Phillips, H. I., 290
Picard, Henry, 164, 276, 286
Pierce, Frank, 263
Pignon, Fred, 101, 164-65
Pilgrim's Village, Michigan, 6
Pine Valley, Clementon, N. J., 320
Pinehurst Country Club, N. Carolina, 54, 83, 110, 126, 136, 290, 297, 320
Plum Hollow Country Club, Mich., 227, 321
Pomonok Country Club, Flushing, 164, 255
Portland, Oregon, 78
Powers, Francis, 321
Powers, John, 17, 23-4
Powers, Walter, 17
Prestwick Links, 79, 82
Prince's Links, Kent, 79-80, 198, 233
Probasco, Scotty, 124
Probasco, Mrs. Scotty, 295
Probst, R. Otto, 289
Professional Golfers' Association, 48, 51, 137, 168, 208, 210, 325
Professional Golfers' Association Championship, 102, 138, 159, 181, 182, 183, 186, 241, 255, 262, 275, 280, 289-90, 325
    1921 Inwood, 98, 137, 139-40
    1923 Pelham, 128, 186
    1924 French Lick, 106, 137
    1925 Olympia Fields, 144-45, 148, 173, 177-82, 326
    1926 Salisbury, 156, 182
    1927 Cedar Crest, 163, 164, 183-186, 258
    1928 Baltimore, 201
    1929 Hillcrest, 224, 239-40
    1930 Fresh Meadow, 250
    1931 Wannamoisett, 279
    1932 Keller Links, 279, 289
    1936 Pinehurst, 297
    1938 Shawnee, 269
    1939 Pomonok, 164, 255
Providence, Rhode Island, 111-12

Pulsifer, Fred, 88-90
Pulver, F. F., 125
Quier, Edith (Mrs. H. Flippen), 295
Radix, Harry E., 176, 320
Randall, Jim, 108, 177
Ray, Ted, 18, 25, 27, 28, 31, 32, 37, 47, 80, 93, 158, 208, 228, 268, 276
Red Cross exhibitions, 19, 48, 50, 61, 288, 321
Red Run Golf Club, Detroit, 287, 288
Reid, Wilfred, 28
Revolta, Johnny, 276, 286
Rice, Grantland, 34, 64, 105, 121, 155-56, 255
Rice, Lester, 286
Ridgewood Country Club, N. J., 211, 292
Riley, Polly, 295
Ripley, Robert, 78
Riviera Country Club, Los Angeles, 272
Robertson-Durham, A. W., 218
Robeson, Irving S., 229
Robinson, Ray, 86
Robson, F., 208
Rochester, Country Club of, 3, 9, 13, 14, 16, 17, 19, 21, 22-4, 25, 33, 34, 39, 48, 55, 56, 65, 228, 229, 258, 265, 287-88, 296, 315-17
Rochester Ramblers, 19
Rochester Red Wings, 258-59
Rockefeller, John D., 161-62, 317
Rogers, Johnny, 202
Romack, Barbara, 295
Roosevelt Family, Quentin, 225
Roosevelt, Theodore, 296, 315
Rosedale Golf Club, Toronto, 21
Rosenbloom, Maxie, 86
Ross, Alex, 268
Ross, Ike, 322
Royal Cinque Ports Golf Club, Deal, 62-3, 64, 67, 68-71, 72, 73, 74, 79-80, 82, 220, 233, 238, 254
Royal Liverpool Links, Hoylake, 82, 130-35, 197, 249, 250, 265, 271
Royal Lytham and St. Anne's Golf Club, Lancashire, 4-5, 7, 82, 156, 194, 213, 241
Royal St. George's Golf Club, Sandwich, 67, 79-80, 82, 99-102, 196-198, 214, 233, 267
Runyan, Paul, 209, 269, 276, 286
Ruth, Babe, 7, 9, 96, 121, 202, 258, 286, 291
Ryder, Samuel, 207, 210
Ryder Cup Team, 19, 186, 203, 205-211, 212, 213, 217, 238, 280, 292, 298, 299, 302

Sage, Leon, 279
St. Andrews, Scotland, 67, 69, 81-2, 210, 213, 280
St. Cloud Club, Paris, 220, 299
St. George's Hill, England, 9, 67, 171
St. Mary's Church, Rochester, 48
St. Paul Open Championship, 104
Salant, Gabriel, 88-90
Salisbury, Rhodesia, 234
Salisbury Golf Club, L.I., 156
Salsinger, H. G., 2
San Antonio, Texas, 130, 202, 270
San Francisco, Cal., 45
Sandwich Links, see Royal St. George's Golf Club
Sanford, Florida, 104
Santa Barbara, California, 316
Sarazen, Gene, 9, 47, 81, 84-5, 86, 102-5, 123, 128-30, 131, 147, 158, 186, 188, 189, 194, 197-98, 200, 206, 208, 209, 211, 212, 214, 216, 217, 218, 233, 235, 239, 272, 274, 276, 287, 288, 291-93
Sargent, George, 21, 38, 268, 271, 300
Sassoon, Sir Philip, 211, 220-22, 238, 248
Savannah Country Club, 316
Savoy Hotel, London, 62, 90, 164, 171, 186, 189, 194, 220, 281, 299, 300, 302
Sayers, Benny, 47
Scioto Country Club, Columbus, Ohio, 156, 194, 208, 241
Scott, Randolph, 242
Sebring, Florida, 79
Selfridge Field, Michigan, 227
Sennett, Mack, 239-40
Shanghai, 240, 248, 315
Shawnee Country Club, on the Delaware, 269
Shawnee Open Championship, 269
Shenecossett Club, New London, 110
Shute, Denny, 209-10, 218, 276, 280, 286
Sixty, Billy, 161
Skokie Country Club, Illinois, 47, 49, 110
Smith, Alex, 21, 44, 45, 47, 110, 207, 268, 271, 275, 277
Smith, Bob, 320
Smith, Horton, 106, 201-3, 209, 212, 239, 276, 286
Smith, MacDonald, 28, 32, 131, 132, 135, 210, 212, 273, 277
Smith, Walter, 218, 233
Smith, Wiffi, 295
Snead, Sam, 86, 109, 218, 265, 269, 272, 276
Snyder, Carl, 278-79
Somerville, C. Ross, 159

Sorensen, Charles, 300
Souchak, Mike, 269-70
South Central Open Championship, 202
Southport, England, 205, 208-9, 292, 298, 299
Spalding, A. G. & Bros., 45, 140
Speaker, Tris, 321
Stein, Joe, 207
Stiles, Wayne, 120
Stirling, Alexa, 295
Stranahan, Bob, 320
Stranahan, Page, 320
Strong, Harry, 17-8, 23-4
Suggs, Louise, 295
Sullivan, Ed, 86, 291
Sweetser, Jess, 159
Swinley Forest Club, England, 220-23
Sydney, Australia, 243-44, 245, 298

Tacoma, Washington, 28, 44
Takarazuka Golf Course, Japan, 247
Talmadge, Constance, 62, 242
Talmadge, Norma, 88, 242
Tam O'Shanter Course, Chicago, 235
Tanganyika, Nairobi, 234
Tarpon Springs, Florida, 33
Taylor, J. H., 5, 67, 79, 82, 100, 132, 206, 212, 213, 218, 268, 280
Taylor, Jack, 118-21, 125, 130, 146, 147
Tellier, Louis, 28, 32, 207
Texas Open Championship, 98-9, 130, 202, 270
Thistle Club, Rochester, 13, 14, 22
Thompson, E. E. (Red), 256, 278-79, 298, 310
Thomson, Jimmy, 287, 321
Thursday Island, 246
Tilden, Bill, 182, 202
Tinker, Joe, 141
Toda, "Torchy," 158-69
Todd, Thelma, 242
Tokyo Golf Club, Japan, 234, 247
Tolley, C. J. H., 136
Topping, Henry, 124
Toronto, Canada, 20-1, 277-79
Towel, Tom, 321
Travers, Jerry, 46, 47, 158
Traverse City, Mich., 322-23, 327
Travis, Walter, 67, 80, 268
Trevor, George, 205
Troon Links, Ayrshire, 82, 126-28, 130, 135, 213, 234
Trosper, Harry P., 143
True Temper Open Championship, Detroit, 121
Truss, Jack, 256, 257, 278-79
Tufts, Dick, 320

Index

Tunney, Gene, 7, 182
Turnesa, Joe, 159, 185, 186, 208, 212, 258

United States Amateur Championship, 156, 159, 182, 235, 272
United States Golf Association, 19, 42, 47, 50, 51, 59, 81, 156, 251, 271
United States Open Championship, 18, 20, 46, 149, 157-58, 207, 235, 251, 271, 272, 275, 321
   1901 Myopia, 271
   1902 Garden City, 271
   1906 Lake Forest, 21, 271
   1909 Englewood, 38, 271
   1912 Buffalo, 20-1
   1913 Brookline, 25, 27-32, 35, 37, 39, 40, 67, 68, 163
   1914 Midlothian, 34-8, 39, 44, 46, 52, 56, 60, 84, 115, 163, 226, 254, 271, 278, 286-87, 300
   1915 Baltusrol, 46-7, 321
   1916 Minikahda, 47, 271
   1919 Brae Burn, 75, 86, 254
   1920 Inverness, 80, 81
   1921 Columbia, 47, 98
   1922 Skokie, 47, 49, 110
   1923 Inwood, 128, 145
   1924 Oakland Hills, 146
   1925 Worcester, 77-8, 144-45, 177
   1926 Scioto, 156, 194, 241
   1930 Interlachen, 241, 250, 278
   1931 Inverness, 287
   1933 North Shore, 104-5
   1935 Oakmont, 85
   1936 Baltusrol, 271
   1937 Oakland Hills, 272
   1938 Cherry Hills, 316
   1939 Philadelphia, 164
   1948 Riviera, 272
   1952 Northwood, 272
   1953 Oakmont, 219, 241
United States Women's Amateur Championship, 295
United States Women's Open Championship, 295
Utica Golf Club, New York, 235

Vail, Eddie, 322
Van Wie, Virginia, 295
Vardon, Harry, 25, 27, 28, 29-30, 31, 32, 37, 40, 47, 67-8, 72, 80, 82, 93, 100, 212, 218, 228, 268, 270, 276, 319, 320
Vare, Glenna Collett, 295
Versailles, France, 72-5, 136, 207
Virginia Beach Open Championship, 201-2
Von Elm, George, 156, 159, 182

Wales, Prince of, 2, 80, 99, 165, 198, 205-6, 209, 211, 220-24, 237, 305
Walker, Cyril, 125, 136, 146-47, 158, 159, 207, 276
Walker, Jimmy, 199-200
Wall, Bernice, 169, 295
Wallace, Al, 54-5, 60, 87, 142, 169, 256, 271
Wallace, Henry, 166
Walsh, Frank, 227
Wannamoisett Country Club, Providence, 279
Washington Post, 166
Waterloo Golf Club, Brussels, 281-82
Watersmeet, Michigan, 183
Watrous, Al, 159, 178-79, 207, 208, 212, 217, 276, 277, 322
Webber, Jerry, 257
Webber, Tom, 55, 257
Webster, Tom, 189, 194
Weiss, Seymour, 261
Weismuller, Johnny, 242
Wells, Ort, 124
Wentworth Golf Club, Surrey, 9, 171
West, Mae, 87
West Coast of Florida Open Championship, 61, 98, 99, 156
Westchester-Biltmore Club, Rye, 90, 102, 114, 199-200, 275
Western Open Championship, 48, 60, 99, 156, 164, 186, 275
Wethered, Roger, 81
Whalen, Grover, 102
Whitcombe, Charles, 208, 209, 292
Whitcombe, Ernie, 131-34
Whitefield Estates, Sarasota, 147-55
Will, Walter, 12
Willard, Ernest, 34-5, 36
Williams, J. W., 233
Wilson Sporting Goods Co., 143
Wind, Herbert Warren, 25, 146
Windsor, Duchess of, 224, 288
Windsor, Duke of, 7, 288-89
Wiswedel, Fred, 288
Wiswedel, Loraine, 288
Wolf Hollow, 156, 173
Wood, Craig, 202, 209, 210, 272, 276, 280
Worcester Country Club, Mass., 77-8, 144, 177, 207
Worsham, Lew, 276
Wrigley, William, 201, 203

Yasuda, Kokichi, 247
Yelland, Starr, 289
Young, L. A., 139, 142-44, 200

Zaharias, Babe Didrikson, 295
Zeder, Fred, 55